Issues in Teaching using ICT

Issues in Teaching using ICT explores the communicative potential of new technologies. The book addresses the key political and philosophical issues of using ICT in schools, its implications for teaching approaches and children's learning and the wider issues for the educational community.

The issues discussed include:

- making and using multimedia: a critical examination of learning opportunities
- developing a sense of community on-line
- setting authentic tasks using the internet
- special educational needs issues and ICT
- the teacherless classroom: myth or reality
- lifelong learning in the electronic age
- building on-line communities for teachers

This book encourages students and newly qualified teachers at both primary and secondary level to consider and reflect on the potential of using ICT in schools and in new ongoing professional development and make reasoned and informed judgements about the part it should play in their own teaching.

Marilyn Leask is a Principal Research Officer at the National Foundation for Educational Research (NFER). She has worked on a number of innovative national and international educational projects exploring and developing the use of ICT and the internet in education.

Issues in Subject Teaching series
Edited by Susan Capel, Jon Davison,
James Arthur and John Moss

Issues in Teaching using ICT

Edited by Marilyn Leask

London and New York

First published 2001
by RoutledgeFalmer
2 Park Square, Milton Park, Abingdon, Oxon, OX14 4RN

Simultaneously published in the USA and Canada
by RoutledgeFalmer
270 Madison Ave, New York NY 10016

Reprinted 2003

Transferred to Digital Printing 2005

RoutledgeFalmer is an imprint of the Taylor & Francis Group

© 2001 selection and editorial matter Marilyn Leask,
individual chapters the contributors

Typeset in ITC Goudy by Keystroke, Jacaranda Lodge, Wolverhampton

British Library Cataloguing in Publication Data
A catalogue record for this book is available from the British Library

Library of Congress Cataloging in Publication Data
Issues in teaching using ICT / edited by Marilyn Leask.
    p. cm. – (Issues in subject teaching series)
    Includes bibliographical references and index.
    1. Educational technology. 2. Information technology.
    3. Computer-assisted instruction. 4. Internet in education.
    I. Leask, Marilyn, 1950– II. Issues in subject teaching.

    LB1028.3 .I89 2001
    371.33'4–dc21   00-062757

ISBN 0-415-240034 (hbk)
ISBN 0-415-23867-6

Printed and bound by Antony Rowe Ltd, Eastbourne

Dedication

This book is dedicated to the memory of **Sally Tweddle**, a teacher, researcher and an innovative educational thinker who has led the way in her research and development work based on the use of the internet for educational purposes.

Her work in IT in school-based education provided the foundation for her innovative work to develop Cancer Help UK, an internet-based resource for cancer patients and clinicians. The project is located in the Institute for Cancer Studies at the University of Birmingham.

Cancer Help UK provides an example of how in her words 'education and learning theory can be harnessed in the medical world's quest for evidence-based practice'.[1] The model she developed provides an example for others concerned with evidence-based practice in different professions to follow.

Marilyn Leask
Christina Preston
Michelle Selinger

1 S. Tweddle (1998) 'Development and use of a theoretical model for understanding how Internet texts are used in learning', Occasional paper, CRC Institute for Cancer Studies, Clinical Research Block, University of Birmingham, B15 2TA.

Contents

Figures

Tables

Contributors

The editor

Marilyn Leask is a Principal Research Officer at the National Foundation for Educational Research (NFER). As TVEI co-ordinator she had email in her classroom in 1985. She has since worked on a number of educational projects focused on the use of IT and the internet in education. She co-ordinates the pedagogical research on the EU funded European Schoolnet Multimedia project. She is also the chair of TeacherNetUK, a professional organisation concerned with the effective development of the internet to support teachers' professional development and a MirandaNet Fellow. As part of a professional commitment to disseminate findings from research directly to teachers, she has published a number of texts in initial teacher education, management and quality issues. She is joint series editor of the successful Routledge *Learning to Teach in the Secondary School* series covering all subject areas. Recent texts include *Learning to Teach with ICT in the Secondary School* with Norbert Pachler and, with John Meadows *Teaching and Learning with ICT in the Primary School*. These report the work of innovative teachers, pupils and lecturers. Her particular research interests are in the development of internet-based resources to support teachers' professional development. She has directed and been adviser to a number of national and international projects in this area sponsored by OECD for example the DfEE, British Council, European Schoolnet.

Contributors

Steve Bruntlett is Senior Lecturer in Art and Design Education at De Montfort University. He teaches on the PGCE and MA (Art and Design Education) courses where his teaching and research focuses on new technologies in art and design education and multicultural multimedia. He is currently working on web materials for the Contemporary and Traditional Black and African Artefacts project at DMU and the Portuguese Patrimony project which he is co-ordinating with a colleague at Coimbra University. He is currently running NGfL and NOF Art and Multimedia training and working as a member of the BECTA Curriculum Consultation group for Art.

Niki Davis is Professor of Information Technology in Education in both Iowa State University of Science and Technology in the USA and the University of London's Institute of Education in England, where she leads the creation of a global degree programme for leadership in educational technology. She has collaboratively developed and researched information and communication technologies in teacher education for over a decade, mainly as the first UK professor of Educational Telematics in the University of Exeter School of Education. In 1999 she was awarded a prestigious Marie Curie Research Fellowship to assist her native country Ireland's oldest university to establish a centre in this field. She is President Elect of the International Society of IT in Teacher Education. Niki edits the UK Association for IT in Teacher Education's scholarly refereed journal of *IT for Teacher Education* and has spoken and published widely on paper and electronically.

Lyn Dawes works at BECTA. Previously she was a Research Student at De Montfort University, researching the impact of the National Grid for Learning and the introduction of ICT into schools, with a particular interest in the professional development of teachers. She taught in schools for many years and as science co-ordinator at a middle school, carried out action research with staff from the University of East Anglia and the Open University evaluating the quality of children's talk whilst working in groups at the computer (Spoken Language and New Technology (SLANT) Project). This research developed into the Talk, Reasoning and Computers (TRAC) Project and continues in the Raising Achievement Through Thinking with Language Skills (RATTLS) Project. Publications include chapters in: Wegerif, R. and Scrimshaw, P. (1997) *Computers and Talk in the Primary Classroom*, Clevedon: Multilingual Matters; Grugeon, L., Hubbard, L., Smith, C. and Dawes, L. (1998) *Speaking and Listening in the Primary School*, London: David Fulton Press; Monteith, M. (ed.) (1998) *IT for Learning Enhancement*, Exeter: Intellect Books.

Glendon (Ben) Franklin is a special needs co-ordinator at Plume School, the largest comprehensive school in Essex. He is a MirandaNet fellow where his main interest has been in encouraging teachers to use computers and developing their use as a special needs administration tool. He is looking at ILS products as a way of improving literacy. Glendon has been a keen advocate of portables since his first Z88. He is an active contributor to the SENCO Forum run by BECTA and is constantly being surprised by just how useful the internet really is.

Philip Langshaw is head of art and design at a large comprehensive school in north-east Essex, where he is principally responsible for A Level, vocational education and ICT within the art department. He has been teaching for 20 years, most of which has involved the latest developments within ICT. Work is regularly undertaken with local businesses by the students themselves, which reflects the standard of work produced. This work has included graphic design, photography, digital animation, video production and web design.

In April 1998, Philip, with four students, had the honour to attend the launch of HRH Prince of Wales's 'Young Artist's Britain Award'. Follow up work included students working with one of the Princes's artists, James Hart Dyke, during a field trip to 'Constable Country' at Flatford Mill, Suffolk. A recent OFSTED Inspection recognised that the art department was a major leader in the country with regard to the application of ICT to art. Indeed the ULTRALAB project itself was awarded an OFSTED Commendation of Excellence.

Philip has been awarded an OFSTED Certificate of Excellence in recognition of his commitment to quality and innovation within art education. Work in progress involves integrating digital animation and live action video, together with music and sound design. Philip's art department was selected as one of only ten schools in the UK to develop material for a major exhibition of art in schools for the Royal Academy Outreach programme, London, March 2000.

Darren Leafe has worked in both the primary and secondary sector and has been involved in a number of national and international curriculum projects using ICT e.g. the British Council Montage Project http://.av.Org/montage. His interests include the effective use of new technologies in education and he is currently responsible for all content development at NETLinc, Lincolnshire's response to the UK government's National Grid for Learning (NGfL) initiative. He is vice-Chair of TeacherNet and his work on planning and implementing internet based curricular projects is reported in Leask and Meadows (2000) ibid.

Richard Millwood is a Reader in Educational Technology and Deputy Director of Ultralab, at Anglia Polytechnic University, Chelmsford where he has been involved in a wide range of innovative projects for many years. Ultralab undertakes development work for many commercial and government agencies. His particular research interests are in the development and applications of interactive work spaces on the web and profiling software which would mean that individuals could use the web in such a way that it responds to individual needs. Ultralab are the prime movers behind the TescoNet 2000 project, support for the Learning Zone in the Greenwich Dome, and the government impetus to place all school pupils on-line with their own learning community and email address through the Oracle Millennium Project – Think.com.

Norbert Pachler is a Senior Lecturer at the Institute of Education, University of London, with responsibility for the Secondary PGCE in Modern Foreign Languages and the MA in Modern Languages in Education. His research interests include modern foreign languages teaching and learning, comparative education as well as the application of new technologies in teaching and learning. He has published in these fields.

Christina Preston has long been an advocate for using advanced technologies as a catalyst for change in teaching and learning. She established a non-profit making professional development model, MirandaNet, in 1994 which is supported by partnerships with industry including Oracle, BT and Xemplar. Before founding MirandaNet, Christina Preston spent 15 years teaching English, drama, media and ICT. She was then adviser in ICT in Croydon LEA and London.

Christina advises on ICT teacher-education issues with governments including Chile, Brazil and the Czech Republic; Christina Preston and the Chair of Czech Miranda, Bozena Mannova won the 1998 European Women of Achievement Award for their humanitarian ICT projects. She is Chair of the Board of Directors of the Learning Circuit, a south-west London community regeneration ICT project supported by Aztec and the Roehampton Institute, She is a visiting fellow at the Institute of Education, University of London. She writes for the educational press and has published 'Scoop', a best-selling education adventure game and 'Newsnet', an international newsroom simulation with BT and King's College, London.

Michelle Selinger is an education specialist at Cisco Systems. She was previously the Director of the Centre for New Technologies Research in Education (CeNTRE) which is a research and multimedia centre dedicated to research and development in ICT at the University of Warwick. Michelle's own research interests are in telematics, particularly text-based computer conferencing, and in defining effective pedagogies for ICT. Michelle was chair of ITTE (the UK Association for IT in Teacher Education) (1997 – September 1999), and is consulting editor for *InteracTive*, a journal for the management of ICT in schools, and co-editor for the *Journal for IT in Teacher Education*. She is currently leading a project funded by RM plc to explore effective pedagogies with ICT and looking for ways to encourage teachers to use ICT.

Alastair Wells heads the information and communication technology department at the Netherhall School, a local education authority comprehensive school in Cambridge. The school has a sixth form centre and 1,450 pupils aged 11 to 18. Currently Alastair teaches GCSE and sixth form students as well as co-ordinating cross-curricular ICT for all pupils. Netherhall has a whole school ICT policy with all teachers using computers during lessons. Some of the teachers have very high levels of expertise. Resources include Acorn, Macintosh and PC computers, including multimedia work stations, a weather station and satellite receiver, data loggers, scanners and internet access to over 100 computers via an ethernet, fibre optic, and an ATM network.

Alastair designed and now edits the school's website which was created by a student. Alastair provides the INSET training for staff and oversees a multimedia authoring team of 40 sixth form students who are producing interactive television and world wide web materials.

He has been in teaching since 1976 and involved with information technology since 1978. During that time he has designed many educational software programmes, interactive video and interactive television materials, multimedia CD Roms and ICT curriculum support materials including assessment software for National Curriculum Key Stages 3 and 4. He also lectures on aspects of ICT both in the UK and Europe and currently has a one day a week industrial placement to develop on-line learning materials. His main aim at the moment is to extend the school ICT resources into the community and make on-line learning a reality in the homes of students through networked computers.

Netherhall School website can be found at http://www.netherhall.cambs.sch.uk

Lawrence Williams is Director of Studies at Holy Cross Convent School, Surrey. He has been Guest Lecturer at Baylor University (Texas, 1996); at Osaka Kyoiku University (Japan, 1997 and 1998); and the University of Wroclaw (Poland, 1999). Lawrence has given presentations at conferences in the UK (Media '98, CAL '99, and Association for Science Education, 1999); in the Czech Republic (Webwise, 1998, and Poskole, 1997, 1998, and 1999); in Japan (Schools and the Internet, Tokyo, 1998); and in Poland (Informatyka w Szkole, 1998 and 1999). He has also been a frequent speaker on post-graduate courses at the Institute of Education, London, under Project Miranda, where he is an Honorary MirandaNet Scholar. His work in cross-curricular and ICT methodology is published as part of the National Education Centre's guidelines for headteachers throughout Japan in Mizukoshi, T. (1998) *Unique Educational Methodologies in Foreign Countries*, Tokyo: National Education Centre; in Murakawa, M. (1998) *Exhortation towards a Cross-curricular Learning Model*, Japan Educational Publishing; in Vosatka, K. (1997, 1998, and 1999) Poskole, Czech Technical University, Prague; in Syslo, M.M. (1998 and 1999) *Informatyka w Szkole XIV, and XV*, Ministry of Education, Poland; in Leask, M. and Pachler, N. (1999) *Learning to Teach Using ICT in the Secondary School*, Routledge; and in Milosevic, L. (1999) *School Improvement in the UK*, British Council. Lawrence has also acted as adviser for ICT education to the ministries of education in Poland and in Japan (1998 to the present). In 1999 he received a Guardian Award for the 'Most Creative Use of ICT in Secondary Schools', and his pupils' work has been seen on television programmes made by the BBC (Blue Peter), by Anglia (ICT on TV), and by NHK Japan (Media and Education).

Sarah Younie is Senior Lecturer in Education at Montfort University. She has experience teaching BA, PGCE and MA courses where her teaching and research focuses on the impact of ICT in education, in particular the opportunities ICT provides for innovation in teaching and learning. Previously she was a secondary school teacher in a city comprehensive and rural community college with experience of teaching KS3, KS4 and Post 16. She is currently involved in delivering NOF ICT training to teachers. She is Research Officer for 'The Learning School' project, which is part of the EU funded European Schoolnet Multimedia project supported by 20 ministries of education. At De Montfort University she was involved in the Electronic Campus project and is currently working on the SOURCE project (Software use, Reuse and Customisation in Education) in partnership with the Open University. She has delivered research papers at international conferences and published articles on ICT and education.

Introduction to the Series

This book *Issues in Teaching Using ICT* is one of a series of books entitled *Issues in Subject Teaching*. The series has been designed to engage with a wide range of issues related to subject teaching. Types of issues vary among subjects, but may include, for example: issues that impact on Initial Teacher Education in the subject; issues addressed in the classroom through the teaching of the subject; issues to do with the content of the subject and its definition; issues to do with subject pedagogy; issues to do with the relationship between the subject and broader educational aims and objectives in society, and the philosophy and sociology of education; and issues to do with the development of the subject and its future in the twenty-first century.

Each book consequently presents key debates that subject teachers will need to understand, reflect on and engage in as part of their professional development. Chapters have been designed to highlight major questions, to consider the evidence from research and practice and to arrive at possible answers. Some subject books or chapters offer at least one solution or a view of the ways forward, whereas others provide alternative views and leave readers to identify their own solution or view of the ways forward. The editors expect readers of the series to want to pursue the issues raised, and so chapters include suggestions for further reading, and questions for further debate. The chapters and questions could be used as stimuli for debate in subject seminars or department meetings, or as topics for assignments or classroom research. The books are targeted at all those with a professional interest in the subject, and in particular: student teachers learning to teach the subject in the primary or secondary school; newly qualified teachers; teachers with a subject co-ordination or leadership role, and those preparing for such responsibility; mentors, tutors, trainers and advisers of the groups mentioned above.

Each book in the series has a cross-phase dimension. This is because the editors believe it is important for teachers in the primary and secondary phases to look at subject teaching holistically, particularly in order to provide for continuity and progression, but also to increase their understanding of how children learn. The balance of chapters that have a cross-phase relevance, chapters that focus on issues which are of particular concern to primary teachers and chapters that focus on issues which secondary teachers are more likely to need to address, varies according to the issues relevant to different subjects. However, no matter where the emphasis is, authors have drawn out the relevance of their topic to the whole of each book's intended audience.

Because of the range of the series, both in terms of the issues covered and its cross-phase concern, each book is an edited collection. Editors have commissioned new writing from experts on particular issues who, collectively, will represent many different perspectives on subject teaching. Readers should not expect a book in this series to cover a full range of issues relevant to the subject, or to offer a completely unified view of subject teaching, or that every issue will be dealt with discretely, or that all aspects of an issue will be covered. Part of what each book in this series offers to readers is the opportunity to explore the inter-relationships between positions in debates and, indeed, among the debates themselves, by identifying the overlapping concerns and competing arguments that are woven through the text.

The editors are aware that many initiatives in subject teaching currently originate from the centre, and that teachers have decreasing control of subject content, pedagogy and assessment strategies. The editors strongly believe that for teaching to remain properly a vocation and a profession, teachers must be invited to be part of a creative and critical dialogue about subject teaching, and encouraged to reflect, criticize, problem-solve and innovate. This series is intended to provide teachers with a stimulus for democratic involvement in the development of subject teaching.

Susan Capel,
Jon Davison,
James Arthur and
John Moss
January 2001

Foreword

There is a page on the Cancerhelp UK website headed **Hope**. It carries a reproduction of a 12 year old's painting and is accompanied by a written and spoken description of the painting recorded 18 months after the boy's Father dies. This page was the first of a site that now has many thousand pages, both literally and metaphorically it is the heart of Cancerhelp UK. When I show the page to visitors, it never fails to connect in some way with their experience, more often than not they cry. The picture depicts a Father's struggle with his cancer and the efforts of Family and Friends to support him. The boy is my Son, his Father was my Husband.

The extract above is taken from the unfinished PhD thesis of Sally Tweddle. The poignancy of these words is heightened beyond feeling by her own death from cancer on 14 December 1999. Sally introduced her thesis this way for a reason. It was to explain why, with the help of many others, she dedicated herself to developing Cancerhelp UK, a website to provide information on cancer to patients and medical professionals. Sally was concerned about the one-sided nature of the patient–professional relationship, particularly in their ability to access information, and Sally had the vision to see that the emerging internet offered 'a new paradigm in meaning making which challenges traditional practices in relation to information-giving and which may also have a potential to modify the focus of power in lay/professional relationships'. Sally goes on in her thesis to identify a similar change in the teacher/learner relationship.

Her work is challenging to all of us who work in education. First, it forces us to recognise that learners come with personal and emotive needs that affect their use of the technology; second, that the technology can shift the power balances that exist in the system; and third, it forces us to realise that lifelong learning is more than government rhetoric. It affects us all and we will all need it at different stages of our lives.

As well as developing the website, she carried out research on its use. She looked at the patterns of usage in considerable detail, tracking individual users, categorising them into different types of readers. She also developed a theoretical framework for the interactive nature of the website based on socio-cultural theory and the work of Engeström, Wertsch and others, extending Vygotsky's 'subject, means, object triangle' to consider the interactive nature of computer based technologies. She created a theoretical framework that took into account the importance of the direct user feedback which these technologies provide, often leading to a blurring of the roles of authors and readers.

Her desire to create a strong theoretical framework for her empirical research was typically brave, far-sighted and much needed; too often developments in the field of educational technology are under-theorised and lead to no new understanding. Sally's work and her vision sets a challenge for all of us to be equally brave and farsighted, we can listen to her message even if we can never overcome her loss. She is desperately missed both personally and publicly.

Peter Avis
BECTA
January 2001

Preface

Contributions in this book focus on the exploring the *communicative* potential of new technologies through addressing a number of themes. In their different ways and from their different perspectives, contributors examine issues related to:

- **developing a sense of community on-line** with those with whom we can now communicate regardless of time and place. The work of Lawrence Williams (Chapters 4 and 9), Richard Millwood (Chapter 11), and Christina Preston (Chapter 14) is particularly focused on the human factors which have to be accommodated if the technology is to facilitate real human interaction.
- **understanding and identifying new ways of learning** which are facilitated by the technology and issues related to the integration of these into classroom work. Michelle Selinger explores the opportunities provided by the technologies to create authentic learning experiences and she challenges the notion of ICT supporting the teacherless classroom in Chapters 6 and 7. Ben Franklin (Chapter 8) looks at the issues from the point view of teachers concerned with special educational needs. Phil Langshaw's work (Chapter 11) on key skills provides an example of what innovative use of ICT can mean in practice as does the cross-curricular approach at Holy Cross school (Chapters 4 and 9). Both Phil Langshaw and Steve Bruntlett share a vision related to the ways in which the new technologies can unleash creativity and new ways of working and learning (Chapters 11 and 12). Norbert Pachler (Chapter 2) and Sarah Younie (Chapter 15) argue the case for new literacies: 'We need to move beyond traditional notions of literacy in our school curriculum towards critical media literacy, visual literacy, electronic/infomatic and global cultural literacy' (p. 16, Chapter 2) to what Sarah Younie calls a 'cognitively flexible literacy' (Chapter 15).
- **the support needed for change**: innovative practice in the UK is being achieved by visionary teachers who through a variety of means have access to the appropriate supportive infrastructure, technical support, hardware and software and who are supported by the senior management in the school in achieving their vision (see Wells Chapter 10 and Leafe Chapter 13). Evidence from research in which I have been involved (e.g. the Learning School Project within the European Schoolnet: EU funded contract MM1010; Chapter 16;

Chapter 1) indicates that supportive networks within the school and the teacher's own personal and professional community coupled with support for and acceptance of 'just in time' learning is necessary if teachers are to be able to incorporate ICT across the curriculum. Lyn Dawes explores these issues more fully in Chapter 5.

- **the challenge to traditional power structures**: that the technology poses challenges to the traditional power exercised by governments both over teachers and over the community in general cannot be doubted. Chapters 1 and 3 explore these issues. Teachers are now able to discuss ideas and share practice internationally. Moves to make research more easy available to teacher practitioners (e.g. the EU/Socrates funded European knowledge center within the European Schoolnet; the Campbell collaboration) may in time provide educators with a sound and publicly available evidence base in which practice can be deeply rooted and with reference to which practice can be justified. Such a resource may support the depoliticisation of education although clearly the content and form of education must always be a legitimate concern of any government in their role as representing the interests of society.

That the technology now available can potentially offer access to all the knowledge and resources, both print and human, required for an individual to achieve high levels of learning in many subject areas is not in doubt. Virtually anyone, any age, anywhere, at any time will within the foreseeable future be able to access learning resources and on-line expert tutorial support coupled with assessment to enable them to complete programmes of study leading to internationally recognised accreditation. Access to finance may be the most important limiting factor but even this depends on how much of what is freely available on the internet now remains free, and, as new material becomes available whether people decide to charge for this or not. For example there may be sufficient altruistic teachers, lecturers and writers in the world that high-quality materials in a wide range of subject areas can be provided free of charge. It is not inconceivable that benefactors will step forward to fund low-cost virtual international on-line schools/colleges/ universities with perhaps scholarships for those in areas where the costs of connectivity (hardware, software and connection charges) are beyond the reach of potential students. Benefactors have after all in the past undertaken such activities in real environments.

I hope you enjoy considering the ideas expressed in this book. If you wish to have access to more practical ideas about the use of ICT in schools then the companion texts may be of interest to you: Leask, M. and Meadows, J. (eds) (2000) *Teaching and Learning with ICT in the Primary School*, London: Routledge; Leask, M., Dawes, L. and Litchfield, D. (2000) *Keybytes for teachers*, Evesham: Summerfield Publishing; Leask, M. and Pachler, N. (eds) (1999) *Learning to Teach with ICT in the Secondary School*, London: Routledge. Each text in the *Learning to Teach in the Secondary School Series* (Routledge) contains a chapter related to the application of ICT to the specific subject.

Marilyn Leask
January 2001

Acknowledgements

My thanks go to the teachers, student teachers, LEA, government and university staff as well as industrialists with whom I have worked over a number of years, on various ICT projects which provide the foundation for the ideas in this book.

Inspiration and the development of innovative practice has particularly come from colleagues on the TeacherNetUK, MirandaNet, OzTeacherNet and European Schoolnet initiatives. Colleagues who have contributed to this book have played their part in furthering the work of these initiatives.

Marilyn Leask
January 2001

Part I
Political and philosophical issues

1 Electronic professional networks for teachers

Political issues

Marilyn Leask

Introduction

This chapter charts the development of ideas about using the communicative potential of technology to support web-based networks for teachers' professional development in the UK and Europe during the latter part of the 1990s and early part of the twenty-first century. Various developments supported by governments in the area of national and international electronic communications networks in the UK and in Europe are outlined and discussed.

The purpose of this chapter is to provoke a debate about the basis on which such networks are established, developed and funded and to raise the question about the sustainability and usefulness to the teaching profession of networks which are controlled directly by governments.

The suggestion is made that while the teaching profession may benefit in a variety of ways from the establishment of such networks, there may be a tension between their capacity to serve the needs of pupils and teachers and the political needs of government. At the time of writing, the General Teaching Council (GTC) for England is being established and, as part of its provision for members (all teachers), it will develop a website. What professional role could this organisation play given the technologies at its disposal? To what extent is it of value for teachers in England to have a central professional website independent and protected from government intervention and control? Can professional needs be satisfied through government run 'professional' networks? These and other related questions are discussed in this chapter.[1]

Background to UK and European networks

This section focuses particularly on the development of the National Grid for Learning (NGfL) (UK government funded),[2] the Virtual Teacher Centre (VTC) (UK government funded),[3] and the European Schoolnet (Swedish Government funded initially, moving to European Union funding with support of the ministries of education in member states).

Discussions about the foundation of a national professional website for teachers in the UK began to my knowledge in 1996 with a consultation conference funded by the British Council and attended by subject association representatives, teachers and representatives from the various government organisations (Leask and Pachler 1997). A steering group was established with representatives from these organisations and practising school teachers, and several meetings over a two year period were held to develop the ideas.

The government at the time, (January 1996), the Conservative government led by John Major, accepted that the idea was sound but indicated that no money could be made available. The group (by then called TeacherNetUK) then spent many months establishing possible funding options including developing relationships with private companies. Much of the summer of 1997 was spent on establishing funding strategies for what was expected to be a national, independent, financially self sustaining, professional website. The change of government to Labour in May 1997 brought in a government committed to ensuring Information and Communication Technologies (ICT) had a high profile in education and policies were introduced that accelerated the rate of development of national networks and prioritised development of ICT use in schools.

By October 1997 the new Labour government had distributed a consultation paper (DfEE, 1997) about what they called the National Grid for Learning (NGfL) which was intended to encompass many activities through which learning takes place in a society and which was to start with a Virtual Teacher Centre (VTC).

These developments clearly indicated a very positive commitment to education and the notion of a professional website for teachers. However, experience with web developments indicates that what can be developed overnight at a political whim can also disappear overnight. The government organisation now with the brief to develop the VTC (BECTA previously NCET) was unable to act under the previous government as the political will was absent. Hence, when the political agenda changes e.g. if value for money is not demonstrated, current government funded provision may just disappear or alternatively it could potentially be used for overtly political ends. In England, the concerns of teaching professionals are not necessarily directly linked with those of politicians.

The European Schoolnet (EUN), a network of networks for European teachers, is potentially on a much firmer footing. The initiative was funded initially (Yohansson 1997) by the Swedish Government with some start up contributions from the European Commission (following the Cresson and Bangemann (1996) initiative) and matched funding from participants who were drawn from industry, government and universities and other educational organisations. By the end of 1998, various ministries of education had agreed to underwrite part of the cost and the number of ministries involved has continued to grow. Details about those involved can be found on the website (http://www.eun.org) together with the documents related to the initiative. Long term funding may come from an agreement which becomes part of each member state's commitment to the EU. At the time of writing this is yet to be decided.

Philosophies and purposes of networks

If the values and beliefs and purposes behind the establishment of a national/ international network are not explicit then there are likely to be unresolved tensions between developers of the network and the users.

Different approaches across Europe are summed up by the co-ordinator of the European Schoolnet in an interview:

> What we would like to do (with the European Schoolnet) is to establish an infrastructure for co-operation at a European level. In a way **putting tools and instruments in the hands of teachers of schools to (enable them to) do things on their own.** . . . there are several approaches in Europe. The philosophy in Sweden and I think all of the Scandinavian countries is very much that a network of this kind, a School network, puts tools at the disposal of teachers . . . It is not a matter of distributing ready-made lessons or modules. That might be a good way to disseminate or facilitate access to teaching materials, but more as elements in what the teachers need to use to build up their own teaching and learning . . .
>
> (Co-ordinator EUN project March 1998 interview)

The co-ordinator goes on to use the analogy of the network being similar to the 'trunk of the tree' .

> **A tree** which teachers could go to and enjoy some of its fruits. But you could also go there to decide to put on some leaves, or to put on some fresh branches and I think this analogy is very important. To me the European Schoolnet or the website of the European Schoolnet, the internet platform is the trunk of the tree and some of the essential branches. The second element in this philosophy is to help to fertilise the soil in which the tree is growing. That is to help at a European level member states and schools to use information technology and to use it more efficiently.
>
> (Co-ordinator EUN project March 1998 interview)

The EUN platform developers are working with 500 innovative schools across Europe in order to find out more about the EUN's impact on teaching and learning as well as to examine questions relating to the development, design, and management of an on-line educational resource. Details of the development of the EUN are available from the website (http://www.eun.org).

The philosophy behind the Virtual Teacher Centre in the UK is yet to be spelt out fully (Poole 1998; Dawes 2000). To my knowledge there is no widely available document which sets out the structure, the process of development and how the input of teachers will be managed. For example, when details of good practice are placed on this site – as recently on the topic of literacy, what is their status? Who has vetted them? Is this the government approved/recommended approach? Is there an issue in that material on government run sites must, by its very nature, have a different status to that on sites which are run by teachers for teachers? History shows that what is espoused as good practice by one government may be derided by the next.

My concern about government run professional sites really serving the needs of teachers comes from the recent history of change in education in England (and a study of history in general). In England, the history of government dictated change in education and regular reverses of policy over the last 20 years has led me to a view about the government's role in education which is different from that experienced by educators in other countries. In Leask (1998) I discuss some of the policy contradictions which have resulted (particularly affecting less academically able children) and in Leask and Goddard (1992) I document some of the unexpected and damaging effects of this direct government intervention.

The added value of working in cross-cultural contexts

Lawrence Williams, in Chapter 4, writes about his pupils feeling part of a world community through video conferencing and his hope that this communication between pupils of different cultures may encourage peace.

In the case of the European Schoolnet, the rationale for qualifying for European Commission funding is that there is some added value to be gained at the European level. Providing enabling structures which support teachers in developing joint curriculum projects across countries clearly satisfies a need which teachers have already and the EUN will do this. What is less certain is the effect on individual pupils and teachers and the curriculum of such developments. Up to date curriculum material which can be used for cross-cultural studies is now available through the internet in a way that previously wasn't possible and the accessibility of newspapers and radio broadcasts are just two examples which enhance the curriculum in a cross-cultural context.

As the co-ordinator of the European Schoolnet initiative pointed out in interview, one of the purposes of the EUN is 'to help at a European level, member states and schools to use information technology and to use it more efficiently'. And indeed the networking the EUN supports is demonstrated by the partners' page of the website which allows access to those networks identified by individual governments as representing their education system. There are of course, other networks operating in many countries.

The context for professional electronic network development in England

At the time of writing, in England, a culture of public exposure of 'failure' of schools and teachers exists and is coupled with publication of non-contextualised results from national tests. Not suprisingly, soon after the introduction of this policy, school exclusions were reported as increasing – children who are achieving below the average academically bring a school's publicly published averages down leading to potential loss of income as parents choose schools with better results. An expensive and extensive inspection procedure exists (reports are publicly available on the internet – you can find them through the NGfL site as mentioned earlier) but the validity of the results is challenged by some academics (the OFSTIN group contactable through Professor Taylor Fitzgibbon at University of Durham).

In this climate, one questions whether web-based tools supporting professional debate about professional issues are appropriately located on a national professional website funded by government. Millwood (2000) identifies a wide range of forms of communication between professionals and his research indicates that trust is an essential part of establishing effective on-line communities. It may be that in other countries, there is such a level of trust and respect between government and the teaching profession that government funding and government control of a national professional site is not considered to be potentially constraining or manipulative.

A whole system approach?

Putting my reservations about the political control and the question of appropriate activities on the VTC to one side, the Labour government did, I suggest, develop a very coherent approach to whole system change with relation to integrating ICT into teachers' professional practice.

As part of the TeacherNet UK initiative, I undertook an analysis of strategies which would encourage whole system change in ICT (Leask 1998). Figure 1.1 illustrates the different influences on teachers' professional knowledge: the areas in which current developments in the UK at government level are likely to make an impact have been referenced.

On the diagram, the following notes indicate this impact.

1   covered by proposals in the document: National Grid for Learning (DfEE 1997)
2   covered by New Opportunities Funded training of teachers (recognised providers provided training from 1999 onwards) and the national curriculum for ICT in initial teacher training (implemented from 1998)
3   provided by funding for portables[4] and personal hardware and software (£20 million allocated 1999–2000)

Local bodies e.g. LEAs		**National bodies e.g. DfEE**
through		through
• policy development[1] • networks[2] • INSET[2] • advice • internal publications • occasional external publications		• circulars[1] • legislation[1] • guidance[1] • resource provision[3] • OFSTED/HMI reports[1]
Influences on the development of professional knowledge of teachers in the school system		
Internal school processes	**Professional associations**	**Media**
through	• publications • conferences • inservice training	through
• school planned INSET days[1,2] • internal procedures • occasional internal and external publications • work with higher education institutions[2]		• newspapers • TV documentaries, etc. • Websites

Figure 1.1 Influences on the development of professional knowledge through which the impact of government policy is felt

As can be seen, there are still a number of gaps in the strategy outlined by government which require LEAs, teacher training institutions, the media and schools to take up the challenge but overall, government support for, encouragement of and insistence on change in ICT use has been substantial. As is to be expected of an undertaking focused on changing professional practice, impact will be patchy for a wide variety of reasons. Dawes (1999, 2000) has charted impact over the period 1997–2000 and provides details of impact during that period at the personal level of teachers' lives. Nevertheless, a reasonably coherent attempt at whole system change has been implemented.

The roles of local education authority (LEA) and school intranets

An interesting development in the UK stimulated by the government drive to encourage a networked society and starting with the teaching community is the development of LEAs' and school intranets (see also Chapters 10 and 13).

It is possible that, in the UK, at this community level, the control of the medium for professional purposes may pass to local teachers in a way which is not possible with the national Virtual Teacher Centre. There are of course many examples on the web where teachers share resources already but for the new entrant, or for the teacher who has not found their own network, the LEA intranet could well be a key resource e.g. through providing reliable access to downloaded sites of educational worth and to local on-line communities. There are a number of questions to be considered in the design of intranets whether for LEAs or schools:

1 What can the intranet add to what is already available in terms of: data and information, access to curriculum applications and on-line communities?
2 What resource deployment is actually appropriate – recognising that the opportunity for endless creation of web pages and for 'play' can get in the way of ensuring that relevance, quality and value for money are high priority?
3 What procedures are needed to ensure quality is delivered, monitored and material on the intranet is relevant to teachers, updated and not replicating work which has already been done elsewhere?
4 What monitoring systems are appropriate to protect adults and children from internet addiction and access to inappropriate material?

Will the General Teaching Council be able to provide an independent professional website?

The results of the TeacherNet members' deliberations about the desirable characteristics of an independent professional website, were presented to the GTC in February 2000. Table 1.1 adapted from a briefing paper prepared for this (Leask 2000b) provides a general outline of the possibilities suggested.

Much more detailed suggestions were made at the seminar and these are published in Leask (2000c).

Table 1.1 Ways in which a website could support the GTC

Key roles of the GTC:	Website: information provision	Website: interactive part: network and community building: tools/provision
a) to speak for teachers b) provide advice on professional issues: to teachers and to government c) support professional development d) disseminate good practice e) disseminate and support research f) support debate g) publicise professional standards h) keep a register of all teachers i) support recruitment	The GTC: Information about GTC's goals purpose and operation, code of conduct, teachers' rights and obligations, register, recruitment and careers (?responsibility of TTA site) PD opportunities: profiling information, courses, networks, conferences, subject associations, teacher-researcher networks, careers, exchange and sabbatical opportunities Web links: govt. and professional organisations, commercial organisations e.g. publishers association, careers, curriculum information (linked with the VTC/commercial providers/ subject associations) PD Resources: Educational Resources Mall, Higher Education Virtual Mall, libraries, access to research, Virtual Library of Educational Case Studies, data collection tools for self analysis of practice	1 **electronic newsletter:** open to all – perhaps different newsletters targeted to different groups 2 **bulletin board:** notifications of: seminars/ discussions; professional projects; professional information; votes – open to all 3 **advice:** professional mentoring/agony aunt 4 **seminars/fora/on-line workshops:** open/ closed discussion groups; entrance vetted for closed seminars; supporting team work, peer-support and co-learning strategies; regional networks 5 **voting/opinion sampling:** identity of voters would have to be verified, electronic questionnaires 6 **projects/research:** related to professional issues e.g. research projects using researcher and teacher researcher networks to identify good practice 7 **profiling:** for purposes of receiving information relevant to the individual and presenting information about oneself. *Establishing trust in the on-line communities is essential. On-line communities may be short-term, long-term, open close, self monitoring or otherwise, vetting needs to be considered for closed communities and protocols about confidentiality clearly established.*

Opportunities available for a website to support the GTC in the realisation of the organisations' 'key roles' (adapted from Leask 2000b). This analysis is split into two aspects of web provision – provision of information and an interactive part focused on a network and community building role through the provision of interactive services.

The creation of the General Teaching Council provides a one-off opportunity to create a professional independent website in England which can support confidential on-line discussion and debate between professionals as well as the provision of resources and further innovative developments. Finance is potentially available through the subscription. Will we, in England, be able to make the most of this opportunity? Only time will tell.

Establishing the financial basis of operation of an independent professional website

In the introduction, the desirability of a website which purports to provide a professional service for teachers being based on an independently sustainable footing was raised and two aspects of management of the provision, in particular, need to be considered if this is to be achieved. First, the development and control of content should be seen to be managed for professional not purely political purposes (though sometimes these two coincide). This issue has been discussed earlier. The second aspect is related to funding being available on a self-sustaining basis. If a national website is to have a life beyond that of the political influence of the politicians who created it, then the funding basis needs to be sound. In this section, models of funding and issues related to these are considered.

Models of funding

The ways in which a website can be funded include:

(a) sponsorship
(b) advertising
(c) subscription

There are pros and cons for each example and indeed a mixture of funding types could be used.

Sponsorship   may be appropriate in the early stages but is a vulnerable form of funding as sponsors can always withdraw their sponsorship.

Advertising   on what is recognised as a national website for teachers is of interest to advertisers – research on the funding of the TeacherNet UK project demonstrated that. But not all forms of advertisement are acceptable. Nevertheless, for a company which sells to teachers, access to the education market is worth a considerable amount.

Subscription   has the potential of providing a steady income but if a purpose of national educational websites is to provide a service and resource to all members of the teaching profession then subscription is not an option.

Questions to be considered in establishing an independent professional site

a) Is the funding base of a proposed website sound enough to be able to sustain the development and maintenance of the site and outlast changes in government policy?
b) Is value for money provided by the service delivered – is the return in learning outcomes or other criteria that are established (e.g. uniformity across the system) worth the investment?
c) If public funding is appropriate, what guarantees are there that public funding will continue to be provided?
d) If private funding is available what are the implications of using this?
e) What forms of partnerships between educators and industrialists are appropriate in this new medium?

Conclusions

The opportunities offered for professional development of teachers through the medium supported by the internet are without parallel in our history. Like all human endeavours, what is achieved is influenced by the developers' values and motives which they themselves may not even recognise. I cannot recall a time when people in apparently all the countries around the world focused so much attention on the same sort of educational activity. The pressure is on all of us to use the medium, and the pressure is certainly on governments in Europe to develop national websites for education. This opportunity will come but once. In the same way the museums built by Victorians have become part of our cultural heritage, the structures being developed which are guiding the further development and management of professional places on the web will provide models for future developments. It is worth pausing and considering the implications of structures and approaches being established now before new patterns become too fixed and too much resource is squandered through lack of planning and forethought. Are the UK national professional websites to be politically controlled and content driven or are they to be developed in a way which empowers teachers to use the technology for their professional growth?

It is essential that where governments are diverting public funds to develop national websites for teachers the benefits related to teaching and learning are apparent and the lessons of good practice not political ideology disseminated. If such 'national websites' are seen to be too politically influenced then they will remain that – potentially political propaganda sites rather than professional sites. Research is being done and will be done to clarify these issues but the ease and rate of change of websites is such that it may be difficult to link findings and development.

In conclusion, I have posed questions in the sections above to stimulate debate about the form of independent professional provision on the web that might support the long term and short term needs of teachers for professional development. Progress in the use of ICT in classrooms is slow and faltering in many cases and not just in the UK (Jakobsdottir 2000; Gibson 2000; Dawes 2000; Cox, Preston and Cox 1999). Effective use of the communicative aspects of the technology may not occur automatically. Any sites wishing to provide independent professional services of value to teachers will need mechanisms to be responsive to those for whom they are creating the service. Noble intentions whether on the part of government or others are no guarantee that a site of value to the teaching profession will be produced.

Notes

1 This chapter is based on research undertaken in a number of funded initiatives and on the deliberations the group of innovative educators taking part in the TeacherNet UK initiative who, over the period 1995–2000, debated such issues and presented ideas to the Department for Education and Employment (DfEE), OFSTED, Teacher Training Agency (TTA) as well as the General Teaching Council for England in February 2000. I write as chair of TeachernetUK (http://www.teachernetuk.org.uk), and as a researcher into the effectiveness of the European Schoolnet in which I have been involved since its beginning (http://www.eun.org), as a founder member of the British Council Montage project (http://www.montageplus.bc.uk) and as a consultant on a number of other projects for both government and private organisations. These are documented in a number of publications such as Leask 2000 a,b,c; Leask and Pachler 1999; Leask and Meadows 2000). The DfEE sponsored Teachernet internet gateway initiative is just starting at the time of writing (http://www.teachernet.gov.uk) with Teachernet UK members advising.
2 National Grid for Learning (NGfL) http://www.ngfl.gov.uk
3 The Virtual Teacher Centre VTC http://www.vtc.org.uk
4 DfEE (1996) Multimedia Portables for Teachers:
   http://becta.org.uk/mmportables/about.htm

Questions

1 Review a range of websites providing professional services to you. What are the values and beliefs underpinning the operation and development of these websites?
2 What purposes do these websites serve for you as a teacher and for those paying for its maintenance and development?
3 How could the web be made more useful to you professionally?

Further reading

If you wish to gain a fuller picture of the development of UK government thinking of the use of the web for education, then the following texts provide useful background:

Cresson E. and Bangemann H. (1996) *Learning in the Information Society: Action Plan for a European Education Initiative*, communication to the European Parliament, Council, Economic and Social Committee and Committee of the Regions.
Department for Education and Employment (DfEE) (1997) 'Connecting the Learning Society: consultation paper', London: DfEE.

Leask, M. and Pachler, N. (1997) 'The background and rationale for the TeacherNet UK initiative – harnessing the potential of the internet for improving teachers' professional development and pupil learning', Information Society Open Classroom II Conference Proceedings, Lambrakis Foundation, Greece.

Poole, P. (1998) 'Staff development in ICT: Can a National Grid for Learning work?' mimeo, Canterbury Christ Church College.

Stevenson Report (The independent ICT in Schools Commission) (1997) 'Information and Communications Technology in UK Schools: An independent inquiry', 78–80 St John Street, London, EC1M 4HR.

References

Cox, M., Preston, C. and Cox, K. (1999) 'What motivates teachers to use ICT?' paper presented at the British Educational Research Association Annual Conference, September 1999, Brighton.

Cresson E. and Bangemann H. (1996) *Learning in the Information Society: Action plan for a European Education Initiative*, communication to the European Parliament, Council, Economic and Social Committee and Committee of the Regions.

Dawes, L. (1999) 'First Connections: teachers and the National Grid for Learning', *Computers and Education*, Vol. 33, pp. 235–53.

Dawes, L. (2000) *The National Grid for Learning: Outcomes of an Opportunity for Change*, PhD thesis, Bedford: De Montfort University.

Department for Education and Employment (DfEE) (1997) *Connecting the Learning Society: Consultation Paper*, London: DfEE.

Gibson, I. (2000) 'At the intersection of technology and pedagogy: considering styles of learning and teaching', ESRC Seminar Series Paper, January 6, Keele University.

Jakobsdottir, S. (2000) 'Effects of information and communications technology (ICT) on teaching and learning in Iceland', ESRC Seminar Series Paper, January 6, Keele University.

Leask, M. (1998) *The development and embedding of new knowledge in a profession*, De Montfort University, PhD thesis.

Leask, M. and Goddard, D. (1992) *The Search for Quality: Planning Improvement and Managing Change*, London: Paul Chapman/Sage.

Leask, M. (2000a) 'Ways in which a website could support the GTCE in the realisation of the organisations key roles: views from TeacherNet members' Briefing paper 2 for the 17 February 2000 seminar, mimeo, Bedford: De Montfort University.

Leask, M. (2000b) 'The GTC website: Purposes, content, services, stages of development', Report from the Seminar 17 February 2000, mimeo, Bedford: De Montfort University.

Leask, M. (2000c) 'European Knowledge Centre within the European Schoolnet', Seminar 2 Report: 'Classroom practice and educational research: using ICT to build European networks for innovation and change', mimeo, Bedford: De Montfort University.

Leask, M. and Meadows, J. (eds) (2000) *Learning to teach with ICT in the Primary School*, London: Routledge.

Leask, M. and Pachler, N. (1997) 'The background and rationale for the TeacherNet UK initiative – harnessing the potential of the internet for improving teachers' professional development and pupil learning', *Information Society Open Classroom II Conference Proceedings*, Lambrakis Foundation, Greece.

Millwood, R. (2000) 'Presentation to the European Knowledge Centre UK', Seminar 2, 7 March 2000 published in Leask, M. (2000c ibid.) Seminar 2 Report: 'Classroom practice and educational research: using ICT to build European networks for innovation and change', mimeo, Bedford: De Montfort University.

Poole, P. (1998) 'Staff development in ICT: Can a National Grid for Learning work?' mimeo, Canterbury Christ Church College.

Stevenson Report (The independent ICT in Schools Commission) (1997) Information and Communications Technology in UK Schools: An independent inquiry. 78–80 St John Street, London, EC1M 4HR.

Teacher Training Agency (TTA) (1998) *Curriculum for ICT training in ITT*. London, TTA.

Williams, M. and McKeown, L. (1996) 'Definitions of the Net that Teachers Experience', *Australian Educational Computing*, Vol. 11, No. 2, pp.4–9.

Yohansson, Y. (1997) 'Towards a European Schoolnet', paper presented by the Minister for School and Adult Education, Sweden, to the informal Education Council in Amsterdam, 2 March 1997.

2 Connecting schools and pupils: To what end?

Issues related to the use of ICT in school-based learning[1]

Norbert Pachler

Introduction

In this chapter I aim to delineate the impact of ICT on pupils as members of the information society. I will argue that, in order to become successful members of our digital culture, pupils need to be furnished not only with the basic but also the higher-order skills required to part take in the fundamentally different ways in which members of our society are beginning to work, shop, play, form relationships and communicate. Digital culture I deem to be a linguistically mediated discourse community in which the semiotic specificities of computer-mediated communication as well as electronic/informatic, visual and critical media literacies are important higher-order skills; an environment which is characterised by a novel interplay of text, sound and pictures requiring, amongst others, new text construction, composition and decoding skills as well as new navigational strategies. I consider school-based learning to have an important role to play in the acquisition of and learning about these skills and strategies by providing all young people with access to ICT and thereby counteracting the potential digital divide between information haves and have-nots, despite the fact that the very existence of new technologies in general and the internet in particular calls traditional schooling and traditional approaches to learning into question.

The socio-cultural context of learning in the information age

Developments during the 1990s in the field of new technologies, in particular interactive multimedia and the internet, brought about an 'information revolution' which can be seen to lead to changing cultural practices by reshaping the way we work, study, play, form relationships and communicate (see e.g. Tapscott 1998 or Warschauer 1998). Access to and the ability to manipulate information have become important preconditions for success in economic and political as well as personal terms: 'the central factor in producing wealth and power is the ability to access, adapt, and make intelligent use of new information technology' (Warschauer 1998: 2). The world is becoming a much smaller place characterised by globalisation and internationalisation of the economy and society. The changes in cultural practices entailed by these processes, in turn, have considerable implications for compulsory and post-compulsory education. New technologies make it possible for us as educators to do new things in new ways and require of us to re-examine the epistemologies of what to teach (see Noss and Pachler 1999). We need to develop in young people, abstraction, system thinking, experimentation, collaboration and learner training, allowing them to meet the challenging requirements of the information society and equip them with the ability to be flexible, change and learn new skills for emerging contexts (see also Warschauer 1998: 2–3). I would argue, therefore, that we need to move beyond traditional notions of literacy in our school curriculum towards critical media literacy, visual literacy, electronic/informatic and global cultural literacy; away from the transmission of information towards analysis, judgement and interpretation within the framework of a school-based education.

Seymour Papert rightly points to the increasing importance of the act of learning as 'the most important single issue facing society as we move into the next millennium' and argues that the important question is about not simply changes in curricula but 'changes in the human relationships most closely related to learning – relationships between generations in families, relationships between teachers and learners and relationships between peers with common interests' (1996: 18). In other words, Papert questions traditional modes of school-based learning as the most effective paradigms. The concern that traditional notions of schooling are performing inadequately is also in evidence in writing about educational leadership and management. David Hargreaves, for example, argues that, in response to the so-called postmodern fragmentation of society,

> (the) traditional 'education system' must be replaced by *polymorphic* educational provision – an infinite variety of multiple forms of teaching and learning. Future generations will look back on our current sharp disjunction between life and education and our confusion of education with schooling as a barrier blocking a – perhaps the – road to the learning society.
>
> (Hargreaves 1997: 11)

J. Lemke (1998), another critic of the status quo, calls the prevailing 'curricular learning paradigm' into question, since it 'assumes that someone else will decide what you need to know and will arrange for you to learn it all in a fixed order and on a fixed schedule' (p. 293), and argues instead for an 'interactive learning paradigm', which

> assumes that people determine what they need to know based on their participation in activities in which such needs arise, and in consultation with knowledgeable specialists; that they learn in the order that suits them, at a comfortable pace, and just in time to make use of what they learn. . . . It is the paradigm of access to information, rather than imposition of learning.
>
> (ibid.: 294)

Indeed, new technologies are increasingly being seen by policy makers as a viable option (see e.g. DfEE 1997a, DfEE 1997b, McKinsey and Company 1997, Stevenson 1997). However, rather than looking to new technologies to replace school-based education in the hope they make education more cost-effective, I would argue that we need to look to educators to prepare young people for the challenges of an adult life which increasingly requires the capability to work effectively with new technologies. Not only should formal, school-based education, in my opinion, continue to play an important social function in society, it should also, for the foreseeable future anyway, continue to ensure access to new technologies for pupils as home computer use remains heavily contingent upon social class and socio-economic factors and the interrelationship of access with attitude appear to be of significance (see e.g. Millard 1997: 2). I would, further-more, argue that it is our moral obligation as educators to prepare young people adequately for their adult lives in today's and tomorrow's world, so that they can take part in social and entertainment activities made possible by new technologies not only as passive recipients and consumers but as active and empowered participants (see also Leask and Pachler 1999: xix). New technologies must not be allowed to become a vehicle of containment but must become a vehicle of education (see Hargreaves 1997: 15).

'Independently', I fear, young learners would find it very difficult to acquire all the requisite skills and become aware of all the – often hidden and embedded – moral and ethical issues around ICT use, some of which I shall discuss in the remainder of this chapter. However, Seymour Papert's argument (1996: 25) that computers should be used differently in school-based settings in order to maximise their potential, warrants serious consideration:

> (the) **cyberostriches** who make school policy are determined to use computers but can only imagine using them in the framework of the school system as they know it: children following a predetermined curriculum mapped out year by year and lesson by lesson. This is quite perverse: new technology being used to strengthen a poor method of education that was invented only because there were no computers when school was designed.

Nevertheless, school-based education remains vital in ensuring that future generations of young people are well prepared for adult life in a world strongly influenced by new technologies, not least because of the potential and value of the pedagogic mediation of teachers in the learning process (see e.g. Mortimore 1999). My experience as a teacher and educator strongly suggests that the role of the teacher, despite pressures to change towards that of a facilitator and creator of didactically prepared web-based learning material, remains absolutely central in rendering the experiences and work of pupils with and at the computer coherent (see e.g. Crook 1994, Noss and Pachler 1999 or Pachler 1999b). I believe effective learning takes place through social interaction and interpersonal support (see Pachler 1999b) and I would argue that in the context of learning with and about new technologies the social environment of the classroom and schools can be

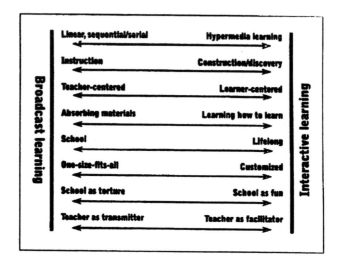

Figure 2.1 The shift from broadcast to interactive learning
© Don Tapscott 1998 (permission obtained)

helpful. Equally, the role of teachers in identifying appropriate learning outcomes, choosing appropriate software and activities and structuring and sequencing the learning process is imperative in the acquisition of and learning about the higher-order skills necessary to understand fully the social, cultural, political, ethical and moral issues which are often only implicit in new technologies and their use.

Don Tapscott (see 1998: 143) suggests a new learning paradigm, from broadcast to interactive learning (see Figure 2.1) which illustrates well the complexity of learning in the information society.

Whilst clearly demonstrating the shift from learning based on transmission and information transfer to a more learner-centred approach built around interactive multimedia material, in my estimation the complexity of Tapscott's model underlines the importance of school-based education as one important mode of learning and of teachers as important facilitators in the learning process, albeit with a focus on individualisation and learner training, i.e. teaching pupils how to learn.

New technologies and new cultural practices

Dieter Wolff (1998: 8) rightly asserts that new technologies are media created by humans to store information and to interact with others. As such they play an important role in the cultural practices of society.

Traditionally, two definitions of culture are distinguished, one coming from the humanities, the other from the social sciences. In a discussion of culture, teaching in the context of modern foreign languages education at advanced level, I argue:

that (the) one 'focuses on the way a social group represents itself and others through its material productions, be they works of art, literature, social institutions, or artefacts of everyday life, and the mechanisms for their reproduction and preservation through history'. (Kramsch 1996: 2)

The other refers to 'the attitudes and beliefs, ways of thinking, behaving and remembering shared by members of that community'. (Kramsch 1996: 2).

Traditionally the notion of 'material culture' has prevailed which manifested itself in . . . teaching in the study of written sources, particularly literary texts, or that of 'time-honoured institutions' (Kramsch 1996: 2) such as the political or education systems of (a) country etc.

(Pachler 1999a: 77)

Whichever definition of culture one might adopt, and the two definitions are not necessarily mutually exclusive, it soon becomes clear that, given their characteristics – which I shall delineate briefly below – new technologies have a considerable impact on groups of people, how they present themselves and communicate and share ideas, thoughts, memories, attitudes, beliefs etc. with each other.

Internet-based culture, according to Tapscott (see 1998: 80–1), is characterised by everyone being a producer of and participant in culture; the personal nature of so much internet content can be explained by it often being written within an intimate environment for an anonymous audience where the producer and the user have a relationship with the information rather than with each other.

Some characteristics of new technologies and their implications for teaching and learning

The main characteristics of new technologies can be said to be:

- interactivity and communicative potential,
- non-linearity and provisionality of information,
- distributed nature, as well as
- multimodality.

Interactivity is seen by many commentators as a defining feature of new technologies in that users are no longer passive recipients – as with television, for example, where a few people have control over content and where content is broadcast – but active participants and creators of content which they can publish to a vast audience. Web-based resources, for instance, are not held in one central location, but are **distributed** across the world.

Time spent on the Net is not passive time, it's active time. It's reading time. It's investigation time. It's skill development and problem-solving time. It's time analyzing, evaluating. It's composing your thoughts time. It's writing time. (*Cynics might interject here that time spent on the Net currently is often also still waiting time*, NP.)

(Tapscott 1998: 8)

Tapscott (1998: 7) argues that by controlling rather than passively observing the new media, child development may accelerate. This, according to him, includes the evolution of motor skills, language skills and social skills, as well as the development of cognition, intelligence, reasoning, personality and the development of autonomy. The danger, for Tapscott, lies in the digital divide between 'the information haves and have-nots – those who can communicate with the world and those who can't' (Tapscott 1998: 11) and in the fact that children without access to the new media will be developmentally disadvantaged (see Tapscott 1998: 7). Should this assertion be borne out by research, and it should be stressed here that Tapscott's views are not universally shared – e.g. in her book *Failure to Connect,* Jane Healy, for example, posits that very young children who use computers may be impaired in their ability to learn (see also Haughton 1999 and Johnston 1999), it would furnish a very powerful argument in favour of an entitlement to computer literacy and computer use through formal schooling. This despite the fact that, as I discussed earlier, in the new digital age school-based education is by no means the only place for learning.

One might argue, however, that Tapscott's discussion of the virtues of new technologies lacks a certain critical edge and acknowledges potential problems and shortcomings insufficiently; such as the lack of direct human interaction and face-to-face communication, which might lead to an ineptitude in non-virtual, i.e. 'real-life' social contexts; or health implications, such as repetitive strain injury caused by excessive typing or eyestrain caused by viewing a flickering screen. Furthermore, Tapscott appears to take the positive outcomes of the use of new technologies for granted. It might, therefore, be advisable to relativise some of the claims he makes. In this way, time spent on the internet *can* become active time, *can* become reading time, *can* become investigation time etc.; once again, the role of the teacher in facilitating these outcomes takes centre stage.

New technologies allow users to create and distribute their own work and become active participants in the culture creation process. In order to make full use of this potential and to understand all the implications users need to be taught the respective basic and higher-order skills such as electronic/informatic, visual and critical media literacies.

The interactive potential of new technologies does, of course, lend itself not only to the skills, knowledge and understanding of educational contexts. Indeed, young people tend to encounter and exploit this potential in the context of play and entertainment rather than education.

There exists, particularly in this context, the real danger of young people being exploited by software producers and distributors in whose commercial interest it is to 'control' users by getting them to buy all of their products if possible. Given a sound educational rationale, the use of new technologies for purposes such as simulations, hypothesis testing, modelling and role-plays as well as social interaction through on-line chats and discussion groups can yield considerable learning gains and allows 'kids to try on the world for size' (Tapscott 1998: 8), provided the activities are appropriate. Careful reflection by users, parents and teachers on the educational value of software is, therefore imperative (see p. 23).

New technologies can be seen to make a considerable contribution to the social qualities of our lives by making accessible to us new (virtual) ways of socialising, networking and of communicating, which can meaningfully supplement, and at times replace, face-to-face modes. Computer-mediated communication (CMC), be it synchronous, i.e. real-time (e.g. IRC[2], MOOs[3]), or asynchronous, i.e. delayed-time (e.g. email, bulletin boards), opens up previously unknown opportunities to interact with individuals and groups of people beyond the here and now, and create and share with them social conventions across traditional linguistic and cultural boundaries in so-called virtual communities. This notion is supported by Tapscott, who sees a new culture emerging 'defined as the socially transmitted and shared patterns of behavior, customs, attitudes, and tacit codes, beliefs and values, arts, knowledge, and social forms' (Tapscott 1998: 55). Membership of virtual communities, amongst other things, allows users to

> construct and project different social identities for themselves – freeing them from the 'tyrannies' of face-to-face communication in which their personality and social status will be signalled through physical attributes such as body shape, skin colour and interactional style, accent, and clothing.
>
> (Yates 1996: 108)

One important aspect of membership of this new culture and of virtual communities is the need to learn about the new writing culture which characterises them. CMC, with the exception of video conferencing and voice recorded emails takes place by way of written language but with a considerable affinity with the spoken word in terms of often informal and colloquial style, new semiotic systems and multi-strand interchanges (one-to many and many-to-many conversations). Given that extralinguistic clues such as gestures, intonation and other contextual information tends not to be available (other than in video-conferencing), compensatory strategies have developed including

- 'posing', i.e. metatags denoting the speaker's mood or actions etc.,
- smileys, e.g. :-) for smiling, :-] for smirk,
- acronyms/abbreviations, e.g. *lol* = laughing out loud (with * representing a physical action in non-virtual space) or f2f = face-to-face, or
- neologisms, e.g. c-girl = cyber girlfriend.

These linguistic developments have considerable implications for educators, particularly in the field of languages in education and literacy. If we take literacy to be about the (linguistic) skills necessary to function in society, there clearly lies an important task of realignment and redefinition ahead. It is interesting to note, incidentally, that these new semiotic conventions are gradually finding inclusion in 'mainstream' language use: one widely used commercial word processing package, for instance, has included a number of smileys in its auto-correct tool, automatically converting, for example, :-) to ☺.

CMC can be open, i.e. freely accessible, or closed, i.e. accessible only to members. Often there is a degree of monitoring and moderation in place to ensure certain 'cultural practices' (rules of conduct) called 'netiquette' are adhered to so as to ensure appropriate conduct of members and to avoid antisocial behaviour such as 'flaming', i.e. the submission of unsuitable, inaccurate, inflammatory or obscene material or 'spamming' the distribution of unwanted mailings (see also Pachler 1999c and Tapscott 1998). CMC requires complex new skills on the part of teachers in relation to moderating and facilitating discussions in on-line learning environments (see Salmon 2000).

Ease of access to information, I have already pointed out, is an important feature of new technologies. Of particular interest, in the context of this chapter, is the need for users to develop the skills relating to identifying relevant information sources. Because all users can create content, there is a vast repository of information available, much of which is of little or no use to many users and some is even unsuitable or offensive. There is the real danger of information overload and of quantity of information being mistaken for quality of experience. Whilst so-called search engines are at hand to help with this task, selecting the right search engine for a particular task and inputting appropriate search-strings to yield maximum success are higher order skills which need to be learnt or acquired.

The particular challenge of locating relevant information through new technologies arises from the provisionality of the information available. Because of the flexibility of the medium and the ease with which alterations can be made, Uniform Resource Locators (URLs) and their content tend to change frequently. The openness of the system means that there is no or little editorial control; publishing houses and their scrutiny procedures are no longer needed. This, in turn, requires the ability on the part of users to discern reliability, validity etc. of content. The higher order skills of evaluation of web-based material, therefore, become central to the effective use of new technologies (see e.g. Pachler 1999b and 1999c) and there is the need to develop in learners the ability to locate, analyse, manipulate, reflect on and reuse information.

Talking about educational software, Seymour Papert (1996) warns of the influence of software barons on the minds (and culture) of children (see p. 2). Whilst the computer allows homestyle, i.e. independent and out-of-school, learning it is important that parents (and teachers) get to know how technology works and don't mystify it (see pp. 9–10). There is also the danger of technology being used 'mindlessly or for the profit of corporations rather than for the benefit of children'. Papert deems a common weakness of educational software to be that it 'sets out to teach the facts and skills of a subject like grammar (or math or geography) much as human teachers and textbooks have traditionally done' (p. 24). This, in his view, neglects the fact that, rather than teaching, '(its) contribution (is) to dissolve barriers to learning grammar (or other subjects, NP) by allowing (the learner) to find meaning for it as a powerful idea – one that she could use, and in a project she had invented herself' (p. 24). In other words, Papert is weary of a didactic mode of (educational) software which replaces the guiding contribution of the teacher by prescribing highly structured paths through the software-based 'learning experience' and which imposes considerable limitations on learners in terms of their ability to shape and structure their way through the material.

Papert (1996: 50–4) identifies three objectionable features of the educational software culture he sees developing:

- it gives agency to the machine, not the child;
- it is deceptive and proud of it; and
- it favours quick reactions over long-term thinking.

The first of his three objections posits that we see children as '"answering machines" – hoping to instruct them by putting questions to them and correcting the answers given' instead of ensuring 'children retain control of their intellectual process, developing their innate instincts to pose and pursue their own questions' (Papert 1996: 50).

The second suggests that 'learning is a nasty pill that must be sugarcoated with fun and games' instead of ensuring 'learning is embraced and enjoyed' (Papert 1996: 50–1).

The third refers to the tendency of a problem/answer construct and to provide feedback in the form of right/wrong comments instead of encouraging children to construct meaning and solve problems. In his research and development work Papert uses the construct 'microworld' to embrace this notion. (see e.g. Pachler 1999b for a more detailed discussion of this concept).

From all this follows that the critical evaluation of the use of technology for educational purposes is imperative. Young learners, I would suggest, may lack the independence of mind to critically evaluate educational software unaided.

> In fact, what has been revealed is that pupils tend to surrender their respon-sibility for learning as a result of using computer assisted learning programs. They tailor their responses and initiative according to the task. Moreover, this places pupils in a purely reactive role.
>
> (Heath 1995: on-line)

This observation by Joanne Heath with reference to M. Guillot (1994) does, of course, not negate the fact that new technologies can make a valuable contribution to the learning process. It does, however, underline that teachers and educators continue to have an important role to play in the learning process.

Another important aspect of much new technology is its non-linear nature. Hyperlinking breaks up traditional conceptual notions of narrative such as the display, in Western cultures, of text from front to back and from top left to bottom right, and in terms of beginning, middle and end. Hyperlinking brings with it the need to become socialised into new ways of 'reading' and processing 'text'. We tend to be determined, in part, in our reading and in how we arrange our ideas by the order that is commonly understood (see e.g. Purves 1998: 237). In hypertext, information is stored and displayed in new ways: 'text' is electronic and has less semblance of permanence than its hand-written or printed predecessor and pages or units of text are linked not in a linear manner but in information webs through which the 'reader' can determine her own path, allowing for exploration and unplanned and unintended learning outcomes, with no two 'readers' proceeding the in same way and with even a single 'reader' having difficulties in retracing her own journey (see Purves 1998: 238).

Reading, writing and critical thinking, therefore, are extremely important:

> (while) N-Geners do have all the world's information at their fingertips, it isn't accessed simply by pointing the mouse over the right link and clicking. It is accessed by choosing the right link to click on from a menu of items in the thousands. Never before has it been more necessary that children learn how to read, write, and think critically. It's not just point and click. It's point, read, think, click.
>
> (Tapscott 1998: 63)

As is the case in the comic strip and comic book, new technologies allow for multimodality, i.e. the combination of text, (moving) images and sound. This characteristic and potential has huge implications in terms of visual and (critical) media literacies as multimodality is characterised by the interplay of different semiotic systems. Electronic and multimedia text is governed by different discourse and composition rules and patterns from traditional text. Conventions of navigating through computer screens with their new and unfamiliar iconic interfaces need to be learnt.

> Hypertext therefore sharpens the question of the relationship of a reader with the text by raising and holding as paradox that the reader is both passive and active; the reader both makes meaning of the text and takes meaning from it.
>
> (Purves 1998: 244)

Preparation for adult life

The changes brought about by new technologies in general, and the internet in particular, are beginning to affect learners significantly in terms of their personal and professional adult lives:

> the way we create wealth, the enterprise, the nature of commerce and marketing, the delivery system for entertainment, the role and dynamics of learning in the economy, the nature of government and governance, our culture and arguably the role of the nation-state in the body politic.
>
> (Tapscott 1998: 3)

New technologies have transformed the workplace in recent decades and will continue to do so in the foreseeable future:

> (new) technology permeates the work activities of nearly half the adult population and creates new literacy demands for communication,

gathering information, solving daily work-related problems, and monitoring performance.

(Mikulecky and Kirkley 1998: 304)

These new demands, according to Mikulecky and Kirkley (see 1998: 304–5) are brought about by participation in the global marketplace, democratisation of workplace decision making, synchronous production (just-in-time target delivery, statistical process control, self-management teams) and multiple roles on most jobs leading to the requirement of higher level literacy, communication and computation skills as well as the use of technical tools for processing and communicating information on the part not only of high- but also of low- and middle-level occupations. Employees need to be able to access and comprehend information presented on computer screens, analyse the use and reliability of information, transpose information from one structure and context to another and apply it to solve problems (see Mikulecky and Kirkley 1998: 313). In addition, the authors point out that these demands keep changing as newer technologies appear, and that this results in a perpetual challenge to keep up with changing technical and literacy skills surrounding these new technologies (see Mikulecky and Kirkley 1998: 310).

Clearly, the focus on learner training, i.e. the ability of learners to know how to learn, and the training in thinking and problem solving skills and not on computer skills per se has important implications for school-based education: 'people will need to learn and apply higher order thinking skills such as inquiry, investigation, organization, reflection, reasoning, analysis, and problem solving' (Mikulecky and Kirkley 1998: 314) in the context of simulation and problem-based learning in which new technologies play an integral part.

One aspect of the use of new technologies in the workplace that makes headlines is the use of the internet and email for personal and private purposes as many companies are becoming increasingly concerned about employees using their working hours and resources for personal use. Many companies are starting to monitor their employees' on-line behaviour and more and more employees are being caught out leaking information or distributing unsuitable material costing them their jobs and marriages:

> (people) think email is private, but it's the most exposed form of communication on earth. Unless you have a strong and well-defined framework of what is acceptable and what is unacceptable, you are bound to have problems.

(Julian Stainton quoted in Waldman 1999: 4)

Young people, therefore, need not only be taught the skills necessary to make the best use of new technologies in their adult lives and in the 'traditional' workplace but also to understand the new possibilities for commercial activity afforded to them by new technologies, i.e. electronic commerce (e-commerce), as well as the implications for them both as consumers and service/information providers. They need to become familiar with the working practices characteristic of today's workplace, such as file sharing, group editing and collaborative writing.

Jeff Kuppermann and Raven Wallace (1998), for example, propose an interesting framework suggesting learners should engage in writing projects which pursue meaningful learning goals such as:

- engagement;
- consideration of purpose and audience;
- evaluation and synthesis of information;
- developing of personal standards for writing;
- cultural awareness; and
- participation in a literate community.

Furthermore, they identify seven activities as being characteristic of potentially successful projects:

- publishing;
- friendship exchanges;
- data sharing;
- collaborative artefact creation;
- peer critiquing;
- mentoring; and
- question asking.

Don Tapscott identifies ten themes of what he calls 'N-Gen (Net-Generation) culture' which, in turn, he considers to lead to a new enterprise culture (see Figure 2.2). This 'new culture of work' is characterised by features that young people need to be taught during their formal education.

Figure 2.2 The relationship between N-Gen culture and the new culture of work
© Don Tapscott 1998: 211 (permission obtained)

Stephen Pritchard describes the internet as 'one of the world's greatest egalitarian forces' (1999: 6), allowing individuals and small companies with limited capital to compete with large multinationals and young entrepreneurs are continuously able to find new ways of income generation via the use of new technologies.

However, Pritchard points out, fraud and misrepresentation are serious concerns. Caution and requisite skills are necessary to ensure consumers do not fall victim to rogue traders. Once again, schools can be seen to have an important educational role in this respect: how can one ascertain that the company one buys from is doing business legitimately and that they operate satisfactory standards of security, for instance in how they deal with personal data?

In Tapscott's words (1998: 247) we face the problem of '"little brother" and "dataveillance"'. We leave a 'trail of digital crumbs' (Tapscott 1998: 247) when we use the internet, i.e. we are often required to provide personal detail by an increasing number of content providers in return for accessing their site or accept so-called 'cookies', files containing information concerning our on-line habits and profile (often including username and password) when accessing many sites.

Bertram Bruce and Maureen Hogan (1998) describe how technologies embed themselves in everyday discourse and activity and how we lose sight of the way they shape our daily lives (p. 270) and that we need to remain alert to the ways in which technology affects our lives despite the fact that we often cannot see it directly. For them, '(literacy) means not just reading and writing texts, but "reading" the world, and the technological artifacts within it' (Bruce and Hogan 1998: 272).

As educators we face the challenge of making these implicit aspects of new technologies explicit to young people in order to allow them to become emancipated users of, and prevent them from being abused by, new technologies. Other issues to be considered in the context of the use of new technologies are ethical in nature, such as copyright matters, pornography or plagiarism, which, as educators, we also need to give due consideration in our curricula.

In case I am misunderstood: I don't, of course, place an emphasis on new technologies and related skills, knowledge and understanding simply in order to make education subservient to the needs of UK plc but because of my belief in our moral duty as educators to prepare young people as best we can for the demands of adult life, to make maximum personal and professional gains in life and to allow them to play the fullest possible part in the societies and cultures they live in.

Conclusion

In summary, then, the following can be seen as the main motivations for including new technologies in the curriculum:

1 that it will improve the economy by producing young people able to work in modern industry and commerce (the economic imperative);

2 that it involves activities that accord with progressivist or constructivist views of learning (its value to learning);

3 that it has some intrinsic value through its unique concepts and processes that are essential to the development of all individuals, in the same way as the study of mathematics, science, history, humanities, etc. (its intrinsic value);

4 a modern citizen has to have an understanding of technology to be able to function, and to be collectively in control of the development of society that is increasingly driven by technology (education for citizenship).

(McCormick 1999: 217)

Notes

1 Thanks to my colleague Dr Douglas Allford, Institute of Education, University of London for his constructive comments on a draft of this chapter.
2 Internet Relay Chat. IRC is a virtual meeting place where you can 'meet' and talk to people from all over the world. To use IRC you need internet access and a program such as MIRC available at http://www.mirc.co.uk.
3 Multi-user domain, Object Oriented; see e.g. Café Mooland available at http://www-moolano.berkeley.edu. To use a MOO you need internet access and a telnet program on your computer which tends to be standard specification of newer computers.

Questions

In this chapter I argue the case for the development of higher-order ICT skills through school-based learning:

1 What are the main reasons for the need to develop higher-order ICT skills and why do schools provide relevant contexts for learning of this kind?
2 What do you consider to be important features supporting effective ICT-based learning in school environments? What approaches are less conducive?
3 Which out-of-school experiences can be used to achieve effective higher-order ICT skills development? How can they best be integrated into school-based learning?

Further reading

Leask, M. and Pachler, N. (eds) (1999) *Learning to Teach using ICT in the Secondary School*, London: Routledge.
This edited volume offers a collection of contributions from researchers and practitioners dealing with the implementation of ICT in secondary education and with ways ICT can be employed in teaching, learning and professional development.

Papert, S. (1996) *The Connected Family: Bridging the Digital Generation Gap*, Atlanta, Georgia: Longstreet Press.
An inspirational book about the impact of ICT on traditional learning paradigms by one of the pioneers of ICT use in teaching and learning.

Reinking, D., McKenna, M., Labbo, L. and Kieffer, R. (eds) (1998) *Handbook of Literacy and Technology: Transformations in a Post-typographic World*, Mahwah, NJ: Lawrence Erlbaum Associates.

This handbook brings together a range of interesting, research-based contributions exploring the impact of new technologies on notions of literacy.

Tapscott, D. (1998) *Growing Up Digital: The Rise of the Net Generation.* New York: McGraw-Hill.

An interesting account and evaluation of the impact of ICT on aspects of socialisation of young people.

References

Bruce, B. and Hogan, M. (1998) 'The disappearance of technology: toward an ecological model of literacy', in Reinking, D., McKenna, M., Labbo, L. and Kieffer, R. (eds) *Handbook of Literacy and Technology: Transformations in a Post-typographic World*, Mahwah, NJ: Lawrence Erlbaum Associates, pp. 269–81.

Crook, C. (1994) *Computers and the Collaborative Experience of Learning*, London: Routledge.

DfEE (1997a) *Connecting the Learning Society, National Grid for Learning: The Government's Consultation Paper*, London: HMSO.

DfEE (1997b) *Preparing for the Information Age*, Synoptic report of the Education Department's Superhighways Initiative, London: HMSO.

Guillot, M. (1994) 'A word of caution', *Computers and Education* vol. 23.

Hargreaves, D. (1997) 'A road to the learning society', *School Leadership and Management*, Vol 17. No. 1, pp. 9–21.

Haughton, E. (1999) 'Look what they've done to my brain, ma', *The Independent Education*, June 3, p. 2.

Healy, J. (1999) *Failure to Connect*, London: Simon and Schuster.

Heath, J. (1995) 'When interactive media is not truly interactive', in *Active Learning 3 Teaching with Multimedia*, CTISS Publications. Available at http://www.cti.ac.uk/publ/actlea/issue3/heath/

Johnston, C. (1999) 'Infants warned off computers', in *TES*, June 18, p. 7.

Kramsch, C. (1996) 'The cultural component of language teaching', in Zeitschrift fur interkulturellen Fremdsprachenunterricht 1, 2 on-line: http://www.ualberta.ca/~german/ejournal/archive/kramsch2.htm

Kupperman, J. and Wallace, R. (1998) 'Evaluating an intercultural internet writing project through a framework of activities and goals', Paper presented at the annual meeting of the American Educational Research Association, [on-line] Available: http://hice.eecs.umich.edu/papers/aera98/

Leask, M. and Pachler, N. (1999) 'Introduction', in id (ed.) *Learning to Teach using ICT in the Secondary School*, London: Routledge, pp. xvii–xix.

Lemke, J. (1998) 'Metamedia literacy: transforming meanings and media', in Reinking, D., McKenna, M., Labbo, L. and Kieffer, R. (eds) *Handbook of Literacy and Technology: Transformations in a Post-typographic World*, Mahwah, NJ: Lawrence Erlbaum Associates, pp. 283–301.

McCormick, R. (1999) 'Curriculum development and new information technology', in Moon, B. and Murphy, P. (eds) *Curriculum in Context*, London: Paul Chapman Publishing in association with The Open University, pp. 212–29.

McKinsey and Company (1997) *The Future of Information Technology in UK Schools*, London.

Mikulecky, L. and Kirkley, J. (1998) 'Changing workplaces, changing classes: the new role of technology in workplace literacy', in Reinking, D., McKenna, M., Labbo, L. and Kieffer, R. (eds) *Handbook of Literacy and Technology: Transformations in a Post-typographic World*, Mahwah, NJ: Lawrence Erlbaum Associates, pp. 303–20.

Millard, E. (1997) 'New technologies, old inequalities – variations found in the use of computers by pupils at home with implications for the school curriculum', Paper presented at the British Educational Research Association Annual Conference, University of York. Available at:
http://www.leeds.ac.uk/educol/documents/000000362.htm

Mortimore, P. (ed.) *Understanding Pedagogy and its Impact on Learning*, London: Sage.

Noss, R. and Pachler, N. (1999) 'The challenge of new technologies: doing old things in a new way, or doing new things?' in Mortimore, P. (ed.) *Understanding Pedagogy and its Impact on Learning*, London: Sage, pp. 195–211.

Pachler, N. (1999a) 'Teaching and learning culture', in id (ed.) *Teaching Modern Foreign Languages at Advanced Level*, London: Routledge, pp. 76–92.

Pachler, N. (1999b) 'Theories of learning and ICT', in Leask, M. and Pachler, N. (ed.) *Learning to Teach Using ICT in the Secondary School*, London: Routledge, pp. 3–18.

Pachler, N. (1999c) 'Using the internet as teaching and learning tool', in Leask, M. and Pachler, N. (eds) *Learning to Teach Using ICT in the Secondary School*, London: Routledge, pp. 51–70.

Papert, S. (1996) *The Connected Family: Bridging the Digital Generation Gap*, Atlanta, Georgia: Longstreet Press.

Pritchard, S. (1999) 'Would you buy a used car on this website?' *The Independent on Sunday*, June 6, p. 8.

Purves, A. (1998) 'Flies in the web of hypertext', in Reinking, D., McKenna, M., Labbo, L. and Kieffer, R. (eds) *Handbook of Literacy and Technology: Transformations in a Post-typographic World*, Mahwah, NJ: Lawrence Erlbaum Associates, pp. 235–51.

Salmon, G. (2000) E-Moderating: The Key to Teaching and Learning On-line, London: Kogan Page.

Stevenson, D. (1997) *Information and Communications Technology in UK Schools. An Independent Inquiry*, London.

Tapscott, D. (1998) *Growing Up Digital: the Rise of the Net Generation*, New York: McGraw-Hill (See also http://www.growingupdigital.com).

Yates, S. (1996) 'English in cyberspace', in Goodman, S. and Graddol, D. (1996) *Redesigning English: New Texts, New Identities*, London: Routledge, pp. 106–40.

Waldman, S. (1999) 'Beware the mail detectors', in *The Guardian*, April 29.

Warschauer, M. (1998) *New Media, New Literacies: Challenges for the Next Century*, Plenary address at the annual conference of the English Teachers Association of Israel, Jerusalem. Available at http://www.boker.org.il/eng/etni/etaitalk2.html.

Wolff, D. (1998) 'Fremdsprachenlernen in der Informationsgesellschaft: einige Anmerkungen zu gesellschaftlichen und medialen Rahmenbedingungen', in *TELL&CALL*, No. 4, pp. 6–13.

3 The Virtual Community of Teachers

'Power stations' for learners nationwide?

Niki Davis

Introduction

What counts as a 'good education' for citizens of the information age? What do young people need to prepare them to move beyond 'immigrant' status within the emerging Learning Society? One potential for information and communications technologies (ICT) is to change the profession of teaching, so what can the UK National Grid for Learning mean for the teaching profession? Can teachers join to form a virtual community that acts as an interconnected grid supporting learning across the nation? This chapter attempts to draw upon developments and research of the 1990s around the world, real and virtual, and to move beyond them into the future. The author acknowledges that such an attempt is risky in the extreme given the increasing speed of change in educational and social systems and their interaction. To predict a year ahead may be reasonable, but to attempt a view that will be of use to teachers in the future may well prove to be foolish!

Schoolteachers have always tended to teach a historically based curriculum in order to impart their society's cultural norms, presumably with the hope of instilling respect into students for their elders. If such an aim is too contentious for the reader, perhaps it can be accepted that students have much to gain from the knowledge that previous generations have stored. Also that they, as citizens, will be more comfortable and better able to contribute to society if they have been prepared to make use of the accumulated skills, information and systems.

This chapter takes a critical view of a number of initiatives and projects to identify pointers to describe the 'good education' that teachers may seek using ICT themselves in their communities. The chapter will then attempt to anchor these against theoretical perspectives, before taking the final risk to give the reader the author's current view of what will count in 'good education' for the citizens of the information age. A major initiative that will be critically examined is the embryonic British 'National Grid for Learning'.

Is a national grid for learning possible?

In January 1998, the British Government announced a major initiative: the building of a 'National Grid for Learning' (NGfL).

In January 1999, Charles Clarke, the Education Minister responsible for ICT in schools, announced a major upgrade of the National Grid for Learning with the statement that:

> The Government is fully committed to improving ICT in schools in its aim to raise educational standards
> * it is developing a National Grid for Learning to deliver high quality educational content and other resources to teachers, pupils and other learners.
>
> (http://www.dfee.gov.uk/bett/bett.htm)

The analogy of a national grid takes on many aspects of the promises that developers of information and communication technologies (ICT) in education have promoted over the years. Optimists have promised individualised and flexible learning opportunities at anytime and in anyplace. The restrictions that come with this particular analogy also highlight for me the way in which an increasingly political agenda is influencing deployment of ICT. Exploration of this analogy for the information society's major support infrastructure may therefore inform our view of 'good education'. This critical examination of the NGfL could also be applied to other analogies. It therefore also illustrates for us ways in which computer simulations and other analogies are useful despite their inaccuracy, providing that we examine them for both the value of the model, as well as its limitations and inaccuracy.

What is a national grid for learning? First, the words will be discussed one at a time.

National

The NGfL is a set of initiatives to make use of the internet for education and training. One of the major strengths of the internet is that it is international: it is as easy to send and receive messages with those the other side of the world as it is with people in the local community. Similarly documents and multimedia are available from many countries. Even economically disadvantaged countries are determined to find their way forward using the internet. So why is the first word of the NGfL 'National', leaving out the prefix 'Inter'? My guess is that the answer lies in politics and national economics. It would be inappropriate in the 1990s to suggest that one government would be undertaking a major initiative on behalf of education in an international context. Indeed the task ahead is big enough for one country, but I suggest that 'good education' is a more likely result if the designers do not limit their vision to this one nation. Environmental education is an example of one key area that could benefit from an international approach.

There are major initiatives to support schools and other sectors of education in many countries on all continents. Many of their titles also imply similar geographical limitations. For example, European Schoolnet implies limitation to Europe. The structure and style should be suited to users in European schools.

Perhaps it is just as well that such initiatives are limited to an audience that may be defined. I know that European Schoolnet is facing major challenges in its attempt to link up the information and communication for schools and educationalists across regions and countries. The challenges and benefits of communicating across disciplines and phases of education should also be acknowledged, as well as communities and regions, and I will return to that later.

Grid

The word grid is puzzling unless the analogy with the supply of electricity in the United Kingdom is understood. The UK's national grid links up the power stations and it also has some international connections, for example into France. These connections permit a power station, which experiences demands for electrical current in excess of ability to generate, to draw additional power from another power station in the grid. The pattern for demand of electrical supply can described as 'bursty' at times. For example, when many people in a city such as Manchester cook lunch at 1 pm on Sunday, there is a 'burst' of demand. A much larger power station would be required to service this demand if the national grid were not available.

Let us get back to the NGfL: Can it become possible to have 'power stations' generating 'energy' for learning? And, if so, will they be prepared to link together to support each other such that they can respond to bursts in demand for 'good education'? I suggest that it is teachers who must be the power stations creating and responding to the demand for learning and they who will provide the energy for learners. The appliances which will be 'switched on' (the cookers in the analogy of cooking a Sunday lunch above) will be both the traditional forms of educational resources such as textbooks and pencils and artist materials and newer forms which incorporate ICT, such as the web pages from the internet, desk top publishing software and digital cameras. Teachers' 'stored energy' will also become available in the form of integrated learning systems and computer assisted tutorial software disseminated by publishers. Publishers are already adapting to a developing electronic market where authors continue to be involved in the updating and development of their material accompanied by a team of multimedia designers who understand the ways in which information must be adapted across media and communication systems. Research indicates that teachers are the key to effective use of ICT in schools: how else can the variability be explained (Wood 1999; available on-line at http://telematics3.ex.ac.uk/erf/present/lecture4/wood1.htm)? Teachers must remain the key actors to facilitate 'good education' given the volume and range of interaction and resources that must be organised and developed for education: the power stations of the NGfL.

There are clear signs of the acceptance of the key role of teachers in Europe and in other continents. Guy Weets, in his briefing paper for the current European Commission research plan known as Framework V, stated: 'Preparing teachers is perceived as the main critical success factor in deploying information and communications technologies in education'. In the USA the President's Panel on

Educational Technology in 1997 made six recommendations, including 'Give special attention to professional development', which included 'ongoing mentoring and consultative support', time and 'mobilisation to help our national schools of education so that they are capable of preparing the next generation of American teachers to make effective use of technology' (Panel on Educational Technology Report 1997). In 1995 the United Nations Commission on Science and Technology examined the benefits and risks of ICT for the development of poor countries and came to the conclusion that, although the costs are high, the costs of not embracing them are even higher. Veen and Dhanarajan (1999) suggest that teacher training is a critical factor in societies where high quality education is needed and traditional systems cannot meet the demand.

So the question becomes: Will teachers be prepared to link together to support each other such that they can respond to bursts in demand for 'good education' using the NGfL?

Early practice seems to suggest that this might be the case. More than 10 years ago I was employed in creating a forerunner of the Information Superhighway. As 'Development Officer for Micro Awareness' for the whole of Northern Ireland I was almost overwhelmed with the task of supporting teachers' use of ICT in prevocational education. I resorted to ICT as a tool and ended up leading a service for teachers across the UK called ResCue. It supported the adoption of resource based learning in vocational education, accessed through British Telecom's (BT's) on-line service for education, and provided a forerunner of websites. ResCue (Resources Cue) had three main sections: catalogues, full-text resources, and notice boards with related course information from the 11 Regional Curriculum Bases across the UK (Davis 1987). Resources came in two forms:

1   Assignments, which could be saved and edited by teachers using a word processor, thus enabling them to adjust assignments to the local contexts and resources. A working group of Regional Curriculum Base staff, from across the UK, selected and catalogued the assignments from those contributed by teachers. Contributions from less than 10 per cent of teachers provided a wealth of material for all teachers who had been challenged with a new curriculum.
2   Relevant published resources were selected and catalogued by a librarian to ensure that teachers could search for resources according to their perceived educational need. The changed curriculum included development of students' basic skills, so my librarian colleague developed a new cataloguing system permitting searches for assignments that developed a core skill (e.g. reading) in particular vocational areas (e.g. mechanical engineering).

There are other examples of teachers sharing their skills and knowledge through electronic networks to develop professional practice. A well known example in America is LAB Net in which science teachers were supported by the Technology in Education Research Consortium (TERC) in Boston and they also supported each other to adopt a problem based learning approach to science education

(Ruopp *et al.* 1993). A more recent example originating in the UK is MirandaNet, where teachers and others support professional and schools' development as well as research (http://www.mirandanet.com). Regional services have also evolved to support teachers and schools. An interesting side effect of one such service in the state of Victoria in Australia is that students can have a 'learning account' in more than one school through which they take responsibility for their use of resources and links between courses and teachers who are in different schools.

The answer is therefore yes, some teachers are prepared to link together to support the profession, when given appropriate leadership and support. However whether they can respond to bursts in demand for 'good education' using ICT is a more complex question. In the examples given above, an agency provided the stimulus, structure, management and quality control for teachers. Teachers are likely to need to be organised into some form of grid that provides them with some form of reward for the energy they provide to the grid. In the examples above the agencies were government funded. With an increasingly 'free market' approach to education, an expansion in the variety of agencies is likely to emerge. A proportion of these agencies will be seeking financial reward rather than the altruistic development of education accompanied by recognition of their contribution to society.

Therefore good education must increase the care (both support and scrutiny) for the quality and source of energy supplied though a NGfL. Such a national initiative requires ongoing funding for infrastructure plus considerations of issues of security and safety. Services are likely to need the equivalent of:

- a fuse or filter in each appliance, similar to an electrical plug;
- protection for the 'substations' and organisations; and
- consumer protection to ensure quality and reliability are as advertised.

Learning

The NGfL, like electricity, is available from many sources and the flow of energy is in two directions. Education can therefore become less bound to time and space. Already there are good examples where ICT is used to de-restrict access to school due to social or geographical exclusion. An example of the former is the use of videoconferencing in the Strathclyde region of Scotland where pupils in small relatively isolated schools, including those on islands, use the video-conference to link with expertise in other schools and communities. The Open School in the South West of England supports the education of many pupils who are excluded from school due to health or behaviour. Open School started with more traditional paper communication complemented with fax and phone for tutorial support. Pupils across the UK are now enthusiastically using more ICT and they are likely to support their tutors' growing skill with ICT.

The use of ICT also encourages collaboration between and beyond classrooms. In 'Computer Based Learning: Potential into Practice' we describe putting the potential of electronic communications into practice in primary and secondary schools (Davis 1994). The primary schools were small schools that found the communications with other small schools across the UK valuable to extend their pupils' curriculum and participation. It was led by my university at that time and focused activity on one theme and one day for the group of small schools. For example pupils in participating schools shared information on playground games on the first of May in 1994. Unfortunately the small schools did not take over the co-ordination for themselves and the application died away, despite its value to them. The secondary school example focused on a foreign language Newspaper Day, organised as part of the Campus World service provided by British Telecom PLC, and supplemented with additional supporting activities for and with student teachers developing their practice in school with university support. More formalised support had also emerged in the form of an educational service marketed by a telecommunications company in the USA. AT&T now market a successful service for schools which promotes the strategy of 'learning circles' where pupils, supported by their teacher, lead a small project within a common theme which gathers its information with the support of pupils in other classes (Riel 1994). The service introduces and supports teachers to adopt this pedagogy and links them with other schools in the circle. Note this partnership across sectors (a university professor and a telecommunications company), who have developed a new educational service for schools, with integral teacher training, which is marketed by teachers now working for the company.

All of these examples emerged prior to the NGfL and are likely to proliferate as it becomes more accessible. It should also be noted that every one of them challenges the traditional curriculum's split into subject disciplines and the timetable that puts the curriculum into regular slots of time, classroom and teacher. Every one of them engages the core skills of literacy and numeracy adding to them learning skills and ICT. This is not simply an extension of the old foundation of the 3 Rs, but an acknowledgement of lifelong learning (see also Chapter 14). These core skills will remain the core for the pupils' development throughout their life and will need continuous nourishment and support.

It becomes clear that ICT has many roles to play in education and will continue to develop three dimensions through this century:

- ICT aspects of core skills;
- ICT as a theme of knowledge; and
- ICT as a means of enriching learning

We could say the same of language, of course. One further option is a curriculum organised along the lines of projects and themes, though which learners develop their values, skills and knowledge in a way that is meaningful to their interests under the guidance of their many teachers. It is likely that ICT will be applied to underpin the organisation and assessment of this curriculum using instructional information management systems, such as that described by David Carter as applied to supervision of student teachers in Australia (Carter 2000; forthcoming at http://www.triangle.co.uk/jit/).

Who are the teachers in the information society?

This critical examination of the NGfL has concentrated on teaching. Although it is recognised that learning and the learner are the centre of education, teaching remains the key to a 'good education'. However, it is necessary to expand the notion of who is 'the teacher'. Clearly teacher educators and school teachers are experts in this role. Other teachers who are joining the force in increasing numbers are the learners, when they become peer tutors. Parents and community workers such as librarians, social, church and health workers also facilitate learning and can be teachers at times. School pupils may also teach these adults. Members of the work community also take on the role of teacher when they provide work experience and other forms of apprentice education. This expanded view of teachers will now be illustrated with examples from our work on the emerging NGfL. Many more examples and related issues will be found in the synoptic evaluation report of the twelve superhighways for education projects edited by Peter Scrimshaw (1997).

Teachers are beginning to work with many colleagues and the NGfL opens up such collaboration across the world, however, perhaps the most important collaborating teachers are those closest: the learners themselves. In the largest superhighways for education project, the Bristol Education On-line project (BEON) created by ICL with BT, the most important change in teaching strategy that was promoted was the use of peer tutoring. The schools were faced with so many new ICT applications that the Telematics team from Exeter University recognised a need for a coping strategy. Bruce Wright evaluated practice in a school where a wide range of ICT was employed in good educational practice, Robin Hood primary school in Birmingham, looking for the key to this. He identified that peer tutoring was the key, because it freed up the teacher to provide higher-level support. Peer tutoring was also recognised as an important way of extending pupils' skills in learning and communication and their self esteem. The quality was ensured though participative training of peer tutors with the award of status and a community of practice. It became an important part of the school ethos. In doing so the school showed clear evidence of having become a 'learning organisation', which was able to promote learning within it, in addition to its published status as an organisation to educate pupils. The Telematics Team identified two schools and teachers within the BEON trial group of 12 schools, who would be able to deploy the strategy with minimum disruption and maximum support. The concept was introduced and training supported with video and print materials. Most importantly, a videoconference between BEON teachers and those in Robin Hood school was used to give BEON teachers reference information from their peers. This assured them that such a strategy was achievable and enabled them to examine the stages that experienced teachers had adopted as they developed what turned out to be a whole school policy. Teachers in Robin Hood school had trained their peer tutors using role play of good and bad teaching. Through this the pupils set out their approaches to peer tutoring, such as the peer tutor was not to touch the mouse, but could point to relevant points on the screen.

These were captured over the videoconference along with an example of peer tutoring. The accreditation of peer tutors is also formalised in Robin Hood school such that peer tutors are: identified by a badge; awarded a certificate, and the approach is noted where appropriate within school policy. The adoption of peer tutoring within the BEON project was evaluated as highly successful (Sharp, Still and Davis 1998).

Peer tutoring with ICT is not uncommon today, but it is rarely recognised and promoted. Perhaps this is related to the need to accept 'just in time' learning for all, including teachers and support staff. Recent in-service courses with practising teachers, led by the author and delivered on-line, have explicitly changed our approach to one that promotes peer tutoring. In this way we provide a model for teachers to follow with greater comfort, having experienced it personally. The first step is to recognise individual strengths and to build confidence in those and the ability to teach peers. Too often supporting others has resulted in a 'take over' strategy where the difficulty is resolved by 'doing it for them', possibly even reducing the ability for those who asked for help in perceiving what was done. Training peer tutors involves them in reflecting how to tutor such that their learner is able to perform the task independently on other occasions. Training teachers to develop and support peer tutoring takes this further into the sphere of training trainers, celebrating achievement and co-ordination.

Experts other than teachers are also important in education. Informal contributions of visitors and visits often provide important motivation and resources, including the relocation of an expert onto the school premises. One example is the artist in residence scheme. The Telematics Centre in Exeter adopted this idea and transferred it to a virtual approach; first with a business expert offering advice on pupils' project work through desktop conferencing. Later, as images became accessible over communications technologies, an 'artist in non residence' successfully supported curriculum development, extending pupils' art appreciation and the continuing professional development of their teacher. Our first collaborating artist, Nick Eastwood, has an international reputation for his abstract work and, as a university media librarian, also has access to a very large set of images to share with pupils in schools. His approach is to agree a topic with a teacher and to work, over videoconference link, with a small group of students extending their skills and knowledge. The pupils' brief is to undertake the work, to operate the videoconference sessions, and to share what they have learned with their class. The teacher manages this as one of the activities in her classroom and in addition has access to expertise and support to develop her knowledge and skills. She does not expect to become proficient in all the new techniques or art history, but her knowledge naturally grows as the topic progresses (Sharp, Davis and Still 1998: 34–39).

Adults other than teachers may also be associated with museums and art galleries. The Royal Albert Memorial Museum in Exeter commissioned a totem pole, which was carved 'live' in June 1998 in the museum by a master craftsman of the Nuu-chah-nulth Nation from Vancouver Island in Canada. Alongside the live exhibition schools discussed the project, spanning almost all subjects in their curriculum. Several schools designed and carved their own totem poles, one of which now proudly stands high in the school playground. Although many visited the museum in person, other visits were made virtually using the complementary Telematics Centre website on the internet, which supported both teachers and pupils to engage with the experience and build a relationship with the First Nations' people. The quality of these relationships, together with the supporting www resources and discussions undertaken and archived on the web, has reinforced the understanding of the meaning and values inherent in Nuu-chah-nulth culture. It also forms the context within which the English pupils begin to further the understanding of their own personal values, meanings and beliefs and those of the communities within which they live. The additional teachers who joined in the educational process included crafts people and museum staff. The interview data from the discussion has been integrated into the website complemented by curriculum guidance and professional video, images and audio clips. Researchers believe that this project exemplifies best practice in how the NGfL can extend and enrich the curriculum and participation. Further pupil and festival activities will be required to continue to keep the museums exhibitions lively and educational (Exeter University projects led by Penni Tearle and Dominic Prosser are publicly available at http://telematics.ex.ac.uk/projects.htm).

Activities such as these are 'fertilising' the growth of a wealth of resources that are transformed into new resources and media. These will shorten the learning curve for teachers who follow. Many teachers will also demand their own mediator to assist the development of their practice, a development of both knowledge and skills. The author believes that the community of practice that is needed will be best supported through courses that establish appropriate practice and provide the stimulus for further development. Such courses will need to model good practice and The Telematics Centre has created and piloted several approaches, two of which will now be contrasted. They are for two key NGfL participants: librarian and teachers who join these accredited courses provided by the University of Exeter. The librarians' course acknowledges that librarians' working practice in libraries often focuses on books and assignments to locate information and advise readers on such library skills. The Exeter course for librarians getting to grips with information and communications technology therefore has an interface that develops as follows:

1   they enter through a picture of a library door;
2   a plan of their library study centre provides spaces for communications and for self study;
3   the resources are organised onto book shelves of topics and chapters; and
4   each chapter provides an overview in text, explanation and web links and a task.

The other important features of the course are:

5   the tasks build up their knowledge of the internet and good practice;
6   links are established with other librarians with complementary interests;

7   the assignment for assessment develops the practice within libraries; and
8   the assessment is linked to recognised postgraduate qualifications for librarians.

Most recently we have built a University of Exeter Virtual Study Centre that takes a contrasting analogy for teachers, putting them in a classroom for their learning and actively fostering peer tutoring and action research. The plan of the classroom in graphic form provided the interface, and prompted appropriate study behaviour. It was designed to include all the facilities that students have when attending a course on site. The author's classroom placed teachers into groups with common interests such as 'special needs' or 'communication in education'. Although users do not hear the buzz of a busy classroom, the conversation threads could be seen in text form by clicking on a person in the classroom (for class-wide discussion) or clicking on a table to access to each group's shared working area (it also included plans and shared web links). Audio was used in the 'lecture theatre' where lectures are available as an audio file dynamically linked to change the slides at the correct time. In May 1998 the class, who were studying together virtually while located in several English counties and overseas, debated the application of educational theories, then applied these to their favourite ICT applications and contexts. Following this directed study, the teachers developed and evaluated their own practice in ICT. Selected assignments have been archived for public use in the ICT Educational Research Forum (e.g. Megan Dick and Al Reynold's joint assignment is available on http://telematics3.ex.ac.uk/erf/library/curric/reynolds.htm). The ICT Educational Research Forum is itself a later attempt to engage more practitioners in research into IT in education through the medium of the internet. These teachers are better prepared for the rich experiences and resources developing within the NGfL. In ways such as this, teachers' continuing professional development may start to take on a new dimension when supported by teacher educators on the NGfL.

Theoretical views

ICT can be considered in the Vygotskian sense as a wide range of intellectual tools that permit learners to develop their knowledge (Somekh and Davis 1997: Chapter 1). The word processor helps the individual produce clear and complex writing though a variety of stages and today's word processors are also starting to support collaborative writing. These ICT tools can be strategically important in developing written language providing the teacher guides learners in their use to support growth and fluency. Such tools could also be used as a 'crutch' which would obstruct proper growth of 'muscles' and the 'skeleton', for example by insisting that all pupils use a computer for best copy. Already the key role of teachers in this process is recognised and training is underway in initial teacher education and, for practising teachers across Britain, it has been linked to the NGfL initiative. However, given the tight set curriculum, such training is unlikely to promote the best traditions of teacher education: reflective practice that permits teachers to critically re-examine pedagogy and support changes within and across their practice. In addition, such changes, and ICT use, are not only an individual process: the advent of the NGfL raises the importance of social dimensions and organisational development too.

Bridget Somekh warned of the social and organisational constraints to the concept of ICT tools. Education is essentially a social process in which both teachers and learners are constrained by time and space and particularly by established practice. Perhaps the most constraining of these practices relates to assessment. Peer tutoring brings with it a threat to assessment of individuals. Where learners collaborate, the assessment of individual contributions and achievement can be difficult to untangle and validate, unless the learners too are empowered to collaborate in the assessment process. However risky this may appear, such risks are only an extension of the traditional control of cheating by copying. Changes to assessment are needed to encourage pupils to develop appropriate skills and work practices, including communication and teamwork.

Saloman (1996) takes this further, pointing out that undue attention to an individual's learning environment in order to research and evaluate the effect of ICT on learning with rigour causes major problems. Each individual's environment changes when ICT is introduced. The examples given above illustrate that the changes that are occurring with the introduction of an NGfL will be wide ranging. As several systems are changing simultaneously it is impossible to predict the outcomes. Recently a pump engineer told me it was difficult to analyse the flow resulting from two sets of three pumps linked in parallel because the flow is likely to become chaotic. Introduction of the NGfL into schools, homes and business plus the associated changes in education and training are much more complicated and will inevitably result in chaos at times. Saloman gives us hope that the profession will be able to cope. In setting new research questions, he notes that more innovative ICT using classrooms tend to have the opposite pattern to traditional classrooms:

> social and learning climate, interaction, mindful engagement and more innovative assessment of achievement at the core with ability and teacher behaviour at the outskirts.
>
> (Saloman 1996)

Although the teacher's behaviour is at the outskirts, it is the thoughtful support and scaffolding of the pupils' learning activities that makes the difference. Saloman also calls for research using a complex systemic approach. Such research evidence would also be valuable to guide the chaotic development of education. There are many teachers and support staff who can be guided to contribute to the enrichment and stabilising of education and they could be connected to each other through the NGfL. Therefore the information age also brings us back, from mechanical individualised approaches to learning, to a more complex understanding of the social systems and contexts that bind knowledge with skill and content with process.

Technology is relentlessly promoting change, so it is helpful to have frameworks through which to inform that change. The need for informed development of institutions, individuals and the curriculum has been described above. Three frameworks are worth briefly noting because they can permit teachers and educational organisations to promote effective development in education in these fast moving turbulent times. One framework is provided for each of the three levels.

The MIT'90s framework shown in Figure 3.1 informs organisational change. It lays out five stages that organisations commonly move through: Exploitation, Integration, Process redesign, Network redesign and Scope redefinition. Reflection on the changes to the organisation of banks serves to illustrate this framework: they moved from paper into electronic banking and diversified into financial services. Schools across the world are in the early stages of localised exploitation and internal integration. Very few have felt the forces that demand Scope redefinition, as yet. Note that careful planning will be required to achieve educational aims.

A framework for individual professional development associated with innovations is the Concerns Based Adoption Model (CBAM). It was an implicit strategy within project INTENT to develop IT in UK initial teacher training (Somekh and Davis 1997). The key feature of this model is the recognition that innovation needs to start with the concern of the individual. For this reason the concerns pass through stages. The first stage is linked to personal individual concerns and its features are a developing awareness of the potential of the innovation accompanied by seeking information. The next stage is of management and tends to parallel the MIT'90s stage of institutional co-ordination. The final stage reported focuses on the impact of the innovation though developing an understanding of its consequences, collaborating with colleagues and refocusing work. It is therefore important to give teachers access to new technologies in a way that addresses their concerns and needs. In addition, agencies have promoted change by instituting additional demands that establish new concerns for teachers to address.

---

1   Localised Exploitation

2   Internal Integration

** Nearing revolution **

3   Educational Process Redesign (internal)

4   Educational Networking Redesign

** If you're here you are ready for new partnerships **

5   Educational Scope Redefinition

Figure 3.1 The phases of organisational transformation according to the MIT'90s project (adapted from NCET 1992)

It is also possible to use a framework for the reconstruction of curricula. A holistic set of principles was developed and researched in a collaborative international process during the European Telematics for Teacher Training project with support from teacher educators, policy makers and commercial organisations (Davis and Tearle 1998). Figure 3.2 shows the principles embodied in the T3 core curriculum for ICT in teacher training. The use of principles set in a holistic framework permits curricula to be responsive to the rapidly evolving national and local infrastructure, culture and context as well as individual interests and needs. Principles remain more relevant than itemised competencies as new developments are forged in ICT and education. Detailed description and exemplars are provided on-line in the T3 Showcase at http://telematics.ex.ac.uk/T3

Major changes are expected in the systems within and beyond education as interactions increase. The multiple systems undergoing change suggest chaos points ahead. Readers fearing an apocalypse should reflect that our weather systems are also chaotic and yet we enjoy a green and fertile land in England. Change, even continuous and chaotic change, can be a good climate for growth providing the inhabitants are prepared to adjust to the conditions. Education will be an important preparation for all citizens' ability to adjust and to contribute to stabilising processes. Politics and business will also play their part, as I have already indicated, so consumer education will also be important in the consumption of education and associated resources.

What counts as a 'good education' for citizens of the information age?

This final section will now take an ambitious look into the future in an attempt to answer the question: What counts as a 'good education' for citizens of the

Figure 3.2 T3 holistic principles for ICT in teacher education
Source: T3: permission obtained

information age? In doing so the author is assuming ongoing transition to a learning society. One in which each member enjoys the responsibility of learning throughout their life and, having read the previous sections, the reader will also appreciate that learning involves teaching using strategies such as peer tutoring. Today's citizen is akin to a 'settler' of new territory where everything is strange and the appropriate behaviour requires continued conscious adaptation. In the next century learners will have grown up in the information age with habits which assume ICT and related access to information. ICT should have become part of the core or key skills of young people, especially in the UK where the government's initiatives appear to have been designed to accelerate this process.

In addition the technology will have continued to mature and to integrate computers, telephony and broadcast media. Net stations (known as dumb terminals in the first phase of computing) are likely to be used widely because they will allow individual users to centralise stores of information, thus permitting ease of access from multiple locations for multiple users with differing of levels of security. Already small file servers may be carried into the home and plugged in like any other electrical appliance. Digital TV is already available and the analogue signal will be switched off within a decade, thus pushing TV companies to market added value with digital services and appliances, including computers. It is possible that this move will have been complemented with the proliferation of managed services for education, home and work. Indeed the boundaries between places, times and activities are reducing all the time. British Airways has purchased a service from International Computers Ltd. (ICL) which permits employees to do their food shopping from work and the goods are delivered to the work address by the supermarket chain. This example shows the development of strategic partnerships between businesses: an employee's firm, an IT service company and a supplier of goods. In this case the goods are groceries, but in future the goods can be expanded to include educational resources and processes for learning at home, on the job and at school.

Curriculum

Turning to the curriculum: What counts as a 'good' curriculum for citizens of the information age? The boundaries between individual learners, phases and subject disciplines will reduce and possibly disappear, at least in terms of the school timetabled periods of 20–40 minutes that were so prevalent and ruled each day and year. ICT will pervade education in the curriculum and it will add a new dimension to core skills, including the 3 Rs (e.g. Soetaert 2000 for one discussion). ICT will also be an increasingly important resource with which to manage the curriculum.

A curriculum will be organised along the lines of projects and themes, through which learners develop their values, skills and knowledge in a way that is meaningful to their interests under the guidance of their many teachers. This should sound familiar to some teachers, especially those in the earlier years of education, although mixing age groups is less common. In addition this education may take place in many locations and parents, plus significant others, are likely to play an increasingly important role as support staff and mentors. These 'significant others' will include experts and learners in other countries. These adults and co-learners will also gain new knowledge and skills in this process, which will hopefully result in the recognition that age is only one factor in the ability to learn, teach and collaborate with others in a learning society.

ICT is also likely to become more important to the underlying systems of curriculum organisation and quality appraisal including assessment. Our experience between Exeter and the Queen's University of Belfast has validated the effective use of the internet, phone and videoconference, complemented with reduced numbers of visits, for the processes of external examination. Electronic profiles, possibly associated with the UK initiative for learning accounts, are likely to develop such that evidence of the abilities, knowledge and experience of learners as individuals and within groups may be documented. Decentralisation of records is possible with appropriate validation and security. This can support a healthy growth of diverse practices suited to communities and the needs of the individual, which will continue to change over time. The embryonic approach of such software may be seen in the core of some Integrated Learning Systems and school Management Information Systems. These will require addition of records profiling learners which link to evidence, perhaps through a relational database of curriculum, resources, learners and teachers as described by David Carter and his colleagues. Information and resources can be made accessed in whole or in part by different people, thus adding value. For example, access to elements of individual learning profiles may enable employers to recruit staff more efficiently.

Teachers

The blurring of boundaries continues when we consider teachers. The discussion of teachers above expanded the range of people falling into this category and even their location and source of reward! Most important of all the walls which isolate teachers in their classrooms are breaking down. Many have already become team workers within and across educational institutions. This blurring of boundaries across institutions and the reach into home and business will expand. So too will the collaboration of teachers of all sorts such that they become a virtual community. Teachers will be expected more than ever to become lifelong learners, undergoing continuous professional development. They will also act as superb role models for workers in other professions and their own pupils (Davis 1996).

Education for the future

A 'good education' for the citizens of the learning society will come in many forms and require active participation of all, including an acknowledgement of the responsibility to learn and to tutor. Although education is likely to remain a right for all, it will continue to be impossible to provide an equally good education for all. The upheavals of an increasingly unstable world are likely to take their toll and the vision of education in 2010 that the Association for IT in Teacher Education stimulated in 1989 still suggests a range of possible scenarios (Keeling and Whitman 1989). The most important strategy will be to ensure that all citizens recognise that education is a central process to life in an information age and that they, with their social groups, can benefit and contribute, and that the value of all levels of contribution are recognised and respected. For these reasons the marketing of education needs to increase. This may be the biggest change of all, giving rise to a host of other changes, as learners become customers and suppliers in their own right!

Acknowledgements

The author wishes to acknowledge the support and teamwork of the University of Exeter Telematics Centre, especially the Deputy Director Penni Tearle.

The Telematics for Teacher Training project (T3) was supported by DG XIII-C of the European Commission under the auspices of the Telematics Programme. Sponsoring partners include ICL, Olivetti UK, UK Open University, Dutch Telecom, Telecom Finland, Videra Oy, CET Portugal, Parque National da Peneda-Geres.

The ICT Educational Research Forum is made possible though support from BECTA, the University of Exeter, and the educational research community.

BEON was funded by ICL and BT, with some support from the University of Exeter.

Questions

1 What counts as a 'good education' for citizens of the information age within and beyond your discipline(s)?
2 What do people need to prepare them to move beyond 'immigrant' status within the emerging Learning Society?
3 Can teachers join to form a virtual community that acts as an interconnected grid supporting learning across the nation?
4 Can research into ICT in education be made more accessible to teachers, enabling the profession to influence the policy and research agendas?

Further reading

1 R. Keeling and S. Whitman (eds.) *Education 2010*. Newman College, Birmingham.
   This short publication was designed to provide materials to stimulate student teachers' views of the future. Consider how many of the future scenarios have elements that are already true. You may also find useful workshop materials to provoke others' views of possible futures for education.

2 ICT Educational Research Forum: Professor David Wood's presentation on 'Worldviews of learning, software and associated research findings'.
   http://telematics3.ex.ac.uk/erf/present/lecture4/wood1.htm. This 'reading' is on-line

in multimedia. Professor Wood provides an overview to teachers and others of research into ICT in education organised around common views of learning. Join in the discussion to identify research that teachers wish to use.

3   Soetaert, R. and Bonamie, A. (2000) 'Reconstructing the teaching of language: A view informed by the problems of traditional literacy in a digital age.' *Journal of Information Technology for Teacher Education*, 8, 2 pp. 123–47. See also the view from America in the current issues in *IT in Teacher Education*: http://www.citejournal.org from August 2000.

Also available in due course on-line at http://www.triangle.co.uk.

Soetaert and Bonamie's guest editorial provides a view of new literacies required for and with new information technologies. Ronald's international literary background informs his colourful writing. Go further with the final paper in the same journal issue written by the creative Guy van Belle who works with Ronald in the University of Ghent.

References

Carter, D.S.G. (2000) 'Extending "supervisory reach" using new information management technology in the teacher education practicum', *Journal of Information Technology for Teacher Education*, 8, 3, 321–33.

Davis, N.E. (1994) 'Superhighways for teachers AND teachers for superhighways', *Proceedings of Ed Telecom'96*, AACE: Boston. 80–85.

Davis, N.E. (1987) 'ResCue for vocational preparation', *Educa*, No 69, p. 8–11.

Davis, N.E. (1999) 'Teacher Education and IT: Challenges for Education and Society', Proceedings of conference.

Davis, N.E. and Tearle, P.A. (1998) *A core curriculum for Telematics in teacher training*. Proceedings of the World Congress in Information Processing, Tele-teaching, Vol. 1, pp. 239–48. Also available at http.//telematics.ex.ac.uk/T3 Accessed October 2000.

Keeling, R. and Whitman, S. (eds) (1989) *Education 2010*, Birmingham: Newman College.

Panel on Educational Technology Report (1997) US Whitehouse Washington DC. http://www.whitehouse.gov/WH/EOP/OSTP/NSTC/PCAST/k-12ed.htm

Riel, M. (1994) 'The SCANS Report and the AT&T Learning Network: Preparing Students for Their Future', *Telecommunications in Education News (TIE News)*, Vol 5, No 1, pp. 10–13.

Ruopp, R., Gal, S., Drayton, B. and Pfeister, M. (eds) (1993) LabNet: Toward a Community of Practice, London and Hillsdale, N.J.: Lawrence Erlbaum Associates.

Saloman, G. (1996) 'Studying novel environments as patterns of change', in Vosnaidou, S., de Corte, Glaser, R. and Mandl, H. *International Perspectives on the Design of Technology Supported Learning Environments*, New Jersey: Lawrence Erlbaum Associates.

Scrimshaw, P. (ed.) (1997) 'Preparing for the information age'. Synoptic report of the Education Department's Superhighways Initiative, London: Crown Copyright.

Soetaert R. and Bonamie. A. (Guest Editorial) (2000) 'Reconstructing the teaching of language: A view informed by the problems of traditional literacy in a digital age', *Journal of Information Technology for Teacher Education*, Vol 8, No 2, 123–47.

Somekh, B. and Davis, N.E. (eds) (1997) *Using IT effectively in Teaching and Learning: Studies in Pre-service and In-service Teacher Education*, Routledge: London.

Sharp, J., Davis, N.E., and Still, M. (1998) 'Continuing professional development via desktop video-conferencing', in Monteith, M. and Underwood, J. (eds) *Supporting the Wider Teaching Community: Case Studies in IT INSET*, Coventry: BECTA. pp. 34–9.

Veen, W. and Dhanarajan, G. (1999) 'Educational and pedagogical issues relating to the use of ICT in open and flexible environments in North–South collaboration', in Maltha, H.W., Gerrisen, J.F. and Veen, W. (eds) *ICT and Third World Higher Education: The Means and the Ends*. Amersterdam: Netherlands Organisation for International Cooperation in Higher Education.

Weets, G. (ed.) *European Commission V Framework Programme: Information Society programme for technologies and skills acquisition. Proposal for a research agenda. Draft for large scale consulting*, October 1997. Brussels: European Commission DG XIII-C.

Wood, D. (1999) Accessed on-line April 2000 in ICT Educational research Forum http://telematics3.ex.ac.uk/erf/present/lecture4/wood1.htm

4 ICFT: Information, communication and *friendship* technology

Philosophical issues relating to the use of ICT in school settings

Lawrence Williams

Introduction: world peace – a ridiculous aim?

First there was Information Technology (IT). Then there was Information and Communication Technology (ICT).

Now there is ICFT. That is, Information, Communication, and *Friendship* Technology.[1]

My own personal aim in working to develop the creative use of the internet and its related technologies is amazingly simple: to bring about World Peace. I am, on occasion, accused of being just a trifle ambitious in this respect, but I counter this challenge extremely effectively with a simple riddle:

> *Question:*   How do you eat an elephant?
>
> *Answer:*   A little piece at a time.
>
> With apologies to vegetarian readers, of course.

If, eventually, every school across the world learns to use the internet to link pupils of all ages, races, cultures and religions, so that they can respect and celebrate the rich diversity of other people's lives, then my belief is that each project, each email message, each image, each music file, each database file, each videoconference, each shared website, is contributing something, however small and seemingly insignificant in itself, to that larger goal of world peace.

War is caused by greed, by ignorance and by fear. Schools can always do something to address the first one of these problems by educating the emotions of children through spiritual development programmes. But the greatest strength of education lies in its potential to counter ignorance and fear, by teaching children to understand, share, and respect ideas and customs from other cultures. It is here, I believe, that the internet and the related technologies can be used to do their most significant and powerful work.

Much is made in the media about the negative aspects of the internet, with the stress on pornography, hate groups and so on, but we must never forget that it is also a powerful tool for bringing people together in very positive ways, for building bridges between societies, and for fostering understanding. In this way, I believe that when our children grow up to be the participants in, and leaders of, our future society, they will not choose to wage war on those people who were once their childhood friends.

We are educated when we have come to care about our own well-being in the extended sense that includes living a morally virtuous life, which itself includes an awareness of the needs of others around the world. Indeed, a number of issues considered in chapters of this book – learning together, the empowerment of pupils with educational needs – can be underpinned and strengthened by the use of the internet and the related technologies. These educational issues can most certainly, and most effectively, be resolved by interaction with other pupils. An example of this comes from my own early experience in the mid 1980s of using the old TTNS email, when I had the privilege of working for three years as an advisory English teacher under the Educational Support Grant initiative. My task was to introduce teachers of English to the creative uses of I.T. (as it then was). I was working, as a visitor, on a project in a mixed London school for pupils with special educational needs. The pupils decided, under my guidance, to email a similar school in Tokyo about how Japanese society treated pupils with physical disabilities. Accordingly, the pupils became engaged in very meaningful research (through libraries only at this time, of course) to discover as much information as they could about such issues as hours of study at school, facilities provided by the LEA, support services in the community, and employment prospects. These questions were then emailed to their partners in Japan, and when the individual replies came in, so that they could make real comparisons, there was enormous excitement, joy, and enthusiasm. They had made contact with pupils experiencing similar physical difficulties on the other side of the world, had shared that experience, had felt that they were recognised as individuals, were accepted, and were understood. They were also able to explore these issues together with their new friends through an exciting new communication medium. My own experience in seeing such joy as the printer rolled out messages with the individual pupils' names, and as they responded so positively to those personal greetings and messages, has stayed with me, indelibly part of my educational experience.

This sense of joyful collaboration has been greatly and continually strengthened by the more recent work with UK pupils working collaboratively via video conference with Japanese pupils. (See Chapter 9.) At the end of each video-conference there is a wonderful sense of having shared in the community spirit of the other country. Emails from Japan speak of the joy and fulfilment of the pupils as they complete the various projects. They tell of the growing confidence of pupils who, at first, looked down and read their notes, but quickly learned to look more directly and confidently at their new friends in the UK. Our own pupils in the UK speak of the excitement of working with their partners across the world, and of the deeper understanding of a culture so different from our own. (See Chapter 9 for some pupils' comments on this work.)

The Kabuki Project work, collaborative drama work between UK and Japanese pupils, which we have shared is a striking example of this cultural difference, but when explored more deeply, some strange and surprising similarities seemed to emerge. Japanese Kabuki Theatre, for example, began at the same time as Shakespeare was flourishing in England. Both theatres began in the pleasure districts of important cities (in Kyoto and London). Both began with men playing the parts of women. Both used music as important elements in the total theatrical experience, and so on.[2] In order to share their understanding of Kabuki with us, the Japanese pupils were inspired to learn in greater detail about their own culture first: to share a knowledge of Shakespeare, our pupils needed the same depth of understanding of their own culture.

Unifying the school curriculum

The integrated model of learning which we have developed at Holy Cross School is based on a philosophical position which regards knowledge as a seamless fabric, a belief written into our mission statement. Recently, the national curriculum has caused our primary schools to shift away from the excellent, integrated approach of the past, and we see it as part of our mission to 'hold the torch' of integrated studies until such a time when these schools can develop new ways of coping with the destructive fragmentation thrust upon them, temporarily we believe, by artificial subject specialisms, targets and levels. We have tried to create some solutions to this problem of fragmentation through a number of cross-curricular projects, the Light Project probably being our most successful example.

The Light Project – one example of how ICT can be used to unite different subjects across the secondary curriculum, around concepts from the science curriculum

For more examples of the Holy Cross curriculum model, see Williams in Leask, M. and Williams, L. (1999) and Pachler, N. and Williams, L. (1999).

The Light Project was initiated by the science department with Year 8. The topics covered would have been explored in the syllabus throughout the year, but they were brought together in the Autumn Term, to allow collaboration and focused cross-curricular work.

The topics included the following:
The eclipse of the sun and the partial eclipse
How to view a partial eclipse with a pin-hole camera
Colour and colour chemistry
Fibre optic light and cable
Neon lighting and gas discharge lamps
Holograms

Shadows/shadow theatres
Light detectors
Camouflage
Radiation
Reflection
Refraction
Lenses
Photosynthesis
Fuels
The changing seasons

In drama, by now a familiar partner in all our cross-curricular work, the pupils improvised short scenes on the theme of good and evil (light and darkness). The drama teacher used the camera to take a picture of a freeze-frame from the play, which the pupils then imported into the computer. They then wrote up what the play was about underneath the picture. Although the picture would only be printed in black and white in their project folders (colour printing is horribly expensive!) the pupils discussed what colour of light could be used in the staging of their performances. Red was seen as an appropriate colour for evil and anger, and white or blue was thought to represent goodness and 'calmness'. Some word-processed a play to go with their Science Shadow Theatre. The moral dimension of the characters in the plays was broadened in the religious studies lessons into moral and spiritual aspects of good and evil. The symbolism of light and dark recurs throughout the Bible and the liturgy, so the pupils studied this, too, and presented attractive work as part of the Light Project.

When the art department started working on the Light Project the pupils already had a far greater understanding of colour, light and shadow than would normally be expected. The subject was infinite when it came to painting and drawing. In English, they spent two double periods in the computer room. They scanned through a slide-show of 100 high quality images installed on the network, and chose the one they most liked to inspire them to write a poem about light. They then printed the poem together with the picture. A pupil teacher was helping with this lesson, and was amazed to see how easily they found it to write something which would have been quite abstract as a normal classroom task. Obviously the finished product gave them a great deal of satisfaction, and they proudly showed her their work the following day. They also used a graphics package to create decorative 'light' vocabulary, and explored the uses of the thesaurus to find more words. Some groups did the same in French.

Later in the term, the new music software 'Sibelius' was deployed on the school network, a music keyboard was added (for faster input), and the pupils were soon able to write both the words and the music for some Christmas songs to do with light, using the pentatonic scale – required for the National Curriculum in Music.

In mathematics, they studied enlargement, reflection, and mirror images. In technology, they made circuits, created stained glass mirror effects, used computer-aided design to make T-shirts with computer-embroidered candles on them. In geography, they studied the sun, the seasons, starlight using CD Roms. A group which went to Germany returned and wrote about the Christmas lights they had seen there. The project culminated in a beautiful Advent service in the church, with carols, dance, and drama, all linked to the theme of Light, and a fitting conclusion to a busy and successful term's work.

Some pupils' comments:

'I like using computers. It gives me more confidence.'

'It made me go to the library more than I normally do . . . I didn't use to stay in the computer room after school, but now I do.'

'I could use a lot of resources on the computer. Talk to other people.'

'I really understand science better now, and enjoy it more.'

'I enjoyed doing this project, and I find the research to be fun, as there are so many different sources of information, and it was inspiring.'

'It showed how different subjects can be linked up.'

We start, then, from this belief – that children learn better when links are made between different subjects, and that the computer provides us with an immensely powerful set of tools, (word-processing, spreadsheets, databases, DTP programs, General Midi files, email, the internet, video-conferencing) which enable us to develop a model of learning which serves this purpose. By focusing on other cultures and traditions, through the study of the Caribbean and Japan, for example, and by bringing into the classroom real and relevant learning materials, sent directly to us by pupils across the world, there is an immediacy about the work which provides a further spur to success.

The integrated model of learning at Holy Cross – the advantage for teachers

In addition to the advantages that an integrated and international approach brings to the learning process, there is the further advantage that working together with colleagues from other subject disciplines through these cross-curricular projects (The Caribbean Project, The Light Project and the Japan 2000 Project) has brought the teaching staff themselves together in a greater understanding of one another's work. As the headteacher, Mrs Mary Watson puts it,

> This integrated method brings all subjects together, all pupils together and all staff together. Our 'Panda Report' (national statistics showing for example, pupil achievements against national averages and averages for similar schools) also shows a rapid rise in pupils' achievements from below the National Average to well above it, over a four year period.

So successful has this method been that, in spite of the current severe restrictions of the timetable, we are nonetheless finding ways of extending the time slots available for these projects, as well as adding new, broad topics on Time, World Citizenship, and Media into Years 8 and 9. Some of this work will also, of course, prepare the pupils for their GCSE studies.

In this development we are now being helped by some of our parents, who are able to bring their own skills, interests and knowledge into the school curriculum. We are therefore creating stronger connections with the local as well as the international communities.

Creativity and commitment – the advantage for the pupils

We have also found that by making a cross-curricular framework of learning, there has been an enormous release of creative energy in the pupils themselves. It seems that, given a balanced combination of clear targets coupled with considerable freedom to choose some aspects of their studies, the pupils are powerfully stimulated to excel; to share their ideas with their friends; to beat their own last level of performance in very positively self-critical ways, and to explore learning and the development of skills for their own sake. It has been very exciting to see the release of this creativity. Recently, for example, I had a group of extremely experienced teachers in my classroom, critically evaluating the work of my pupils who were working on a new curriculum project. I had to inform my visitors that the three most creative ideas seen during the Year 7 lesson that the girls were working on were not in fact mine, but their own. These were: making a board game for other children, created using a combination of word-processing and graphics programs; writing a visually creative poem using an art package, instead of a word-processor; and the use of a digital camera by a group of pupils to support their interviewing skills. I am, however, proud rather than ashamed to admit this. If, by truly understanding the creative uses of computer programs, my pupils can create for themselves better and more imaginative tasks through which to develop their English skills, so much the better. They have learned how to be creative.

Another unexpected outcome of this way of working is the amazing confidence and clarity with which the girls are able to explain what they are doing to our many visitors. They develop enormous pride in their work, and are delighted at opportunities to share their enthusiasm with others. As Christina Preston, Director of Project Miranda at the Institute of Education, London, (formerly an English teacher, and currently an OFSTED ICT Inspector) said after her visit to the school, 'The innovative cross-curricular use of ICT is unique in my experience. It seems to develop in the children a real understanding of their work. I have spoken at length to the pupils, who are articulate and self assured in explaining what they have learnt, and the value that their lessons have had for them.'

Teacher training issues – a model for the future

What follows here is a model of how the two schools, Holy Cross Convent School, Surrey, UK, and Ikeda Junior High School, Osaka, working with two universities, London University in the UK, and Osaka Kyoiku University in Japan, have explored together some of the issues related to teacher training, through the 'Kabuki Project'. It seems to all of us who are involved that strong links between the schools and the training institutions are essential if good practice is to be shared and developed. The Project has therefore developed very rapidly on many levels.

Strand 1: Academic links

This has involved the sharing of academic expertise regarding telematics and the new ICT technologies, through 'Project Miranda' at the Institute of Education, London University and the 'Konet Plan' through the 'International Exchange Project' chaired by Hiroyuki Tanaka, at Osaka Kyoiku University, Osaka, Japan. Papers on this project have been presented under Project Miranda at the Institute of Education, London in the 'Media 98' International Conference, and an update was given at the 'CAL'99' Conference. Related papers have also been presented at the International 'Poskole' Conference in Sedmihorky; in Osaka; at the Marie Curie- Sklodowskiej University; at the University of Wroclaw; and at the 'Informatyka w Szkole' Conference in Katowica.

A joint paper will be published at the end of the project by Lawrence Williams and Professor Tanaka, examining the impact and the educational implications of this work, based on the experiences of the teachers, pupils and the learning institutions involved in both countries.

Strand 2: Teacher training links between the Institute of Education, London, and Osaka Kyoiku University, Japan

These links involve the sharing of classroom teaching practice and curriculum development, through lectures, talks and workshops given both by Lawrence

Williams in London and by the Holy Cross team while visiting Japan. This was strengthened at the 'CAL'99' Conference, when two teachers from Ikeda JHS, Ryuzo Tanaka-san, Head of Music and Yoshinobu Yamamoto-san, Head of English, gave a shared presentation about the link with Holy Cross. Introduced by Professor Hiro Tanaka, this presentation explored some of the benefits to the pupils of working with partners from another culture.

Strand 3: Teacher education in the two sister schools, Holy Cross New Malden and Ikeda Junior High School, Osaka, Japan

This entails the exchange of practical teaching ideas through the project, especially regarding music, art, dance, drama, the nature of Kabuki Theatre, and curriculum management issues. Teachers in the two sister schools are constantly working together to devise new programmes of work for their pupils. Indeed, we were delighted to learn that, as a result of the success of the 'Kabuki Project', Ikeda JHS was accepted by the Japanese Ministry of Education as a National Pilot School for introducing drama lessons into the curriculum in Japan, for the very first time. (See below)

Introduction to the play, 'Kabuki Gift', by Douglas Love

We wrote a special Introductory Scene to the play in order to inform the audiences in both countries about what is actually happening in the drama, and about why there were contrasts of style, dancing, and singing, for example. We wanted also to exploit the virtual reality aspect of the videoconferencing technology, by showing how the two countries could be imaginatively linked by the technology itself, through what we hoped would be an amusing visual trick. Judge for yourself . . . Here is the introduction:

Extra introductory scene to the play:
Agata Grela, a Year 9 pupil at Holy Cross School, enters. She is wandering about the Holy Cross School Hall, when she sees the large 29 inch colour monitor in a corner of the set. On the screen there is the image of an empty room in Ikeda JHS, Osaka, Japan. The video-cameras in both countries are pointing at Japanese symbols of peace, on what are otherwise blank walls. No-one is in sight at Ikeda, at first. Agata approaches the camera, looks at the monitor with curiosity, and through it into the empty room in Osaka. She calls out:

Agata: Hello! Is there anyone there?

From Japan comes the disembodied voice of Go Fujita, a pupil at Ikeda Junior High School, Osaka.

Go: Hi. Who is that?

He then appears in front of his camera, and looks at Agata. They look at each other in amazement.

Agata: I'm Agata. Who are you?
Go: I'm Go. Where are you?
Agata: I'm in my School Hall.
Go: Where is that?
Agata: It's in England. South London. Where are you?
Go: I'm in Japan. Osaka.

They pause for a moment, obviously deep in thought.

Agata: You know, this has got possibilities. We could use it to perform a play together.
Go: That sounds interesting. How?
Agata: Well, we could do some scenes in English and you could do some scenes in Japanese. Then the audience could see the same play in two countries simultaneously, and in two languages!
Go: Great idea! Do you have a particular play in mind?
Agata: Well, we are studying Japan at the moment, and there is this play which we found called 'Kabuki Gift'. (She shows Go her copy.) How about that?
Go: Sounds OK. Can you pass it to me, so that I can have a look at it?
Agata: Yes, here it is. Careful, now!

She pretends to pass the copy through the camera lens, by holding the play up close to the camera. Go Fujita reaches up to his camera lens and takes the copy from her hand. A bit of trickery is needed here. He actually has a second copy of the play hidden by the side of his camera in Japan, and slides this copy into the path of the camera lens to create the illusion that the copy has travelled from one country to the other! He looks through the pages of the play for a few moments.

Go: Looks good, but I don't think I like the names of the characters very much. I'm afraid they are not very Japanese. Also it's not traditional Kabuki, you know, in spite of the title. But we can get round that somehow.
Agata: Please change the names, if you think that would be better. We could then do our scenes in a Modern English contemporary style,

and you could add as many Kabuki elements as you like. Two different styles, too!

Go: OK. We will perform some scenes, then you can do the next few scenes, and so on.

Agata: We can add some dances, to it, as well.

Go: Fine. We could also send you some design work for the front of your costumes. My friend here at Ikeda, Naomi, is really good at art. I'm sure she will help us.

Agata: And we could get our school choir to sing at the end of the play, and both groups could dance to the music, while they are singing. A sort of symbol of the union between the two schools. There's a lovely song from the film 'Titanic' which would fit in with the love element of the play, and it's quite popular here in England. Do you know it in Japan?

Go: Yes. Great idea. Suggest a date, and then let's go and practise.

Agata: See you on, let's say, (She pretends to think up a date) 29th June!

Go: Fine. Bye, Agata. Nice meeting you.

Agata: Bye, Go.

End of introductory scene

Then, on to the first scene of the play 'Kabuki Gift', by Douglas Love

Following a trial period, it is likely that drama will now become a part of everyday lessons throughout Japan. We are all very proud of this.

In a second school link, with Hikari JHS, Miss Misa Manabe, a Japanese Shodo Master, very kindly sent Holy Cross several sets of Shodo equipment (special brushes and inks for writing Japanese symbols). These were for use at our fifth Video Conference when she taught Japanese calligraphy techniques to the Year 9 pupils of Holy Cross, live from Japan, over the ISDN 2 videoconferencing link. This idea was later featured by the BBC's 'Blue Peter' team in a Japan Special edition of the programme.

Strand 4: Pupil to pupil exchanges through videoconferencing

Siobhan Clerkin (aged 14, Holy Cross) and Go Fujita (the 'Kabuki Gift' play pupil from Ikeda JHS) were the initial chairpersons of the pupil to pupil links of the project. Together, they explored the use of the new technologies, and helped with the planning and development of many aspects of the project. Drama, dance, music, science and textiles work form the current material for the conference discussions, and email is used for day-to-day communication.

Strand 5: Linked web sites

Through the Konet server (Osaka) and the MirandaNet server, UK, ideas from the Kabuki Project are available to teachers and pupils in both countries.

This, then, has been the development so far of the many levels of communication between the two countries, although the creative use of video-conferencing has always been at the heart of the collaboration. In order to build on this work still further, we have recently completed a further series of videoconferences, which are now being explored by research students in Osaka University, to see in what ways the collaboration and the new technologies are changing social values in the two countries.

Conclusion

I therefore have no reservations whatever about working in this way with computers. It is only our imagination as teachers which limits what is possible. If challenging ideas can be shared across the world through the many new educational partnerships which are springing up, such as TeacherNet, MirandaNet, I*EARN, ENIS, and the Konet Plan[3] then the future for education is very exciting indeed. Teachers now have the tools they need to help them create a better future for their pupils. World peace is no longer a ridiculous aim, but one which we might work towards achieving through the creative use of Information, Communication and *Friendship* Technology.

Notes

1 I am grateful to my good friend Hiro Tanaka, of Osaka Kyoiku University, for inventing this new descriptive title, which he used during our joint presentation at the 'CAL '99' Conference at the Institute of Education, London University.
2 For further details about the Kabuki Theatre and its development, see 'The Kabuki Story' by Michael Spencer at
http://www.lightbrigade.demon.co.uk/Breakdown/story.htm
3 TeacherNet http://www.teachernetuk.org.uk
MirandaNet http://www.mirandanet.com
1*EARN http://www.iearn.org/
ENIS http://www.eun.org
Konet Plan http://www.wnn.or.jp/wnn-s/english/english.html

Questions

1 How can teachers provide effective frameworks for learning in which students from diverse cultures and traditions can learn to respect and celebrate each other's differences?
2 How can this work be developed as part of the new National Curriculum **Citizenship** theme?

Further reading

White J. (1984) *The Aims of Education Restated*, London: Routledge.
This is the definitive text on the principles underlying the education of students as morally autonomous people.

Vygotsky, L. (1962) *Thought and Language*, Massachusetts: MIT.
This text will give you insights into the dynamic nature of language and the need for diversity in approaches to the development of literacy.

Harrison, B. (1979) *An Introduction to the Philosophy of Language*, London: Macmillan.
Harrison provides an excellent survey of issues related to meaning and communication.

References

Leask, M. and Williams, L. (1999) 'Whole school approaches: integrating ICT across the Curriculum' in Leask, M. and Pachler, N. (eds) *Learning to Teach Using ICT in the Secondary School*, London: Routledge.

Pachler, N. and Williams, L. (1999) 'Using the internet as a teaching and learning tool' in Leask, M. and Pachler, N. (eds) *Learning to Teach Using ICT in the Secondary School*, London: Routledge.

5 What stops teachers using new technology?

Lyn Dawes

Introduction

New applications of technology have the potential to support learning across the curriculum, and allow effective communication between teachers and learners in ways that have not been possible before. For this to happen, teachers are responsible for translating into practice the high expectations and the visions of technology enthusiasts. In order for them to do so, a complex variety of key factors must be in place in schools and classrooms. Problems arise when teachers are expected to implement changes in what may well be adverse circumstances. To identify key factors which are barriers to using Information and Communications Technology (ICT) in education, some of the diverse influences on practising teachers are described. Such factors include features of the teacher's work situation, and the external influence of IT firms, specifically through advertising. This chapter suggests some factors which may support teachers as users of ICT, including a model for understanding and evaluating the position of teachers as they move from uptake to proficiency. The ideas are based on research undertaken with teachers during 1997–2000 (Dawes 2000a).

Important influences on educational ICT use

Following Stake (1967) we can evaluate the process of ICT innovation by considering three aspects of the situation in schools:

(a) Antecedents: existing conditions which may relate to the outcomes of change;
(b) Transactions: interaction between people, and between people and contexts;
(c) Outcomes of change.

Antecedents: existing conditions which may relate to the outcomes of change

The history of educational computing reveals that teachers have long been seen by educational technologists to exhibit a range of obstructive behaviours from incompetence to sheer bloody-mindedness, doggedly resisting change; technological reformers have traditionally been 'teacher-bashers' (Cuban 1986;

Boyd-Barrett and Scanton 1991; Selwyn, Dawes and Mercer 2000). However some of the causes of such 'resistance' are identified by the 1997 Stevenson Report, which detailed the state of educational computing in the UK, and provided evidence that ICT use could best be described as patchy. The report was seminal in recommending that teachers should be given access to effective training for ICT, that they should have up-to-date computers for themselves and their classes, and that a network should be set up allowing teachers to exchange professional information. The two key conclusions were that 'the state of ICT in our schools is primitive and not improving', and 'it is a national priority to increase the use of ICT in UK schools' (Stevenson 1997: 6).

The National Grid for Learning (NGfL) proposals were designed to address these issues, and ensure that teachers were well placed to use technology to deliver the curriculum. The NGfL was conceived as a way of organising resources which would enable schools and other institutions to access further digital resources through technology (DfEE 1997a).

Transactions: interaction between people, and between people and contexts

The context for many teachers attempting to assimilate ICT into their practice has been lack of appropriate equipment, training, and time to evaluate new applications. Coupled with uncertainties about genuine pedagogical purposes for computers, these reasons have caused some teachers to remain wary of ICT. The unreliability of school equipment, the expense of repairs and a lack of technical support have been additional problems. Indeed the number of schools using ICT to good effect at the end of the last century could be seen as a tribute to the persistence of teachers in spite of adverse conditions.

The Education Department's Superhighways Initiative (EDSI) report (DfEE 1997b: 28) lists seven *features of institutions* which the evidence indicates might affect the benefits gained from ICT use. (The report points out that there are 'at least' seven such features). Each of the seven features (such as 'quality of management' 'stance towards IT' 'dominant educational and social philosophy') is subdivided into 'markers' – issues that had been found to make a difference (such as 'a prior needs analysis' 'reliablity' 'suitability for the educational purposes of the particular school'). Thirty-two factors were identified as just some of the influences which affect whether direct learning benefits can be gained from ICT use. Table 5.1 summarises these factors. So, although making equipment available is one step towards integrating ICT into educational practice, the EDSI report showed that many conditions had to be met in order to utilise the educational potential of technology in institutional settings. Any or all of these factors may influence what happens in the classroom, and thus whether direct learning benefits are actually gained. Teachers concerned to use pupil time to maximum advantage are therefore likely to avoid ICT use, if they judge that 'markers' such as those in Table 5.1 are not addressed in their work situation.

Table 5.1 Features of institutions which make a difference

Features of institutions which affect benefits gained from ICT use	'Markers' (issues which make a difference)
1 Quality of management	• a high-level supporter for ICT use • one or more effective 'doers' properly resourced and timetabled and with access to senior management • an effective steering group for projects • a prior needs analysis • a development plan for innovation that runs beyond initial stages • an overall development and training strategy into which the innovation fits
2 Quality of other project partners	• effective human networks • establishment of clear management frameworks • clearly articulated roles for all participants • teacher control over curriculum content • relevant training provision • support in creating resources • awareness that the setting up phase is often longer than might be anticipated
3 Stance towards IT generally	• numbers of staff actively using IT • existence of a clear IT policy • percentage of annual income spent on IT • existence of arrangements for prompt and effective technical support
4 Current and anticipated levels of financial and physical resources available and required	• level and predictability of long term running and maintenance costs • moving from temporary trials to permanent provision
5 Quality of new technology available	• ease of use by learners • ease of use by teachers • reliability • the amount of relevant resources available • purchase and maintenance costs and depreciation rate • the immediate obviousness to teachers of the educational potential
6 Dominant educational and social philosophy	• relative emphasis given to vocational education, subject learning, research skills, social development and community involvement aims • approach to obtaining funding (entrepreneurial or public service)

continued

Table 5.1 continued

Features of institutions which affect benefits gained from ICT use	'Markers' (issues which make a difference)
	• approach to developing local, national and international links • stance towards other institutions (co-operative, competitive or self-reliant)
7 Match between the technologies available and the circumstances and priorities of the educational institution	• suitability for educational purposes • compatibility of new resources with old • compatibility with project partners • physical location within the institution

(Adapted from DfEE 1997b: 28)

Outcomes of change

One of the stated conditions for successful outcomes of change (see Table 5.1, item 5) when considering computer use is: 'the immediate obviousness to teachers of the educational potential'. It is evident that the involvement of teachers is instrumental in unlocking potential gains which ICT could offer to learners.

> All students, whatever their ability, stand to have their education enriched by information technology.
>
> (Cockfield 1995: 21)

This hopeful statement indicates the prevailing high expectations for technology. But if the inclusion of computers in classrooms should have a profound effect on learners, why has that not already happened? Computers were in use in various classroom settings from the early eighties. One answer may be that although it is certainly possible that education can be enriched by technology, the provision of equipment is only *part* of what is necessary for this to happen. As the EDSI studies showed, many factors made a difference – crucially including teachers' mediation of learner–computer interactions.

Concurrent with the drive to introduce technology into UK schools is a concern with 'raising standards', that is, a concentration on the aspects of numeracy and literacy that are readily assessed. The British Educational Communications and Technology Agency (BECTA) evaluated uses of Integrated Learning Systems (ILS) and concluded that pupil learning was enhanced by technology, but that 'teaching by other methods is pedagogically necessary' to prepare children for the tests they undertake in schools (BECTA 1999). This provides further evidence that teachers are a necessary part of learning with technology.

> When teachers disengage from the use of the technology and leave pupils to use it and teach each other how to use it, the potential for enhancing learning

drops away steeply. ICT can only achieve the promise it holds for enhanced learning when its use is integrated with the curriculum by effective teachers.

(BECTA 1999: 56).

A further influence on teachers: advertising by IT firms

An external influence on UK teachers during the introduction of the National Grid for Learning has been the print media. As the drive to integrate ICT into classrooms became more pressing, UK newspapers produced supplements designed to convey up-to-date information about the initiatives to an audience of practising teachers. In the late 1990s, access to the internet was not common amongst teachers, and so these supplements were of great importance to those seeking to understand and implement the changes. As Leask (1998) points out, the media remain one of the most significant external influences on the development of professional knowledge of teachers in the school system. National dissemination of new knowledge by this means was therefore crucial to the embedding of innovative ideas in practice.

An examination of educational computing advertisements placed in the press by IT firms wishing to sell goods to the newly lucrative school market by Selwyn, Dawes and Mercer (2000) revealed that the persistent social stereotype of the reluctant or 'technophobic' teacher had become part of marketing strategy. In publications such as TES on-line and Educ@guardian it was possible to discern four images of teachers and technology, all of which could undermine confidence and create further barriers to ICT use. These images are:

a) ICT as a new, futuristic form of education. This well-worn theme depicts the interaction of computers and pupils as inevitably educational, with information transfer always generating new knowledge. The teacher in this scenario is a hindrance, prone to unnecessary interference.

b) ICT as a traditional form of education. The seemingly permanent nostalgia for 'back to basics' education is evoked by advertising copy which depicts familiar technology, such as a bicycle. The computer is presented as a way of linking the productive and now unthreatening past with an unproblematic future. For the present, acquisition of new technologies is the effortless step required of schools: and handing over responsibility for the development of learners to computers is the step required of teachers.

c) ICT as a 'headache' for teachers. This promotion of the teacher/computer relationship surprisingly presents ICT as a problem – but only for the teacher. Having established the idea of the teacher as unable to understand technology, such advertisements suggest that the teacher stand back and allow the IT experts to take over the classroom and ensure that all learners' needs are met.

d) ICT as a solution to teaching problems. This reverses the previous theme. The advertisements seek to undermine the teacher/learner relationship by insisting that access to computers is the best way to ensure that pupils achieve their potential. From mundane administrative tasks to issues of cognitive development, ICT is presented to teachers as providing easy 'solutions' to what they had weakly perceived as quite hard work – teaching.

So, in their advertising rhetoric, such advertisements aimed to sell computers to teachers, to sell the idea of the NGfL, and yet also to offer teachers a reflection of their profession as hopelessly 'behind the times', technophobic, and in need of the assistance of the more expert IT companies. At a time when the UK government wished to enlist teachers as supporters of the NGfL aims, such negative imagery did little to encourage teachers to accept the task of ensuring the educational effectiveness of ICT. That is, the apparent efforts of the IT industry to attract teachers to their products may, ironically, have reinforced the barriers to ICT use which they wished to overcome. I will return to this issue later in the chapter.

The identification of barriers to ICT use in education

Identification of barriers is one of the first steps towards removing them. In an interview study conducted in schools in a city in the Midlands of the UK, teachers were asked to talk about their relationship with technology (Dawes 2000a). Evaluation of the interview data indicated the critical importance to teachers of the following factors:

- Ownership of up-to-date technology
- A sense of purpose for ICT use
- Adequate training
- Realistic time management
- Inclusion in a supportive community of practice

The barriers presented by aspects of these factors will now be discussed in more detail.

Ownership of up-to-date technology

People who have full access to computers become confident in their use. In 1997/8, the DfEE Multimedia Portables for Teachers Pilot provided over 1100 teachers with a portable, internet-capable CD Rom system. The evaluation of the project concludes: 'The portables have made a transformative difference to the teachers, at a personal and professional level' (BECTA 1998).

The personal possession of a computer may well be the single most important factor enabling a teacher to integrate ICT into their professional practice. This fairly obvious fact finally achieved recognition as late as January 2000 when Michael Wills, the Parliamentary Under-secretary of State for Learning and Technology announced that finance (£20,000,000) would be available to subsidise some teachers' purchase of home computers. Primary teachers were not usually given personal access to a computer in their workplace, and in secondary schools teachers in management positions felt that they under-used computers because of lack of time to become familiar with them. It is too simplistic to construe this lack of time as lack of interest or motivation. The Portables for Teachers study showed that given the equipment, and crucially the chance to take it home and learn about it in their own time, teachers made rapid gains in skills. They also acquired commitment and enthusiasm. The study data supported the view that those teachers who have their own computers are more likely to know how to use them with pupils. Tim Brighouse, Chief Education Officer for Birmingham, who had been one of the advocates of the policy of helping teachers to buy their own equipment said:

> The bread would come back buttered if teachers used ICT in the home because people get intrigued by the possibilities technology offers.
>
> (Brighouse 1999: 27)

The following comments were made by a teacher in the research (Dawes 2000a) about her experience of the Portables for Teachers project:

> In the past I was very aware that I was being asked to teach children to use the computer when I really had very little idea myself. I had attended courses to try and improve my skills but the real problem was that any skill I learned was soon forgotten as I did not have a computer of my own. They only way you learn to do anything is to practise it yourself on a very regular basis. I knew I could master computing skills but because of the gaps between 'hands on' I never reinforced the skills. Because I now have a machine which is 'mine' and I use it daily I can now, with some measure of confidence, endeavour to teach the children with IT.
>
> I would say that it is the ONLY way that you will make teachers computer literate. Give them a computer of their own so that they can use their skills. Joking apart I don't consider myself the thickest person on the planet and yet I had a real struggle to get to grips with computing. Now I am confident and undertaking more training so that I can master some new bits and pieces.
>
> I used to have to rely on children who were more computer literate than myself to help me. Now I find I am usually ahead of the game. I hated not being able to manage something that even the least able child had come to terms with. I now recognise that it was simply not having one of my own. Once you own one you improve immeasurably. *In every school I know, the teachers who are computer literate are the ones who have their own systems.* Other staff in the school are all envious in the nicest possible way. They all quite rightly say, 'Why should it be restricted to senior management? We all need this.'
>
> Dawes 2000a: 251 (emphasis added)

Most ICT innovations, however, concentrate on providing computers for pupils; which is an important, but limited goal. The fact that young people enjoy computers does not necessarily mean they can learn everything (or anything) with them. Some pupils are ICT experts. However Selwyn (1998) has shown that the most powerful educational applications of computers are not the ones school pupils tend to use at home. In order to encourage use of spreadsheets, databases, communicative links, and other genuinely educational software for most pupils, the involvement of adept teachers is required. Also, being autonomous with computers (as an increasing number of pupils are) is not always the same as knowing how to help others learn how to use them. Teachers must know how to do things with computers, but must also acquire the more complex understanding of how to ensure that computer use is educationally effective for others. The modern myth that children are 'better' with computers than adults (especially teachers) does not take these additional factors into account. In summary, teachers must first own computers if they are to be able to combine ICT expertise with their teaching expertise. Sharing a computer with colleagues or with pupils is unlikely to engender the sort of enthusiasm described by the teacher earlier who was given a multimedia portable for her personal use.

A sense of purpose for ICT use

Teachers might find themselves in a 'Catch 22' situation by considering these two questions:

(i) How can you decide how to use new technology if you have no experience of what it can do?
(ii) How can you gain experience of what new technology can do if you do not know how to use it?

Teachers require the chance to look at new developments and examples of technology used in educational practice so that they become aware of the opportunities it offers. They also need an awareness of educational purpose for ICT use. There is always the possibility that once provided with experience, purpose, or both, teachers will find the machines themselves fascinating, involving, or simply just useful. Their perception of educational purposes for computers may depend on how effectively those conducting research into practical uses of ICT in education can disseminate their findings – especially if learning gains for children are established. The role of the teacher in classrooms equipped with new technology remains crucial: to frame and structure learning activities which allow the potential of the child and the technology to be realised.

Adequate training

Teachers not only have to teach using ICT, they have to teach *how to use* ICT. Unfamiliarity with constantly changing hardware and software can undermine confidence, especially in the context of the classroom, when teachers are aware that their own time wasted is pupil time wasted.

Effective teacher training includes the following elements:

1　An analysis of the teacher's current level of skills and some indication of what purposes they envisage for ICT use.
2　Unlimited access to the equipment that is to be the focus of the learning.
3　Instruction in the skills required.
4　Consideration of education applications of the technology.
5　Time to practise skills, reflect on new knowledge and consider effective ways of integrating ICT to enhance pupil learning, in discussion with colleagues.
6　The opportunity to continue training, starting again at 1.

(Adapted from TTA 1998)

Realistic time management

It is a while now since anyone confidently claimed that computers would save time. Their processing speed is phenomenal, but that does not mean they decrease the time their operator spends on a given task. Tasks expand to take into account the capacity of the computer, standards rise accordingly, and time gets used at an alarming rate. We now expect computers to make presentation neater, data more comprehensive, information more accurate, layout more attractive, activities more interactive, finished products more impressive – and everything more time-consuming. New tasks arise because the work is undertaken with ICT. The labyrinth of links that is the internet can seemingly absorb infinities of time. Communication generates more communication. So, there are important implications for time management when implementing ICT proposals in the teaching profession. Teachers are used to doing a large part of their planning and administrative work at home. Home computers may streamline this but the disadvantage is that they may come to add to demands on teachers' time, but involvement with new technology inducts teachers into a learning community of users, altering attitudes and behaviour, and seems often to begin or become consolidated at home.

What we do alters who we are.

(Zimbardo and Leippe 1991: 84)

Most practising teachers in the research were determined to organise ICT access for themselves and their pupils. Conflicting priorities such as the implementation of a variety of other changes, professional development in other areas of expertise, large class sizes and increased work load due to the OFSTED inspection procedure were cited as making great demands on the time available. However as the study progressed, those teachers undertaking training for ICT use did not offer 'lack of time' as a barrier to their learning (although they did indicate that the more time they had to practise improved their confidence and their skill levels). This accords with findings reported by Leask and Younie (Chapter 16) who talked to teachers about their uptake and use of the internet: lack of time was not cited as a barrier by those with a sense of purpose for ICT use. Teachers wishing to use ICT to support their work with classes found time to do so.

Inclusion in a supportive community of practice

Research evidence from a study of Australian teachers beginning use of the internet in their work (Williams and McKeown 1996) showed that most of those involved benefited from the on-line support of their colleagues. Electronic communication can allow teachers to transcend their traditional isolation within classrooms, and to begin to develop links with other professionals that allow discussion of common interest issues.

This, and other research, suggests that teachers as learners of ICT may find on-line support offered by tutors and by their peers invaluable. The opportunity to discuss problems or successes, to share information and to ask for help (or offer it) are all easily accomplished by electronic networking – which in itself encourages familiarity with the computer. In a study of Open University students Wegerif (1998) analysed the involvement of individuals with their 'learning community'. One aim of the course was that students learnt collaboratively by discussing ideas with their tutors and one another, using computers to mediate their communication.

> Forming a sense of community, where people feel they will be treated sympathetically by their fellows, seems to be a necessary first step for collaborative learning. Without a feeling of community people are 'on their own', likely to be anxious, defensive and unwilling to take the risks involved in learning. The experience of pupils lends some support to the idea [. . .] that CMC (Computer Mediated Communication) is a naturally effective support for this collaborative learning mode or style of interaction. As one student wrote on their on-line questionnaire form:
> The benefits of collaborative learning were derived from taking part in a developing conversation where many of the replies were much more considered than might have been the case had the same people met and talked together over several hours. Questions were raised, answered, developed, returned to and reconsidered in a much more polite and considerate manner than would have been the case in the face to face situation.
>
> (Wegerif 1998: 48)

The 'sense of community' mentioned may be crucial to the success of training programmes designed to encourage teachers in their use of ICT. Several factors can influence feelings of inclusion or exclusion, which in turn influence how well people learn. Particular barriers are:

- Differential access: those with inadequate access to a computer find it difficult to join in with ongoing discussions.
- Starting points: those who come late to the discussion or training course find it hard to join what is an already established group.
- Confidence: those who find it difficult to join in, lacking confidence initially, lose confidence as time goes on.

Advertising as a further barrier to ICT uptake by teachers

Teaching is a vocational profession. Teachers join the profession for many reasons, but principally because they enjoy the company of young people and like the idea of helping them to develop and grow as individuals (Huberman 1993). But as mentioned earlier, much advertising of school computers has projected negative images of teachers sidelined in this role, made redundant or revealed as unskilled by the inclusion of computers in classrooms (Selwyn and Dawes 2000). The emphasis throughout the advertising rhetoric on individualisation of learners' ICT use and the redundant role of the teacher at the expense of the IT firm mirrors wider debates in education over the nature of schooling and learning. Schools are perceived as institutions not well designed to accommodate ways of learning with technology, and teachers remain a 'nuisance factor' (Bryson and de Castell 1998) delaying the establishment of learner–technology partnerships. The education profession is seen as unwilling to adapt to the changes that developing technology brings, preferring to continue in outmoded styles of transmitting information ('the sage on the stage').

The danger that lies in the construction of such negative images of teachers and ICT is that the persuasive power of advertising may induce teachers to believe that their role will be diminished once technology becomes integrated into practice. It is not just serving teachers who will gather from ICT advertising that the teaching profession is problematic and unskilled, daunted by technology and unable to assimilate change, helplessly waiting for IT firms to step in and 'modernise' education. Parents, governors and prospective teachers may uncritically accept an image which is presented so consistently. Challenging such persuasive themes as ICT as 'dream' and teacher as 'nightmare' is crucial to the removal of this barrier to understanding the reality of the growing working relationship teachers are establishing with technology.

The final frontier: Lack of opportunity

A substantial barrier to integrated ICT use is that of a heavily content-led mandatory curriculum. Lack of opportunity to use technology creatively and for a variety of educational purposes, including communication, because of the requirement to deliver the National Curriculum unfortunately diminishes opportunities.

Supporting teachers

This section looks at two growing areas of support which teachers might expect to find in their drive to integrate ICT into classroom practice. These are:

a)   the assistance of computer-literate pupils; and
b)   a community of teachers as learners of ICT.

Computer-literate pupils

As the National Grid for Learning was introduced in 1997/8, schools and classrooms were the focus for IT initiatives. The print media rarely showed teachers using computers: in one of the few examples found, the caption reads 'A teacher grappling with technology'. Pupils are never portrayed as 'grappling', but shown confidently facing screens, often with an other-worldly enlightened glow on their faces. An investigation of cartoon depictions of teachers at this time revealed that teachers were portrayed as not just inept, but as novices compared to their computer-literate pupils. The possible impact of such cartoons, like the images of advertisements, is not to be underestimated: Warburton and Saunders (1996) examining cartoon depictions of teachers' professional culture, consider cartoons as embodiments of public opinion. Such images gain currency by repetition; repetition coupled with the concise nature of the cartoon provides a powerful means of transmitting ideas.

However, ideas transmitted consistently and repeatedly may nevertheless be inaccurate. The relationship between teachers and computer-literate pupils may well be mutually supportive. Teachers in the interview study insisted on the supportive nature of their relationship with computer-literate pupils. Asked to comment on the perceived wisdom that teachers feel threatened by the expert knowledge of their computer-literate pupils, a secondary teacher said:

> I find it very useful to ask them to help. I have no problem about it when the pupils say to me, 'Oh this has happened' and 'That has happened'. I tend to say, 'Oh Matthew can you help us?' and talk to which ever pupil is good at that particular sort of thing. I know what pupils can do. I don't have any problem with that. I don't have a problem with saying 'I don't understand – I haven't got a clue how to help you, but Sam will –
>
> [QD]

This response was reiterated by other teachers in the study.

> I take pupils in some lessons with IT and I rely on there being one or two with me who can do it too.
>
> [NH]

> Someone will come up, say, with a table and say how do you do this? And someone else will help. And if something goes wrong and you don't exactly know what to do, you say who knows how to get me out of this situation?
>
> [LH]

They are really busy on these things at home, so if somebody gets into problems either you do it or you say, go and ask Jacob –

[QH]

There are so many of them needing help and you can't get round, so you involve the ones who have the skills, on your side.

[TL]

What teachers actually feel threatened by is not the technology itself, or the skills of their pupils, but their own *lack* of knowledge. This is an important distinction. Until recently many teachers may have been excluded from an understanding of the technology by lack of equipment, training and time. The NGfL initiatives (1997 onwards) seem set to enable teachers to equip themselves with the skills and resources they require. Meanwhile although the support of computer literate pupils is valued, teachers recognise the drawbacks of this policy. The learning needs of such pupils are not addressed in such situations, and 'expert' pupils may be sometimes impatient or insensitive with their peers, and tend to take over rather than encourage understanding.

The reciprocal teaching-and-learning relationships good teachers build with pupils might at best remain unchanged by ICT. Teachers have always used their pupils as a stimulating resource as they reflect and refine their practice. Since it allows good communication and encourages equality of opportunity, the inclusion of ICT into this symbiosis may be considered to enhance teacher–pupil relationships rather than threaten them. (Of course this might not make for amusing cartoons!)

A community of teachers as learners of ICT

The government's plans for 'lifelong learning' (DfEE 1998) included provision for teachers as learners of ICT. Training based on identification of individual needs was organised as part of the NGfL initiatives. The training was linked to provision of hardware and connections in schools, and furthered by development of relevant educational content on the web. Such provision reflected a global trend to assimilate new technology into all areas of life. The UK looked to other countries to see how well integrated educational technology might become.

Surprisingly, it seemed that less than a quarter of American teachers have integrated the tools of technology into their everyday practice (McKenzie 1999). McKenzie categorises teachers as either 'Pioneers' or 'Reluctants' in their uptake of ICT, and advocates a separate training approach for 'Reluctants' based on trying to 'turn them on' to technology. Such value-laden categories and divisive training strategies may not encourage teachers. A different approach may be to analyse the contexts in which teachers find themselves, and provide teachers with the means to identify the real barriers to their use of ICT. The number of 'markers' in Table 5.1 indicate that the actions of teachers should not be construed as the main reason why ICT is under used. Labelling the majority of the profession 'Reluctants' and casting them as scapegoats when innovation is not implemented is evidently an ineffective strategy for change.

The next section sets out a framework for analysing the involvement of teachers with ICT. This can provide teachers with a basis for decisions they might take about their professional development and about changes to their work situation, and can provide school management with information for planning. This model is based on the key factors which teachers in the research indicated affected their use of ICT with their classes (Dawes 2000b). The categories suggested here place teachers within a working community of educational technology users. Learning, enabling progression through the categories, is situated in the practice of the community (Lave and Wenger 1991). The boundaries between categories are created by context, and assigning a teacher to any one of the categories is actually intended to help them move into the next category, by highlighting what it is in the work situation that limits their ICT use. So, the categories provide an opportunity to consider the *reasons* why teachers can and cannot use ICT. The model is described here in the belief that practicable change in education systems is encouraged and sustained by the change agentry of individual teachers, as they develop professional expertise within a supportive community.

The questionnaire in Table 5.2 (Situational factors and ICT use) has been designed to elicit some contextual factors which are barriers for teachers. After completion by the teacher, it is intended to act as a discussion document for negotiating change: ticks in the 'no' column may indicate areas requiring planning for change.

The questionnaire can be used by teachers to discuss what planning is required to initiate change. It can also be used to place teachers within the community of teachers as learners of ICT, by matching the responses with the categories described in Table 5.3. If you are a teacher, you might wish to assign yourself to a category as you read through the descriptions. The NGfL initiatives are intended to ensure that every practising teacher joins Category 4 (Adept) or Category 5 (Integral) by the year 2002.

Making a difference

Movement for teachers in terms of increasing professional development is towards Category 5. Table 5.4 (Category Change) summarises what (at least) is required to make a difference, that is, to enable a teacher to move towards becoming an Integral ICT user.

Conclusion

A wealth of information about the implications and uses of new technology in education is becoming available. Changes to existing practice will depend on both constraints and opportunities, but the NGfL initiatives have ensured that the integration of ICT into UK schools is under way. The benefits ICT offers to all learners have at last been extended to those most essential to the success of all the exciting and visionary proposals: teachers. In attempting to harness the technology to support delivery of the curriculum, and to create independent learners, teachers

Table 5.2 Questionnaire: Situational factors and ICT use

	yes	no
1 Do you have a home computer?		
2 Can you use this whenever you wish?		
3 Do you use email at home?		
4 Do you have an up-to-date computer at work?		
5 Can you use this whenever you wish?		
6 Do you use email or the internet at work?		
7 In the coming year: • Will you increase your present use of ICT in school? • Is ICT training a first priority for your professional development?		
8 Within the last year: • Have you had ICT training? • Have you found this transferable to classroom practice?		
9 In school: • do you feel you have adequate ICT equipment to support the work you do with your class? • do you have technical support? • do you have support in your planning for ICT use? • do you have time allocated to plan, prepare or practice using ICT? • does ICT support your delivery of the curriuculum? • do you have time to use ICT with pupils unrestricted by curriculum demands? • do you have an 'ICT buddy' (peer/partner/mentor) who will discuss ICT use with you supportively?		
10 Is technology use fluent and unproblematic for you?		
11 Have you used email: • to communicate with other teachers? • to enable pupils to communicate ?		
12 Is the internet accessible to you? Have you used the internet • to find resources? • to create resources?		

What do you think are barriers to further use of ICT with your pupils?

What would facilitate your use of ICT with pupils?

Table 5.3 Teachers as users of ICT: Categories

---

1 Potential user

Teachers in this category have no personal computer at school or home. They may use ICT occasionally but not systematically. They have not had recent training opportunities nor sufficient time to practise skills or develop understanding of appropriate ICT use. The technology available to them at work may be unreliable and technical support is inaccessible.

2 Participant user

Teachers in this category have a personal computer (not usually a communal one) at home or work, and use it to do work-related tasks. They may use ICT with pupils occasionally but unsystematically. They may feel that they lack the confidence or preparation time to use technology with their classes, or that its educational purposes are dubious.

3 Involved user

(a) Teachers in this category have a personal computer at home or at school, and plan and prepare work using ICT. They may have ICT skills but can not use ICT systematically because of *lack of equipment, or lack of access to equipment*. They may also lack technical support.

(b) Teachers in this category have a personal computer at home or at school, and plan and prepare work using ICT. They may have access to ICT but can not use it systematically because of *lack of training and time to practise*.

(c) Teachers in this category have a personal computer at home or at school, and plan and prepare work using ICT. They can not use ICT systematically because of *lack of training and lack of equipment*. This might include lack of practice time, or lack of access to equipment.

4 Adept user

Teachers in this category have network literacy[1] skills, and an understanding of when and how to use ICT. They have reliable ICT access at home and at work, and technical support. They use ICT for themselves and with their pupils in a planned and systematic way. They may be members of a professional on-line community.

5 Integral user

Teachers in this category integrate ICT use seamlessly into their work practices whenever it is appropriate to do so. They have access to constantly updated resources, and opportunities to undertake further training. Time is allocated for use and preparation of ICT resources in their timetable. They may be members of a professional on-line community.

---

are likely to encounter barriers which thwart their attempts to integrate ICT into their practice. I have suggested that these barriers exist at many levels, including the extent of personal access to computers, aspects of school organisation and management, and the media depiction of the relationship between teachers and educational ICT. Detailed evaluation of contextual factors is one way to establish the real causes of under-use of new technology in classrooms, and to begin to create plans to address problems and ensure sustainable change.

Table 5.4 Category change

Category change	What is required
Potential to Participant (1 to 2)	• personal computer ownership • supportive initial tuition • an 'ICT buddy' – a partner at a similar stage
Participant to Involved (2 to 3) with pupils	• a clear educational purpose for ICT use • knowledge of new possibilities
Involved to Adept (3 to 4)	• up to date equipment • technical support • focused training • access to learning communities (real and virtual)
Adept to Integral (4 to 5)	• continually updated resources • further training opportunities • access to learning communities (real and virtual) • dedicated time for ICT use

Notes

1 NB. The term 'network literacy' is used here to mean the capacity to use electronic networks to access resources, to create resources, and to communicate with others (DfEE 1997a: 10).

Questions

1 What differences might it make to teaching if an analysis of contextual factors were undertaken before developing programmes which involve an integral ICT component?
2 Does the media's portrayal of the teaching profession reflect society's values?
3 Does technology support existing aims for education, constrain them by its limitations, or enhance their evolution by its potential?

Further reading

Warschauer, M. (1999) 'Electronic literacies: language, culture and power' in *On-line Education*, Mahwah NJ: Erlbaum Associates.

Warschauer looks at different definitions of literacy, and considers the social status of emerging literacies engendered by new technologies. Electronic literacy might be thought of as the capacity to use electronic resources autonomously to enable various aspects of personal and community development. Taking the premise that electronic literacies can be either empowering or stultifying, Warschauer examines a range of potential outcomes. He considers the possibility that people may use the internet for everything from creative construction of knowledge to passive reception of multimedia glitz, and uses research to investigate best uses in education. This book details experiences of teachers using electronic resources, drawing conclusions that may increase awareness of what we might lose and gain by the redefinition of education as technology is integrated into practice.

Fullan, M. (1993) *Change Forces: Probing the Depths of Educational Reform*, London: The Falmer Press.

Change Forces tackles the chaotic nature of the forces of change at work in complex systems such as schools, and suggests a way to think about dynamic change. This strategy provides clarity and insights for understanding and coping with some of the seemingly intractable problems of educational reform. Fullan identifies eight basic lessons about why change seems unmanageable and how to make it less so. The book is based on the idea that strong moral purposes underpin our attempts to educate youngsters in schools, and that clear statements of such purposes allow productive reflection on the way changes might be organised. The book is written in a direct and lively style. Its 'message' might have a beneficial influence on individuals, groups, organisations and whole societies: the insights gained from reading this book enable focused change.

Spender, D. (1995) *Nattering on the Net: Women, Power and Cyberspace*, Melbourne: Spinifex.

Spender provides an accessible historical account of the rise of print media and the transfer to electronically held information. Spender analyses the relationship of media to the communities they serve, looking at issues of class, race and gender and the accessibility of all to new information networks. This engaging book allows a fresh perspective on the past and an optimism for a future based on equality of opportunity. Its aim is to ensure that those who populate cyberspace are well informed and have a strong commitment to including one another in continuing development.

References

BECTA (1998) *Multimedia Portables for Teachers Pilot*, Coventry: BECTA.

BECTA (1999) *The UK ILS Evaluations – Final Report*, Coventry: BECTA.

Boyd-Barrett, O. and Scanlon, E. (1991) *Computers and Learning*, Wokingham: Addison-Wesley Publishing.

Brighouse, T. (1999) quoted in *TES ONLINE* January 8th.

Bryson, M. and De Castell, S. (1994) 'Telling tales out of school: modernist, critical and postmodern "True Stories" about educational computing', *Journal of Educational Computing Research*, Vol 10, No 3, pp. 199–221.

Cockfield, D. (1995) *Network Europe and the Information Society*, London: Federal Trust for Education and Research.

Cuban, L. (1986) *Teachers and Machines: The Classroom Use of Technology Since 1920*, New York: Teachers College Press.

Dawes, L. (2000a) 'The National Grid for Learning and the professional development of teachers: outcomes of an opportunity for change', De Montfort University: Unpublished PhD Thesis.

Dawes, L. (2000b) 'First connections: teachers and the National Grid for Learning', *Computers and Education*, Vol 33, pp. 235–52.

DfEE (1997a) *Connecting the Learning Society*, London: HMSO.

DfEE (1997b) *Synoptic Report: Education Department's Superhighways Initiative*, London: HMSO.

DfEE (1998) *Open for Learning, Open for Business*, London: HMSO.

Huberman, M. (1993) *The Lives of Teachers*, London: Cassell.

Lave, J. and Wenger, E. (1991) *Situated Learning: Legitimate Peripheral Participation*, Cambridge: Cambridge University Press.

Leask, M. (1998) *The Development and Embedding of New Knowledge in a Profession*, De Montfort University: Unpublished PhD Thesis.

McKenzie, J. (1999) 'How teachers learn technology best' http://fno.org/howlearn.html.

Selwyn, N. (1998) 'The effect of using a home computer on students' educational use of IT', *Computers and Education*, Vol. 31, No. 2, pp. 211–27.

Selwyn, N. and Dawes, L. (2000) 'Teachers and the dream machines', *Journal of Information Technology for Teacher Education*, Vol. 8, Issue 3.

Selwyn, N., Dawes, L. and Mercer, N. (2000) 'Promoting Mr "Chips": the construction of the teacher/computer relationship in educational advertising', *Journal of Teaching and Teacher Education*, Issue 16.6.

Stake, R. (1967) 'The countenance of educational evaluation', *Teachers College Record*, Vol. 67, No. 8, April.

Stevenson, D. (1997) *Information and Communications Technology in UK Schools*, London: DfEE.

TTA (Teacher Training Agency) (1998) *New Opportunities Fund – The Use of ICT in Subject Teaching: Expected Outcomes for Teachers in England, Northern Ireland and Wales*, London: TTA.

Warburton and Saunders (1996) 'Representing teachers' professional culture through cartoons', *British Journal of Educational Studies*, Vol. 44, No. 3, pp. 307–25.

Wegerif, R. (1998) 'Social dimensions of asynchronous learning networks', *Journal of Asynchronous Learning Networks*, Vol. 2, Issue 1, pp. 34–49.

Williams, M. and McKeown, L. (1996) 'A model for planning for use of the internet', *Australian Educational Computing*, Vol. 11, No 2, pp. 15–19.

Zimbardo, P. and Leippe, M (1991) *The Psychology of Attitude Change and Social Influence*, New York: McGraw-Hill Inc.

Part II

Implications for teaching approaches and pupil learning

6 The role of the teacher

Teacherless classrooms?

Michelle Selinger

Educational institutions can cut teaching costs by using CD Rom courses and computer tutorials to deliver education using support staff rather than teachers to monitor students' progress.

(*Ottawa Citizen* 17 January 1996)

Introduction

Is the relationship that learners have with computers independent of the teacher? Is the teacher in fact superfluous to the learning process as computer aided learning (CAL) and computer-based learning (CBL) of all types enable the learner to develop new understandings and acquire knowledge? Or is the role of the teacher to mediate between computer and learner, to pose questions, and to refocus pupils to support effective learning? Have the definitions of classroom and teacher changed with the advent of ICT? Based on a social constructivist perspective, this chapter will explore the roles of teachers and schools in the information age drawing on the research and dreams of visionaries in the field of changing schools. It will seek to redefine the role of teachers, rather than to dismiss them altogether, and to make a case for the preservation of teachers and schools.

Does the teacherless classroom exist?

At the beginning of his book *The Children's Machine*, Papert describes a hypothetical situation in which a group of surgeons and a group of school teachers from an earlier century are travellers in time. The surgeons do not recognise the operating theatre of a modern hospital, but the teachers find the classroom very familiar in many ways (Papert 1993: 1). Among others, Cooper also describes how little the curriculum has changed and he describes the mathematics curriculum taught in all schools today as almost identical to that taught in public schools in the 1930s (Cooper 1994: 7).

Despite such evidence there is a cultural belief that we are about to witness a complete change in the way schools operate. There is some limited evidence of this taking place. Schools like the Apple Classrooms of Tomorrow (Sandholz, Ringstaff and Dwyer 1996) have developed exciting ways of utilising new technologies, and schools in the UK like Brooke Weston City Technology College in Corby are communicating with all Year 7, 8 and 9 pupils electronically at home through the school's intranet system. Yet fundamentally the structures in schools remain the same. Students are arranged in classes according to their age, perhaps set according to their aptitudes in one subject or another, usually mathematics or English. They are taught in primary schools mainly by one teacher, and in secondary schools by a number of subject specialists in fixed blocks of time.

Cuban (1993: 186) provides an explanation as to why new technologies have not changed schools as much as other institutions:

> First, cultural beliefs about what teaching is, how learning occurs, what knowledge is proper in schools, and the pupil–teacher (not pupil–machine) relationship dominate popular views of proper schooling. Second the age graded school, an organisational invention of the late nineteenth century, has profoundly shaped what teachers do and do not do in classrooms, including the persistent adaptation of innovations to fit the contours of these age graded settings.
>
> (Cuban 1993: 186)

Evidence of this is borne out in interviews I conducted with pupils in a secondary school. When asked to imagine a time when they were sitting at a computer feeling bored, one pupil described an event in which he was 'typing up notes from the board'. The teacher was certainly appropriating the technology to his own view of teaching!

Cuban went on to describe three possible scenarios for the classroom of 2003, ten years after this article appeared in press and which he called the technophile's, the preservationist's and the cautious optimist's. The technophile's scenario of electronic schools of the future is one where an abundance of better machines and software enable pupils to 'learn more and with less difficulty' (p. 192). In this scenario 'students will come to rely on the machines and one another to teach them and that teachers will become coaches to help students with what needs to be learnt' (p. 193). The second scenario is the preservationist's in which the fundamental structures of schools are maintained but schooling is improved. Technology is perceived to be important but only as a tool that teachers use to help pupils be more productive. In this scenario technology is used to support what schools have always done. Cuban calls the third scenario the cautious optimist's scenario and is one in which there is a slow but steady movement 'towards fundamental changes in teaching and schooling' (p. 195). Not even the most visionary and technologically rich classrooms he describes are without a teacher or mentor of some sort. Here I agree with Cuban – the teacherless classroom is a myth; and any change in education will come through how teachers and classrooms change and become defined. It is the advent of ICT that may provide the biggest catalyst to that change. However, Cuban adds caution to this statement: he demonstrates how long other new yet less radical technologies have taken to become commonplace and accepted into classroom practice. He cites as an example the overhead projector which was first introduced in 1932 and only became a 'mainstay' in most classrooms in the 1990s – a tool which 'extends what teachers ordinarily do and is even better than a chalkboard. Teachers can still lecture, explain and ask questions of the entire group at one time' (p. 199).

The overhead projector took nearly 60 years to become embedded in classroom practice yet it was just a tool that enhanced what teachers already did. How long will computers take to become as commonplace? And if they are to change teaching, will the pace of change be slower, or will schools respond rapidly (relatively) to the challenges of the workplace? Cuban examines three 'impulses' for using the latest technology in schools. The first is to bring schools in line with the workplace, so that students are prepared to compete in the job market, and is derived from 'the turn-of-the-century social role of public schools to prepare students for vocations and the proposition that in an increasingly high-tech world graduates must know how to handle electronic machines' (p. 190).

The second impulse is premised on a social constructivist[1] philosophy (Vygotsky 1978) in which computers support students working together on self-directed activities to create understanding. The final impulse is productivity – 'teaching more in less time for less cost' which Cuban traces back to 'the origins of public schools in the early nineteenth century and has been a consistent goal for schooling ever since' (p. 190).

Another reason why schools have changed so little with the advent of new technology is that access within school is hitherto extremely limited. Both Cuban (1993) and Passey (1999) calculate that the amount of time any pupil spends at a computer in school averages between 4 and 6 per cent of their total teaching time. Thus the impact on the curriculum and the way teachers teach is bound to be very small until this percentage increases.

While computers can offer learners models and simulations of real world events, there is also a need for opportunities to have some real rather than virtual experiences. Science practicals, for example, have a place in demonstrating the importance of control, accuracy, error limits, and attention to detail, as well as providing pupils with hands-on experience of appropriate ways of measuring, observing, and controlling variables. Unless learners experience these phenomena first hand, their understanding of the ways in which computer modelled experiments might be set up in reality will be limited. Teachers need to be on hand to support and supervise such practical activity, to set up these experiments in meaningful contexts, and to help learners relate their experiences to computer based simulations.

Are schools authentic learning communities?

We have noted above that schools have changed very little and discounted teacherless classrooms, but we also need to look again at learners to see how the teacher's role might change as new technology is pushed into the arena, and learning gains are continually sought. Will traditional school structures, which have in the main changed very little since the nineteenth century disappear as we move into the twenty-first century? If a social constructivist paradigm is subscribed to, whatever happens, the need for learning to be scaffolded, i.e. supported by a more knowledgeable other, will still exist. According to Vygotsky (1978), in this context a zone of proximal development is created where learners perform within their range of competence while being aided in realising their potential. He defines the zone of proximal development then as

> the distance between the actual development as determined by independent problem solving and level of potential development as determined through problem solving under adult guidance or in collaboration with more capable peers.
>
> (Vygotsky 1978: 86)

But whether it is the teacher who scaffolds the learner, or other adults or peers is an issue that needs to be considered in some depth. There is also a growing recognition of the value of learning that takes place outside the school (Bentley 1998; Nunes, Schliemann and Carraher 1993; Sutherland 1999) and a need to explore whether the beginnings of the change in home–school boundaries are manifesting in increased learning potential and greater motivation. The whole notion of how and where children learn has been the subject of much debate. For many pupils the attractions of school may be lessened as they gain access to knowledge through other means, which are far more dynamic and multimedia in nature. It has been proposed in some quarters that the role of schools in the future could be as institutions whose main function is to provide an environment to develop social skills while real learning goes on elsewhere. Education in schools has a high priority with the government, and schools' role is to seen to be pivotal in providing appropriately prepared citizens of tomorrow. Therefore failing schools are high on the agenda, and this has led to questioning whether it is the nature of schooling itself that is failing. In a series of articles in *The Guardian*, Davies (1999) argues that failure is mainly due to the school's intake of pupils. Poverty and deprivation count as much as the schooling that takes place. Schools are socially polarised and this is reflected in school roles and examination success rates. The government is acting to support schools in deprived areas through the creation of Education Action Zones and its 'Excellence in Cities Programme', which includes new learning centres enabling greater access to ICT and other facilities, thus attempting 'to overcome the big divide between haves and have nots' (Blunkett 1999). All these policies are aimed at preserving the status quo in terms of how schools are organised. Schools are not perceived to be failing because they have not adjusted practices to take account of new technologies and new understanding about teaching and learning in the way that other professions and even industry have.

Many parents work and school provides a stable environment, particularly to children whose home backgrounds include violence and neglect. Abandoning schooling altogether could have huge social and societal implications. The role of schools in the socialisation of children must not be underestimated. This process was recognised in 1997 when the Qualifications and Curriculum Agency (QCA) produced draft guidelines on the promotion of pupils' spiritual, moral, social and cultural development. There was also renewed interest in the social aspect of schooling by the National Forum for Values in Education and the Community and commissions by statutory agencies such as NFER and OFSTED to review research into the social and moral aspects of schooling (see Murray 1998).

Earlier I stated that pupils have access to multimedia and dynamic 'learning tools', but what are they learning, and how is that learning channelled into personal development and career opportunities? Sanger (1997) found that parents and guardians have little active role in supporting or controlling their children's use of screen based technologies (television, video, and computers), and when children go to school they find teachers who are not immersed in the same computer culture. As a result, Sanger argues:

> they are not being educated and supported to develop a critical awareness of their experiences, to explore quality issues relating to them or to understand their role as consumers and users, in the face of powerful commercial forces. The ignorance of adults, regarding children's activities involving computers, computer games, the internet and videos, means that issues involving, for example, gender, emotional impact, aggression, IT skills development, alienation, reading and writing, the interface between reality and fantasy and a whole host of other interrelated themes, documented in this research are not being raised within educational settings.
>
> (Sanger 1997: 169)

Not only do parents need to be educated in the impact of new technologies on their children, but schools also need to adapt to the needs of a new generation for whom learning to use these technologies in the most appropriate ways can support and enhance their learning potential. Network and media literacy sits up there with the old skills of numeracy and literacy and this requires teachers to teach the skills of 'critical awareness and the capacity to exploit technology' (Sanger 1997: 173).

Work on learning styles (Gardner 1983; Litzinger and Osif 1993) also suggests that learners have different needs, and whether a traditional school setting can meet that diverse range of needs is questionable; the fact that school is failing so many young people is testament to this. Gibson (2000) summarises the many theories about learning styles in his quest for understanding how ICT changes teaching and learning, and concludes:

> detailing learning styles with great precision, while important in the sense of understanding how to cater to individual learners and their needs, was not getting me closer to my destination . . . perhaps an analysis of how the use of technology had changed teaching and learning in a variety of contexts would bring me closer.
>
> (Gibson 2000: 7)

New technologies may provide an answer for a radically different organisation, not one that adapts technology for teaching in the same ways. Cuban (1993) debates whether whole class teaching can really be a useful pedagogy if technology infusion is to have a real impact in classrooms. He suggests that primary schools may have more chance because of their (then) current structures of teachers having five hours or so with a class, and the ability to group or pair children to work together, and not being bound by fixed blocks of time as in secondary schools. Of course, he did not know that in the UK at least, in the late 1990s there would be the move back to whole class teaching and numeracy and literacy hours that would put primary schools on the same footing as secondary schools. There are rarely enough computers available in a classroom situation for teachers to plan for all children to use them. However, given the flexibility of the school day in primary schools, lessons can be planned which require all pupils to have some access to the available machines and to work collaboratively to find information, check details, or use the computer to solve a problem. The computer becomes a tool to support learning. But do we know how children learn from their work with computers?

We can start by looking at learning by observing children of all ages playing a range of computer games and consider what we can harness from the way they approach their use of the computer to develop strategies for authentic learning for use in school settings. Papert (1993) and Heppell (1993) have both written about the metacognitive activity that takes place when children are 'playing' with computers. They will learn from their mistakes, they will try moves, question why they have failed; make logical decisions about next moves based on the results of previous experiences; and they will repeat actions time and time again until they reach their desired outcome. They will fix certain variables and change others in ways that they would never consider in mathematics or science lessons. A change in attitude towards school is required not just on the part of learners but also on the part of teachers. School should be seen as places to extend all pupils' capabilities, capitalising on new skills developed and used at home, and linking them with existing skills which teachers support in order to develop more effective ways of learning.

The idea that teachers are fountains of knowledge and that children are empty vessels waiting to be filled with the knowledge and wisdom of their teacher is untenable in the information age. The amount of available knowledge and the breadth and depth of it are far beyond the realms of most teachers as is their control of learners' access to it. The teacher's role must necessarily change to help their pupils learn in the best way they can by recognising different learners' needs, and how and where they access new knowledge. Instead of restricting access, teachers need to encourage skills in which learners seek new information and consider alternative viewpoints, question their sources, and make judgements about the validity and reliability of evidence and information presented to them from a range of sources.

Adapting to computers in teaching

Crook (1996) explores a number of orientations to the technology or 'frameworks for change' that each serve as ' a focal point for arguments about the revolutionary potential of computers for teaching' and discusses whether they have delivered or are capable of delivering the change anticipated.

Computer as tutor

One orientation is 'computer as tutor'; and he compares this with the transmission model of teaching or the 'stuffing in' of knowledge. The flaws with this model are that there is an implicit assumption that knowledge is discrete, stored representations, and that the tutor–pupil relationship with an intelligent tutoring system can simulate the relationship between human tutor and pupil. Humans have intersubjectivity, they are unique at interpreting other humans' psychological states, they can respond to looks of bewilderment, smiles, anger or tears in ways that machines are unable. Teachers can treat each pupil as an individual, they build up an understanding and trust in very different ways to machines. Of course, machines are less judgemental that humans, and sometimes this can be beneficial to pupils who want to battle it out alone, but when they need support or help, they will more likely seek this from a human, whether teacher or peer.

Take for example Integrated Learning Systems (ILS) that are increasingly gaining popularity for teaching literacy and numeracy. Often it is shortcomings in current educational practice that are cited as justification for using this technology. ILS is probably the most researched application of computers to teaching in the UK, yet there is very little evidence to suggest the improvements in learning are substantial, and certainly do not justify the extensive investment that schools are making. However the systems can be shown to be of use when they are combined with teacher input, when pupils work collaboratively, and when work undertaken away from the machines is directly linked. McFarlane (1997) states that 'research supports the view that teachers play a key role in ILS'; their role in making the systems effective is crucial. ICT can also change teachers' views of teaching and learning: Underwood, Cavendish, Dowling, Fogelman and Lawson (1996) reported that teachers saw an ILS as a support tool for diagnosing weaknesses in pupils' understanding, and that an ILS proved to be a tool rather than a substitute for teachers. An understanding of pupils' learning and of appropriate pedagogies is needed to make informed judgements about how best to employ ILS; for which pupils it is most appropriate; and what related work will be needed to ensure the best possible learning gains are achieved. Facts learnt out of context need to be placed in a range of contexts so that pupils understand how to make use of their new knowledge. The teacher's role is to help pupils learn to make links between new knowledge and existing knowledge if new knowledge is to be of any value (see Skemp 1976).

Computer as pupil

The next framework for change that Crook suggests is 'computer as pupil' and cites Papert's contribution to thinking in this area. 'The idea is to regard the computer as a tool which the learner may come to control – or "teach" to do things' (Crook 1996: 80). Papert comments that some children experience learning French in USA schools, yet if they had been brought up in France this would not have been a problem; they would have learnt to speak French fluently. Therefore, as Crook points out, if one wants to learn French one goes to a French speaking country. The idea then is that pupils immerse themselves in microworlds. Logo is one such mathematical world in which children teach the machine to perform various functions – the computer acts a pupil with the child as teacher. However the immersion in a microworld is not enough, some structures may need to be imposed on learners, to ensure that the meaning of what they are doing is clear. There has to be some purpose and motivation for engaging in the activity. Learners need their achievements to be located in broader frameworks of knowledge.

> These are aspects of the learning environment that [. . .] depend upon the intersubjective capabilities of teachers. They depend on sympathetic inter-ventions from more expert people in the learning environment. Such people will build on their own understanding of the learner's experience so far in some knowledge domain: this will entail reacting to perhaps very recent particular experiences but also it will entail making connections with a longer history of what the learner already knows and cares about.
>
> (Crook 1996: 81)

This framework does not make teachers redundant, it merely changes their role in which learners are encouraged to engage in purposeful and creative exploration – one that Papert (1993) describes as 'constructionist'. The goal of a construction-ist teacher would be to teach 'in such a way as to produce the most learning for the least teaching' (p. 139). Papert contrasts this view with that of instructionism, in which 'the route to better learning must be the improvement of instruction' (p. 139). Constructionism is built on the assumption 'that children will do best by finding for themselves the specific knowledge they need; organised or informal education can help most by making sure they are supported morally, psycho-logically, materially, and intellectually in their efforts' (p. 139). The kind of knowledge children most need is the knowledge that will help them get more knowledge and cites the need to develop mathetics (a course in the art of learning).

Computer as resource

Crooks' third framework is the 'computer as resource' and cites the definition of Taylor and Laurillard (1995) as 'open access, self-directed learning from a large information source'. Learners in their interaction with the computer are active, and knowledge is discovered and negotiated. Computers can present information in ways in which teachers are unable; they can present information in multimedia formats allowing users to select and experience new knowledge in text, graphics, sounds or video; and make use of hyperlinks to link concepts together. It allows the learner to make choices about the medium through which they learn and presents them with a wide range of hitherto unimaginable resources. However turning these experiences into meaningful knowledge and understanding relies on the support or 'scaffolding' of another. This other is usually a teacher who has some understanding of the learners' preferred learning styles and can help them make appropriate choices and decisions, can teach the learner to question the validity of new knowledge and help them to assimilate it into existing schema. However, it can also be a peer or group of peers; it could be another adult. The concept of the teacher is changing, and this theme is taken up in the next section.

Who is the teacher?

Teachers need to be more adaptable; more open to alternative teaching approaches, and the use of peer teaching, and adults other than teachers – such as experts in other domains. The access to and availability of information has expanded overwhelmingly since the inception of the internet. Few expect primary teachers in particular to be completely conversant and have in-depth knowledge of all aspects of National Curriculum subjects, especially as pupils can read well beyond the statutory demands, and ask questions that demand knowledge and understanding far beyond current expectations. The same is also true of secondary teachers whose field of specialism within their chosen subject will not cover all they have to teach. A history specialist may have in-depth knowledge of British History but their knowledge of American History may only be superficial reflecting the specialism in their first degree course.

Access to information in libraries has always been recommended to pupils from an early age (study skills), and especially at post-16 level so they could read around and beyond their subject, or undertake an in-depth study. Now with the advent of communication technologies, pupils can not only read around their subject, they can also be exposed to microworlds and simulations, computer generated models, video, graphics, images, audio lectures as well as electronic conversations with experts and others. Teacher control of new knowledge is weakened yet their role does not diminish, it changes to one of supporting and scaffolding learners to assimilate new information, to turn it into knowledge and understanding within a nurturing and supportive environment.

The role of the teacher is broadened beyond the classroom and the school. As school and home boundaries start to blur, the teacher's role will be to support learners through alternative means to traditional face-to-face experiences. Teachers will have to learn how to teach at a distance through virtual learning spaces: email, web-based discussion forums, and computer conferencing systems. The skills of face-to-face teaching will have to be translated into an electronic environment where traditional cues like tone of voice, facial expressions and body language are lost. The benefits of virtual learning spaces are vast; they can bring learners together who may never have met; learners can be exposed to new voices and to new views and they can be presented with an authentic audience for their work. In addition some teachers will have to change their views of pedagogy since the nature of electronic collaboration will not always be between learners and their teachers in schools, but also between pupils and between pupils and adults other than teachers as stated earlier, as the constraints of distance are negated through virtual space. Teachers will have to deal with blurring of the classroom boundaries and for this to happen they will need to be made aware of the possibilities that can exist and the advantages to both teaching and learning.

The classroom can become a metaphor for any learning space in which one or more knowledgeable others support the learner.

> Traditional modes of teaching and learning take place in a group or in a one-to-one situation in the same place, at the same time, in the classroom or lecture theatre, or in a teacher's study. The introduction of distance learning has enabled the learner to work alone or with others on a set of materials but without the opportunity to easily or quickly question the teacher or author of the materials about the content. Electronic communication can be through text, video and audio graphics and each occupies a new learning space: different place, same time, individual or group in an on-line chat, or more commonly in the context of this paper, different place, different time, group (conference) or individual (e-mail). The learning spaces are not mutually exclusive: the opportunities afforded by previous forms of distance learning are now enhanced through the additional spaces provided by telematics and similarly face to face teaching can also be supported and extended.
>
> (Selinger 1998: 25)

When designing any learning experience teachers will need to consider what it is they wish to achieve and then consider the most appropriate approaches to achieving their goals for the learners in question. Whether the technology chosen is face-to-face lectures, print-based distance learning or web-based activities, what is important is that they design the experience to make appropriate use of the characteristics of the chosen technology. Additionally the notion of giving learners a choice of where and how they learn is one that will revolutionise schools. At the moment pupils are 'captive' in classrooms, and rarely given private study time until they are almost at the end of statutory schooling. With the access to so many resources, can the traditional 50–60 minute lesson be maintained? Can schools adapt so that teachers become consultants offering whole class lectures, group seminars or individual tutorials, or pointing pupils to other experts who may be other pupils or other adults in school or available through electronic communications? Can pupils be allowed to make choices about which mode of learning will suit them best for the task in hand? Consider this fictitious account by Jo, aged 14:

> I woke up this morning and thought about my assignments for the rest of the week. I had to find out whether electricity was less efficient than gas for

cooking; write an article for the schools' on-line newspaper; draw up a menu for a meal for a family of four; and perform some mathematical calculations to ensure the structure I made yesterday will not collapse as soon as I apply any force onto it. (I'll need to use the new mathematics program for that – I hope Janie can help!). Hmm, where do I start? I know I'll call Jem and Callum and see if they want to get together on the cooking assignment. We can meet up in the learning resources centre at 10. But first I'll pop in to see my mentor, Ms Basle, as arranged on email yesterday to make sure I have the right structure for the article. I found some great stuff on the Net last night, but I need her to help me put the facts fairly. I think I'll attend the physics lesson this afternoon, as I saw on the intranet that Mr Peel is going to go through forces today. Later on I can use what I learn there to help me have a go on that simulation programme he showed us. . . .

Can schools really offer structures that allow such flexibility and autonomy to pupils, and how will teachers make themselves available in such a scenario? How will *their* days be structured to meet the individual demands of pupils that this mode of operation will require?

Conclusions

Trying to shoehorn the current policies into the new technology is a common approach that does not work and discourages beneficial use of the technology (Turoff 1997). When designing a learning experience, the teacher cannot ignore administrative issues such as how do pupils submit assignments, teaching load, class size and preparation time. Ignoring these considerations can adversely influence the educational outcomes.

The role of the teacher is not redundant, it changes. The teacher either in the classroom or in virtual space is there as a guide and facilitator helping the learner to make judgements about the quality and validity of new sources of knowledge, to scaffold understanding and to help the learner structure new knowledge and demonstrate new understanding and learning. If computers are to make an impact on classrooms then teachers need access to the technology so they can develop their own skills, find out what computers can do to help them in their own learning and in structuring their work, and also give them the opportunity to enter into the world of their pupils. Stephen Heppell at a recent conference in Glasgow organised by the Scottish Council for Educational Technology (SCET) painted a scenario in which teachers would need three computers, one at home, one at school, and one for the family so they could provide a supportive network and environment. At the time of writing a computer is not provided to teachers in the same way as it is office workers, academics and other professionals. Yet access is vital if we are to start to use technology in the ways described above, and so teachers can start to develop and change their understanding of the potential of technology and their use of it in the classroom.

Note

1 Within a social constructivist philosophy learning is believed to be connected with the sociocultural context in which learning takes place. Learners construct knowledge rather than acquire it, and they do so through interaction with others.

Questions

1 Who is the teacher? Should we be redefining the role and who undertakes a teaching role?
2 Is there a place for renaming the 'teacher' to become the 'learning facilitator' or to use some other name?
3 Can ICT really change classroom cultures? What else needs to change if ICT is to have its full impact?

Further reading

Carroll, T.G. (2000) 'If we didn't have the schools we have today, would we create the schools we have today?' *CITE on-line journal*.
http://www.aace.org/pubs/cite/default.htm
This article takes a fresh look at the nature of schools and challenges assumptions about the structure of schooling.

References

Bentley, T. (1998) *Learning Beyond the Classroom: Education for a Changing World*, London: Routledge.

Blunkett, D. (1999) 'Do we want to bus the middle class?', *The Guardian*, 16 September.

Cooper, B. (1994) 'Secondary mathematics education in England: recent changes and their historical context', In Selinger, M. (ed.) *Teaching Mathematics*, London: Routledge.

Crook, C. (1996) 'Schools of the future' in Gill, T. (ed.) *Electronic Children: How Children are Responding to the Information Revolution*, London: National Children's Bureau.

Cuban, L. (1993) 'Computers meet classroom: classroom wins', *Teachers College Record*, Vol. 95, No. 2, pp. 185–210.

Davies, N. (1999) 'Schools in crisis', *The Guardian*, 14–16 September.

Gardner, H. (1983). *Frames of Mind: The Theory of Multiple Intelligences*, New York: Basic Books.

Gibson, I. W. (2000) 'At the intersection of technology and pedagogy: considering styles of learning and teaching', Paper presented at ESRC seminar on ICT and pedagogy: University of Keele, 6 January.

Heppell, S. (1993) 'Teacher education, learning and the information generation: the progression and evolution of educational computing against a background of change', *Journal for IT in Teacher Education*, Vol. 2, No. 2, pp. 229–38.

Litzinger, M.E. and Osif, B. (1993) 'Accommodating diverse learning styles: Designing instruction for electronic information sources', in Shirato, L. (ed.) *What is Good Instruction Now? Library Instruction for the 90s*, Ann Arbor, MI: Pierian Press.

McFarlane, A. (1997) *Information Technology and Authentic Learning: Realising the Potential of Computers in the Primary School*, London: Routledge.

Murray, L. (1998) 'Research into the social purposes of schooling: personal and social education in secondary schools in England and Wales', *Pastoral Care*, September.

Nunes, T., Schliemann, A.D. and Carraher, D.W. (1993) *Street Mathematics and School Mathematics*, New York: Cambridge University Press.

Papert, S. (1993) *The Children's Machine – Rethinking School in the Age of the Computer*, New York: Basic Books.

Passey, D. (1999) Paper presented at MACE conference, July 1999, Coventry: University of Warwick.

Sandholtz, J.H., Ringstaff, C. and Dwyer, C.D. (1996) *Teaching with Technology: Creating Pupil-centered Classrooms*, New York: Teachers College Press.

Sanger, J. (1997) *Young Children, Videos and Computer Games. Issues for Teachers and Parents*, London: Falmer Press.

Selinger, M. (1998) 'Forming a critical community through telematics', *Computers in Education*, Vol. 30, Nos. 1/2, pp. 23–30.

Skemp, R. (1976) 'Relational understanding and instrumental understanding', *Mathematics Teaching*, Vol. 77, pp. 20–6.

Sutherland, R. (1999) 'A new environment for education? The computer and the home', Paper presented at CAL99 Virtuality in Education, 29–31 March, London: Institute of Education.

Taylor, J. and Laurillard, D. (1995) 'Supporting resource based learning', in Heap, N., Thomas, T., Einon, G., Mason R. and Mackay, H. (eds) *Information Technology and Society*, London: Sage.

Turoff, M. (1997) 'Alternative futures for distance learning the force and the darkside', Keynote presentation at Virtual Learning Environments and the Role of the Teachers, Open University, Milton Keynes, April 27–29.

Underwood, J., Cavendish, S., Dowling, S., Fogelman, K. and Lawson, T. (1996) 'Are integrated learning systems effective learning support tools', *Computers and Education*, Vol. 26, No. 1–3, pp. 33–40.

Vygotsky, L.S. (1978) *Mind in Society: The Development of Higher Psychological Processes*, Cambridge, Mass: Harvard University Press.

7 Setting authentic tasks using the internet in schools[1]

Michelle Selinger

Introduction

Research on the benefits of setting authentic tasks to pupils has been shown to increase motivation and improve learning. The introduction of the internet into school culture can increase possibilities for authentic learning. This chapter explores the scope for presenting authentic tasks, examines a number of case studies of pupils working on internet based activities, and makes recommendations about the possibilities of the internet to increase and promote authentic and autonomous learning. Some of the issues and concerns that arise from searching for information, such as the sheer volume of data and the nature of data sources are also explored.

Defining authenticity

The tasks that pupils are set in school tend to be quite different from the situations they find themselves in outside of school, and very different again from the kinds of situations which constitute the everyday practices of adults going about their business. In order to articulate criticisms of the kinds of tasks set to pupils the term *authentic tasks* has been used for:

- tasks which pupils can relate to their own experience inside and outside of school;
- tasks which an experienced practitioner would undertake.

Part of the problem when pupils are given tasks in school is that they do not see the tasks as related, they do not see any driving need to get an answer, and they have a sense that on tasks set in school they are supposed to use methods they have been taught in school, rather than informal methods they have devised or picked up from others. Bruner sets out a number of tenets that guide a psycho-cultural approach to education, one of which is the constructivist tenet which is also implied in all the others. He views education to be conceived as 'aiding young humans in learning to use the tools of meaning making and reality construction, to better adapt to the world in which they find themselves and to help in the process of changing it as required' (Bruner 1996: 19–20). If this tenet is to hold then learning should take place through authentic activity so that pupils learn to construct their own sense of the world in which they live, not solely the world of school. The authentic practice of academic domains like mathematics, history and science should be used in schools to support learning rather than supporting a culture of schooling itself. Brown, Collins and Duigud argue that knowledge is situated, in that it is

> an inseparable part of the activity, context and culture in which it is used and generated.

This is a way of explaining the lack of transfer of knowledge and procedures learned in school. In order to achieve authentic practice, the learner must be engaged in authentic activity.

> Authentic activities, are most simply defined as the ordinary practices of the culture.
>
> (Brown *et al.* 1989: 34)

In the introduction to a book constructed as part of a course on authentic learning, Nicaise explains:

> Authentic learning implies several things: that learning be centred around authentic tasks, that learning be guided with teacher scaffolding, that students be engaged in exploration and inquiry, that students have opportunities for social discourse, and that ample resources be available to students as they pursue meaningful problems.
>
> (Nicaise: 1997)

Many of these tenets are based on theory and research on learning and cognition (Bednar, Cunningham, Duffy and Perry 1992; Gardner 1991; Perkins 1986). Many cognitive psychologists believe that context is an integral element of learning, and research in the field has attempted to show that learning and genuine understanding occurs within pupils' real world experiences. When pupils are given problems and situations that simulate and represent genuine complexity, pupils learn more because the context is appropriate for learning. Thus, knowledge is not independent but becomes the product of an activity, context, and culture in which it is shaped and developed (Brown *et al.* 1989; Resnick 1987). According to many cognitive psychologists then, if pupils are to develop deep understanding and transfer learning, pupils must be presented relevant contexts for learning (Cognition and Technology Group at Vanderbilt, 1993; Collins, Brown and Newman 1988; Lave 1988).

However, having access to the culture of a domain can be problematic particularly for primary teachers who may have no more than two 'specialist subjects'. Teachers can easily plan tasks in the classroom that fit that culture, but it is difficult to find authentic tasks within a domain when your own knowledge of the culture of that domain is limited. It is possible that access to experts beyond the classroom through the internet can support these teachers and others, and this is one of the issues considered in the following vignettes.

Three vignettes

The internet can act as the bridge between school culture and the culture of the community in which a pupil lives, and also beyond. Bos and the UMDL Teaching and Learning Group (1997) have demonstrated that opening up remote access to others outside the classroom can develop writing skills and a sense of audience. Their model for authentic audiences has 'four important dimensions: the knowledge level of the audience with regard to the information given, the relationship between the audience and authors, and the amount and nature of feedback from the audience to the authors, and to a whole variety of sources of information' (Bos et al. 1997: 83). The internet as source of authentic activity is also demonstrated in the following vignettes taken from the 'core' schools in an evaluation project in the UK (Selinger, Littleton, Kirkwood, Wearmouth, Meadows, Davis, Taylor and Lincoln 1998). The 15 month evaluation was undertaken as part of the evaluation of the recent UK Education Superhighways Initiative, and was funded by the Department for Education and Employment (DfEE). At the centre of the evaluation project were four 'core' schools: two secondary, one primary and one special school. These schools were chosen for participation in the project because in their application for inclusion they had indicated that they were already advanced in their thoughts regarding use of the internet in school settings, had a commitment to ICT development in their school development plan and staff had been using the internet during the previous year. Upon being selected as a core school, each site received equipment and resources in the region of £35,000 (supplemented by school resource) to establish a distributed internet network.

Vignette 1

Two 10 year old pupils in the primary school are writing an email to a contact in another country, they have been asked to send some information, the content of which is not significant for this example. The children compose the message together. When they have finished they reread it, they check the spelling, the grammar and the sense of meaning. Their teacher is surprised at the final product which she vets before the children send the message. The attention the children have paid to detail is much greater than would have been the case had the same children written the piece for the classroom.

Vignette 2

Fourteen year old pupils in a geography class in one of the core secondary schools are learning about earthquakes. Their teacher uses the internet to download or bookmark information about the last 20 earthquakes that have occurred across the world. Students are asked to analyse patterns of earthquakes from this internet data. The US Geological Survey site holds information of these earthquakes throughout the world, and from this data the teacher produces a spreadsheet. The pupils work in groups to prepare a report on the pattern of recent earthquakes. The report is to include:

- world distribution referencing latitude and longitude;
- relationship to plate boundaries, e.g. how many were boundaries and to plot this relationship;
- relationships of earthquake incidence to population density using an atlas; and
- a graph to show the differences in earthquake strength and to compare strength and depth.

They discover that the data about the earthquakes gives some measure of the depth of the earth's crust in various locations. The pupils are prompted to select one earthquake and to explore it in more detail. They search websites to look for information about the damage caused, to find out the history and context of earthquakes in a region, and to make comparisons between earthquakes occurring in one part of the world with another. The teacher is excited about the opportunity to find such recent data in such detail. The pupils ask far more questions and are far more engaged than he has noticed when working on the same topic before the availability of internet access in the school.

Vignette 3

An Advanced level chemistry group have to select a topic for an in-depth research study as part of the coursework component of their post-16 studies. Several pupils choose to use the internet to search for information. Two find university research departments who are currently investigating the pupils' chosen area. They both notice an email address for those wanting to make contact about the research and decide to email the university researcher. An email dialogue is struck up and the pupils' projects and understanding of the topic are considerably enhanced. The teacher gives each pupil at least a grade higher than he had expected them to achieve.

Implications of the vignettes

Vignette 1: the email collaboration in Vignette 1 was focused around joint projects and enabled the children to participate in purposeful activities. As Crook (1996) notes:

> this form of communication opens up exchanges between children who are growing up and learning in, perhaps, very different cultural contexts . . . It

can also create real audiences for their work and a real possibility of intellectual co-ordination with peers in pursuit of joint projects.

(p. 221)

The importance of creating real audiences, work and opportunities for intellectual co-ordination must not be underestimated. When children prepare work in the normal classroom situation there is an expectation that there will be mistakes and the teacher will correct it. Although a child may try hard to reduce the errors, the audience is the teacher and the culture of the classroom provides a set of expectations that go with her role that permits errors. When the children prepare material for a different audience, in this case children in another class in a different country, the task takes on a new meaning and more care is taken in the execution of the task to reach the desired goal. The task is authentic in that there is a real audience who will have to act on the information the children send, so there is willingness to invest extra effort to convey meaning in as correct a way as possible. Many classroom based writing tasks involve children writing for different audiences, but so often this audience is fictitious. In the case of email the audience is real.

Vignette 2: illustrates not only the authenticity of the data, but the currency. There are no books that will provide such recent information, and the pupils are accessing the data from a prestigious source. In exploring the data, making conjectures about the earth's crust and the influences that cause earthquakes, they are acting with the same data seismologists would have at their disposal and making conjectures based on facts they are having to search out for themselves. They are engaged with the task because the data is not to hand; the teacher does not have the answers because the data is so recent, and so they can work with him to produce some possible solutions. Their reports are based on authentic activity.

Vignette 3: indicates the possibilities of acting as real researchers in a field that is currently being explored by others who are experts in their domain. Students converse with adults other than teachers who are often more knowledgeable than the teacher in a particular field of work. The potential to be part of that domain as they interact with experts exposes pupils to the methods and procedures by which experts work. The apprenticeship model where pupils' understanding is scaffolded by real experts is motivating and provides a learning context which supports the notion of the constructivist framework within which authentic tasks and situated cognition are set. The opportunity to be exposed to the real culture of the domain rather than the school culture supports pupils in finding a sense of purpose and meaning for their study.

Caveats

So far the potential of the internet seems highly probable as a source and support for authentic learning. However the vignettes described above are examples of practice which has evolved through teachers considering the real value of the internet and the constructive uses to which it can be put. Much internet activity consists of unstructured searches, ill defined tasks, and pupils' work which consists of text and images cut and pasted into a report. Questioning pupils about their reports in these situations often reveals no real evidence of understanding or learning. The email task in Vignette 1 arose as a result of considerable thought and discussion about the nature of collaborative e-mail projects together with some initial trials. As the headteacher of the school reported:

> We soon realised, once the initial euphoria had subsided, that if the project was to progress, some clear objectives needed to be decided upon. It can be very easy for 'keypal' projects of this kind to stay at a superficial level, i.e. an exchange of 'chatty' letters with details of likes, dislikes, hobbies etc. There is very much a place for this kind of exchange, indeed it is probably essential for establishing initial relationships. To extend beyond this to provide deeper learning experiences for the children requires considerable cooperation and planning between the staff involved at each school.
>
> (Flanagan 1997: 36–7)

In Vignette 2, the teacher had spent some considerable time researching the availability and validity of the information on the internet. He had put in many hours of his own time and structured the lessons in such a way as to provide an authentic task. He had been fired and excited by the availability of such rich data, but recognised that he had to invest considerable effort into preparing the work. Had he left the pupils alone to find the same data, then the results might not have been so effective.

This is supported by evidence from another class observed during the evaluation where it was discovered that the search skills of pupils depended very much on their understanding of the topic. The class of 15–16 year old pupils were researching the topic 'space' and had to complete a number of tasks; some were relatively simple questions about seasons, day length; others were more open-ended, for example, they were asked to find out about and describe satellites and comets.

Both groups had started with the Netscape home page and then used some of the standard search engines. Both started by narrowing the search to *education*, then *astronomy*, then *solar system*, etc. Both groups also typed in key words at various stages. But the pupils had very different rates of success. One group of pupils of average attainment just seemed to move backwards and forwards between relevant sites, without spending much time or thought on the data captured. They did not seem sure about when to stop searching and start recording the data. They typed in *year length* and found over seven million entries. Their search technique and general knowledge about space was not advanced enough to know how to extract the information on year length from the data about planetary systems and orbits, and they needed help in making further progress.

The other group was much more successful. Although they adopted the same approach, it seemed that their higher level of scientific understanding and their familiarity with computers and CD Roms helped them in translating the directions from the teacher into alternative key words which the search engine recognised. When the group arrived at *earth*, then went to *earth science*, they discovered this was not a useful link since they were really looking for data about *earth in space*. They quickly realised this and went back, entered *planets* and found what they were looking for.

In the primary school cited in Vignette 1, the teachers encouraged their pupils to search for information on topics of interest to make them aware of the enormity of the task. By giving pupils their interests to pursue, this lent authenticity to what they were doing; they were being their own researchers on their own problems. Students very rapidly discovered that the use of search engines or similar devices to locate material was not a trivial task; it was found to be a time-consuming process and one that can be very frustrating if no suitable sites are found. Unstructured searching of the web made these pupils aware of the real difficulties of finding what they wanted: pupils learned that locating suitable sites was problematic. Again teachers needed to support pupils in developing their search and selection skills, both through helping them to refine their key word searches and, importantly, by encouraging them to evaluate the extent to which sites were useful or appropriate for their needs.

Search techniques and effective data handling are vital skills which pupils need to be taught if they are to make effective use of the vast information sources the internet provides. They have to learn to understand that some sources of data will be more reputable than others, and they have to develop a scepticism far in excess of that needed when research was undertaken in a library in which books had been preselected and vetted by knowledgeable teachers and librarians.

Vignette 3 arose without teacher intervention in the first instance, but once the contact had been made, the teacher supported the pupils in framing some but not all of their questions to the researcher. However the vignette poses another concern. How long will it before university researchers are all so overwhelmed with emails from pupils researching the construction of chemicals, or the design of new board games, and therefore unwilling to enter into the dialogues which prove so effective in motivating pupils and inducting them into the world of expert and authentic practice? Perhaps this will not happen, but if current practice in the UK is examined these concerns are founded. Students all over the UK are engaged in identical projects for one of their public 16+ examinations in which they have to undertake research for a design project and seek information from companies, usually by letters and telephone calls through conventional routes. This usually involves a project on either designing a game, making a toy or an article of fashion clothing. As a result the clothing, toy and games manufacturers have resorted in either sending out a standard fact sheet or ignoring the thousands of requests they receive for information.

Conclusion

There is no doubt from the vignettes presented that access to other sources of information, both human and media, beyond the classroom and the school can provide the basis for much authentic work. However a constructivist philosophy about the nature of the tasks set, a belief in the value of authentic learning and considerable preplanning are vital if the internet is to provide the source for worthwhile activity. Sitting pupils in front of computers and giving them access to the internet will not on its own produce authentic learning. It needs to be structured and supported.

Note

1 Published originally in the Proceedings of the IFIP Conference: Communications and Networking in Education: Learning in a Networked Society: IFIP WG 3.1 and 3.5 Open Conference Finland June 13–19 1999.

Question

1 Recall some of your own learning experiences that excited you or where you felt that you learned something you never forgot. What was special about them and why?

Further reading

The following texts explore the concept of 'authentic learning' more fully.

Selinger, M. (1994) 'Understanding', in M. Selinger (ed.) *Teaching Mathematics*, London: Routledge.
MacFarlane, A. (ed.) (1997) *Information Technology and Authentic Learning; Realising the Potential of Computers in the Primary Classroom*, London: Routledge.

References

Bednar, A.K., Cunningham, D., Duffy, T.M. and Perry, J.D. (1992) 'Theory into practice: how do we link?' in Duffy, T.M. and Jonassen, D.H. (eds) *Constructivism and the Technology of Instruction* (pp. 17–34), Hillsdale, N.J.: Lawrence Erlbaum Associates.
Bos, N. and UMDL Teaching and Learning Group (1997) 'Analysis of feedback from an "authentic" outside-the-classroom audience on high school fiction writing: validation of a theoretical model', *International Journal of Educational Telecommunications*, Vol. 3, No. 1, pp. 83–98.
Brown, J. S., Collins, A. and Duguid, P. (1989) 'Situated cognition and the culture of learning', *Educational Researcher*, Vol. 18, 1, 32–42.
Bruner, J. (1996) *The Culture of Education*, Cambridge: Mass, Harvard University Press.
Cognition and Technology Group at Vanderbilt (1993) 'Anchored instruction and science education' in Duschl, R. and Hamilton, R. (eds) *Philosophy of Science, Cognitive Psychology and Educational Theory and Practice*, NY: SUNY Press.

Collins, A., Brown, J.S. and Newman, S.E. (1988) 'Cognitive apprenticeship: Teaching the craft of reading, writing, and mathematics' in Resnick, L.B. (ed.) *Knowing, Learning and Instruction: Essays in honor of Robert Glaser* (pp. 453–94), Hillsdale, NJ: Lawrence Erlbaum Associates.

Crook, C. (1996) 'Schools of the future', in: Gill, T. (ed.) *Electronic Children*, pp. 75–88, London: National Children's Bureau.

Flanagan, C. (1997) 'Going on-line', *Microscope Early Years Special*, pp. 36–7.

Gardner, H. (1991) *The Unschooled Mind: How Children Think and How Schools Should Teach*, New York, NY: Basic Books.

Lave, J. (1988) *Cognition in Practice: Mind, Mathematics, Articles, and Culture in Everyday Life*, Cambridge, MA: Cambridge University Press.

Nicaise, M. (1997) *Authentic Learning*, http://tiger.coe.missouri.edu/~vlib/Calvin.html.

Nicaise, M. (1997) *Learning through authoring: A student-created book on authentic learning* >http://www.coe.missouri.edu/~vlib/<

Perkins, D. (1986) *Knowledge as Design*, Hillsdale, N.J.: Lawrence Erlbaum Assoc.

Resnick, L. B. (1987) 'Learning in school and out', *Educational Researcher*, Vol. 16, No. 9, 13–20.

Selinger, M., Littleton, K., Kirkwood, A., Wearmouth, J., Meadows, J., Davis, P., Taylor, J., and Lincoln, C. (1998) *Evaluation Report of the Educational Internet Service Providers Project*, London: DfEE.

8 Special educational needs issues and ICT

Glendon (Ben) Franklin

Introduction

ICT is vaunted as the cure to many problems within special educational needs, this chapter explores to what extent, if indeed at all, this is the case? Issues considered include:

- can ICT aid reading recovery? – especially for dyslexics;
- to what extent does ICT help special educational needs with numeracy issues?
- what contribution might independent learning systems make to pupil learning?
- is ICT the answer to curriculum access for the physically disabled?
- the internet and SEN; and
- does ICT really help with the motivation of disaffected special educational needs pupils?

Can ICT aid reading recovery? – especially for dyslexics

The first target on most Individual Education Plans[1] (IEPs) for children with special educational needs is almost always a literacy target dealing with some aspect of reading. Reading recovery has the highest priority for special educational needs coordinators who recognise that unless children can read they will be unable to access the national curriculum. Failing readers by the time they get to secondary school have experienced a variety of teaching tactics, including the literacy hour. Why have they failed and why would using computers make any difference?

Pupils may well fail to learn to read because of irregular attendance in earlier years when classmates were learning to read but equally they may have failed to grasp the necessary concepts when they were taught. The concept of reading readiness has a part to play, children whose pre-school experience is poor will find it harder to learn to read. Fuzzy hearing – a lack of phonological awareness may be the result of inadequate exposure to sufficiently rich language structures early on. These pupils are not able to understand concepts such as phonics since they are unable to hear individual sounds which is a prerequisite for the skill of being able to break the sounds down properly in their own mind. A similar problem will exist for pupils with hearing difficulties such as glue ear (fluid filled middle ear). They are in the position of trying to learn a decoding system for which the key is unreliable. Such children may be unable to distinguish between 'th', 'ff' or 's' for instance which all have a similar sound and which are all fricatives.

Once these pupils have made a poor start it is difficult for them to catch up as everyone else will be making progress and developing reading skills more quickly so they find themselves in the special reading group. Support from home may make a difference but often it is totally lacking or inadequate. By age eleven they may have slipped as far back as three years behind their chronological age on a reading comprehension test. The problem for secondary schools can be compounded by primary schools which measure reading on a word recognition test which gives an artificially high measure of a child's reading ability, thereby reducing the chances of the child receiving an appropriate share of scarce extra reading help.

Dyslexic children present a more serious problem. There is a vast field of research that suggests that dyslexics process information in a different way from the majority of the population. This gives them the potential to be very creative but works against them in an environment where the ability to access written text is regarded as essential. Essentially dyslexics find it hard to process information in a sequential or hierarchical way. This in turn leads to problems for them in knowing which information is important and what may discarded. Parents of dyslexic children frequently state that they can only safely give them one instruction at a time. Memory problems and disorganisation are two key indicators for professionals investigating if a child is dyslexic.

Traditional methods of working with failing readers involve using highly structured activities and careful repetition and over learning. Research done well before the Second World War (Gates 1930) showed that less able children generally benefited from more than double the amount of repetition than was necessary for more able children. A major problem related to this is the difficulty of getting the child to generalise learning from the artificial reading lesson to the real use of text in a wider environment. There is considerable research evidence to show that pupils lose any gains they have made once returned to the normal classroom unless they continue to practise the skills they have learnt. Lunzer and Gardner (1981) were particularly scathing when they looked at this problem in the late 1970s.

A final difficulty when working with secondary pupils is the difficulty of finding suitable reading materials. Teenagers require books with an appropriate interest level and yet a text readability that is accessible without appearing childish. This situation is improving at the moment with publishers actively targeting this market but the choice of modern texts remains very limited. Heavily abridged versions of traditional books will not always answer unless they have been very carefully done to preserve the essence of whatever it was that made it a successful story in the first place. Producing such books is a highly skilled form of writing.

What contribution might independent learning systems make to pupil learning?

Carefully structured computer programs are able to offer an alternative approach which builds on the successful features of traditional teaching methods. First, they can present text in a very highly structured way and can pace the introduction of new concepts and skills depending on the progress the pupil makes through the program. Second, they can provide aural feedback to the pupil and thirdly they will continue to work patiently for as long as the pupil is prepared to keep trying. The patience of computers in these situations is, I am certain, a significant factor, as is the fact that the computer will never belittle the pupil's efforts but will readily praise every success. The facts that the pupil is in control of their learning and that their failures are kept to a minimum are also important.

These then are principles which should apply to reading recovery software. At the time of writing the best known structured programs are those such as 'Success Maker' and 'Global English' which are widely used in English, American and Australian schools. These programs all make claims to help readers recover lost ground and many teachers appear to believe these claims and go along with them but there is an important caveat to this. The research conducted by the National Literacy Association and BECTA both pointed to the importance of teacher input. Using the systems as a substitute for teaching did not produce the same results as when it formed part of a wider structured reading recovery programme. There must also be the concern that when a school has spent a considerable sum of money on a system the teachers and managers are not likely to question too rigorously the gains the software claims children are making. The positive aspect of tests conducted by schools using Success Maker meant significant gains were reported by some and many schools reported on the improvement in pupil motivation.[2]

This raises the question of whether it is the software itself or the changes it creates in the teacher–pupil relationship that results in learning gains. Current reading research points up the importance of reading audience, whether to peers or to a teacher. Some programs recognise this and incorporate it into their modus operandi, for example Carron Electronic Library (details on http://www.Carr. demon.co.uk) where the computer-based activity is designed to form part of a paired reading scheme. The Dyslexia Institute uses a system called 'Units of Sound' (Rooms 1997) which is derived from a cassette based audiovisual programme. This was transferred to CD Rom whereupon a number of advantages were noted. First, audiovisual links were more powerful and direct using the CD Rom which allowed more effective use of them by pupils. Second, the CD Rom allowed pupils to pace their own learning more effectively and motivated them to work better. Third, the multimedia system allowed the initial screening test to be far more precise. Despite all this however the Institute still suggests that the system is dependent on good teacher management in order to be fully effective.

'Talking books' are a new phenomenon that spring straight from the new technology. These can certainly motivate children to take a more positive attitude to books and reading. At the base level children can enjoy having a story read to them when there is no adult available. This can be useful for dyslexic pupils who wish to 'read' such books as *Treasure Island*. These books (presented on CD Rom) often incorporate a feature whereby words can be pointed at and repeated. This can help with both identification and practice of unfamiliar words. At primary level the Oxford Reading Tree stories are a good example of this kind of resource. In this series the computer programs parallel a traditional reading scheme allowing a full integration into classroom activities. Many are produced by American software houses with the text being read in an American accent but this may actually make it more attractive to children and is more of an issue for adults who fear cultural imperialism.

Spelling

Related to reading, but not as closely as a casual glance might assume, is spelling. The prime difference is that the speller does not have any visual cues to go on at all. In addition, because our language is poly-systemic, there are no totally reliable rules for spelling; it all depends on the language the word originally derives from. In English this will mainly be Latin, Saxon, French, or Celtic. To complicate things further, as well as all the oddities acquired during our Imperial past, there was the tendency of scholars to mess around with perfectly good phonic spellings (the Norman insistence on 'wh' rather than the Saxon 'hw' for instance). Finally, some spellings still reflect now extinct pronunciations. Examples here include 'knife' and 'bomb'.

The Fernald method of teaching spelling is still widely used in schools where it is often called the 'Look, Cover, Write and Check' method. This emphasises the visual and memory aspects of spelling. Children look at the word, seeking to find patterns or unusual combinations and shapes that will act as memory hooks. This will allow them to deploy sub skills they already possess, such as recognising syllable breaks or common phonic combinations like 'tch' and to look for hidden words within the wider structure. Once confident they have memorised the word they attempt to reproduce it from memory by covering it up and writing it down. Finally, they check to see if they have got it right. If not they have another try. This is the pattern mimicked by spelling programs and is a method ideally suited to easy programming which is probably why spelling programs were some of the earliest educational software. Within this broad church software may have differing focuses. This normally comes down to whether a strictly phonic approach is to be used or whether a less precise word pattern methodology is adopted. (Though not phonic-based a system designed around legal letter patterns e.g. 'ch' and 'wh' are 'legal' i.e. commonly found as patterns beginning words, can be very effective). Some software makes a game out of learning particular words or letter combinations. Other programs reinforce left right letter orientation and others may produce a combination of these. A good example of a spelling program designed to be effective for special needs children is 'Speaking Starspell'.[3] This program provides the spoken feedback necessary as well as allowing the teacher to customise the word lists. This program is widely used with dyslexic children as is 'Word Shark'[4] which notably includes the full Alpha to Omega wordlist as devised by Dr Bevé Hornsby, acknowledged as the leading British expert on the teaching of dyslexic children.

Spelling programs are effective. The BECTA Senco Forum[5] has debated long and hard over the most effective way to use spelling programs but there is little question over whether they actually work. The reason would seem to be that they build on that particular strength of computers – to tirelessly work at drill in such a way as to make it entertaining for children. Children will play really basic games for hours if allowed to and 'hangman' and 'word invaders' and their ilk fit this bill perfectly.

The foregoing developments have been mainly concerned with skills acquisition but the other way computers work is by enabling children to become more independent in their learning and this is an important feature of reading software. Children who for one reason or another have missed out on the early stages of reading will 'play' with software that is in theory far too young for them. They enjoy the success and they can often be observed playing word games with the software – repeatedly clicking rapidly on the same word for instance so that the computer rhythmically repeats the sound. It may not be too fanciful to compare this with baby babbling which forms part of early language acquisition.

Releasing creativity

There has been a great deal of effort expended producing software that overcomes the difficulties in the way of SEN children who wish to express themselves creatively. Ranging from overlays for concept keyboards to talking and predictive word processors to 'intuitive' spell checkers, these devices and programs all have as their aim the enablement of the pupil as an independent learner. A review of this process is to be found in Chris Hopkins' article in 'Support for learning' (1998).

Multimedia CD Roms are a good example of how computers can be used to empower and liberate children across the wider curriculum. In 'Spinning the discs' Sally McKeown (1997) illustrates the fact that by using video and sound it is possible to make curriculum areas far more accessible to non-readers. This use also applies to children for whom English is not the first language, while English speaking children also enjoy using computer games to help with their language learning. The problem so far as the teacher is concerned is that there are so many CDs to choose from and it is easy to make an expensive mistake. Work currently being done by Teachers Evaluating Educational Multimedia (TEEM) should result in more effective evaluations of software for teachers (http://www.teem.org.uk).

Is ICT the answer to curriculum access for the physically disabled?

Children with physical disabilities: this is probably the least controversial area in special needs work as regards the use of ICT. The benefits are clear and straightforward though there still remain areas where the debate continues on the best way forward. Interesting work has been done by the Virtual Reality Research Group at Leicester University (Stanton, Doreman and Wilson 1997). Using virtual reality software they have been able to enhance significantly the spatial awareness of wheelchair bound children, allowing them to become virtually familiar with new environments prior to experiencing them in reality. This type of work has an implication for the overall quality of life for these children as it increases their independence.

Visual impairment

For visually impaired children the computer at last offers an easy way to produce braille output. It also however can bypass the need altogether with the ever improving speech abilities of computers. Blind people can be taught touch typing using the speech feedback facility and can have text read back to them. Good OCR software used with a scanner can read back letters and other documents. Using speech input extends the parameters even further since the ability to type is side-stepped. Children registered blind but with some vision can use the computer as a low vision aid to magnify print on screen. Concerns at the increased dependence on technology that this all brings have been raised but this essentially has to be seen as a Luddite response to the liberating effects of new technology.

Voice Activated Software

Voice activated software is a field of its own. Most often it is thought of in the context of people or children with progressive mobility diseases who are able to speak but not operate a keyboard. It also has a place with visually impaired and dyslexic children.

Professionals in the field report mixed results with this kind of software (Rahamin 1997) depending largely on the setting and the determination of the people involved to make it all work. At present there is a debate over whether natural speech recognition systems are better than discrete word systems, especially for children with speech or phonological problems (Fine 1998).

Children with motor impairments such as cerebral palsy are empowered by computers. Simple programs such as Clicker[6] allow children to write by using single key presses or through a concept keyboard.[7] As previously mentioned, voice activation allows pupils with very restricted mobility to produce written work of an acceptable standard. In an educational environment where the government and many others are pushing hard for inclusion of all children into the mainstream setting then such devices are going to become far more commonplace and widely accepted.

To what extent does ICT help special educational needs with numeracy issues?

Numeracy takes one back to skills training. If any one area of the curriculum was suited to the use of computers it must surely be a subject such as mathematics where each step logically builds upon the last and where particular skills can be broken down and their components taught first before they are dealt with themselves. If this were all that the teaching of maths involved then there could be an unconditional recommendation of computers as a teaching tool but mathematicians might take issue – there is surely something more needed, for instance the ability to recognise patterns and to formulate rules which can then be tested. Nevertheless, for special needs children it is skills at the basic level which seem to be most needed – concepts such as place value or reciprocals are often still not established by Year 8. Some children are still able to multiply only by repeated addition. Number bonds up to twenty are not yet secure.

For these children it appears the stepped and logical approach of computer maths software is the answer. Children get the chance to over learn concepts and to practice rote skills which are once again accepted as a valid part of the learning process in that higher order activities are more difficult to comprehend if one still has to work through the underlying basics each time rather than relying on an automatic response. The best illustration of this in action is where children are studying area. Children with poor maths skills have at least two tasks to carry out. First they must work out a multiplication sum laboriously by hand, often by repeated counting and then they have to try and grasp the central concept of area which is the measurement of two-dimensional surfaces. They often confuse perimeter with area because superficially both the calculations involved use the same data in the same way (if you do not understand multiplication). These are the sorts of deficits that computers are very good at overcoming since they can demonstrate the principles concerned graphically. Academics who have reservations about the use of ILS systems with reading recovery are much more positive about its use in maths.

The internet and special educational needs

The development of the internet has been exponential. From a military/academic network designed during the Cold War it has metamorphosed into the most powerful communications and information tool ever seen on our planet. It is possible today to develop links and friendships with people all over the world in a way that was never possible in the past. The Stevenson Report makes it quite clear that all teachers and children must come to grips with this and so this must include children with special educational needs. So far this chapter has dealt with the way computer technology can empower and help pupils but it is as well to consider the effect it can have on the teacher. First of all, the internet is the world's biggest library. Because it is so easy to set up a website many individuals and organisations do this, thereby providing a vast repository of expert knowledge to which teachers may turn. For example there are a number of sites with information and advice about dyslexia and dyscalculia, Downs syndrome, Afasia and so on. This free advice makes special needs coordinators much better placed to make informed professional judgements, apart from anything else they will be able to obtain different opinions and overseas advice where expertise may be more highly developed – for example in the case of Attention Deficit and Hyperactivity Disorder (ADHD) and Attention Deficit Disorder (ADD) where American teachers and clinicians are far in advance of Europe.

In Britain BECTA has set up the Senco Forum (Wedell *et al.* 1997). This is a mailing list used by SEN coordinators, educational psychologists and other interested professionals. It provides a huge fund of professional expertise. Threads of discussion have included neurological, biological disorders, the role of art therapy, assertive discipline, Trysomy 8p (a chromosomal disorder) multiple pterygerium syndrome, Aspergers syndrome and dyspraxia to mention but a few that have appeared. Occasionally a thread will stimulate serious debate for an extended period with many opinions being shared and constructive suggestions made – as in the case of the SENCO whose head told him children could not be put on stage three[8] – because the school did not have the resources. Collectively the forum provided chapter and verse to support their colleague.

Does ICT really help with the motivation of disaffected special educational needs pupils?

In the sense expressed above therefore the internet is definitely benefiting children with special educational needs as it is producing a more skilled and competent teaching practitioner but there must surely be a way that the internet is of direct help to pupils as well. This finally brings one to the feature relating to computers which all those involved with them would claim to be the most important aspect of all and that is motivation. From 1988 to 1990 the Palm project explored the effects of computers on pupils' autonomy in learning. The project found that not only were pupils more autonomous but that they were also more motivated. All special needs teachers can give examples of pupils whose attitude to school and learning was turned round through the use of computers. A personal example from my teaching may serve to illustrate this. A Year 8 pupil with cerebral palsy who was otherwise very bright was rapidly becoming a school refuser. It transpired that her shaky handwriting meant she could not keep up with other children with the notetaking involved in her top sets. Although a learning support assistant was available she did not want to appear different by having her notes scribed. Once issued with an Emate computer her attitude and attendance were transformed. Other pupils saw the Emate as 'cool' – they wanted their own in fact and so the pupil now did not mind being different. In fact she would even let her learning support assistant touch type on occasion.

The internet provides children with a stimulating environment which is familiar to them in a way that an older generation does not understand. In the same way that older people understand jump cuts and flash backs in the film media, younger people seem to grasp the concept of a hyper-linked virtual reality with relative ease. For disaffected pupils, particularly boys, this gives them something they are at least as good at as their peers. At present, so far as I am aware, this is an under researched field but it would be interesting to study the effects of computers and the internet in one of the new Pupil Referral Units currently being set up by education authorities.

Banes and Walter (1997) have shown very convincingly how the internet may be used by pupils with complex and severe learning difficulties. They found that the pupils were able to be involved in email and newsgroup communications, multimedia story writing, website making[9] and using the reference material they found on the web.

Conclusion

This chapter has looked at the new technology and its associated software and attempted to show whether there is a significant impact on the independence and learning progress of pupils with special educational needs. The jury is still out to some extent on ILS systems though they should improve and become more effective as time goes on but it seems to this writer that they show up a far more important issue, which is that teachers need to understand thoroughly what the hard and software are capable of doing – and not doing – and be able to bring their professional creativity to bear on how the new technology is used. Computer technology is not just another tool, like language labs or video recorders that a teacher can add to their armoury of pedagogical weaponry. It has the potential to fundamentally alter the way teachers teach. An example of this is the Not School project currently being run on think.com. This allows school refusers, the long term ill and excluded pupils to participate in education and recover lost self-esteem and missed learning opportunities without ever entering a classroom – though interestingly face-to-face meetings with other pupils and their mentors have been held. Computer-based learning projects use the word mentor a great deal, rather than the word teacher, and I think in the medium to long term this indicates a fundamental change in education from the empty vessel model to the learning partnership scenario.

Notes

1 IEPs. Special educational needs provision in England centres upon the concept of the Individual Education Plan or IEP. This is drawn up by the special needs teacher in consultation with parents, subject teachers and hopefully the child concerned. The Code of Practice, issued by the government, makes clear this is regarded as good practice of SEN work and at a certain point, where a child has had a formal assessment and a statement of SEN has been issued by the LEA, this becomes a legal entitlement. This concept will be familiar to American and perhaps other readers.

2 Research Machines Learning Systems Press Pack – includes independent research that shows Success Maker in a favourable light.

3 Speaking Starspell Fisher Marriot Software.

4 Wordshark White Space Software 1998.

5 Senco Forum http://www.becta.org.uk/
6 Clicker, Crick Computing, http://www.semerc.co.uk
7 Concept Keyboard, The Concept Keyboard Company. http://www.semerc.co.uk
8 In England special needs are graded according to the degree of seriousness. Stage one refers to a relatively minor problem. Stage five, otherwise known as a statement is restricted to approximately 2 per cent of SEN pupils and refers to severe learning or behavioural problems.
9 Scope site http://www.scope.org.uk

Questions

1   If, as seems likely, ICT can enable greater inclusion of Special Educational Needs (SEN) children into the mainstream, should schools actively pursue that goal?
2   How might you use ICT to help you convince a conservative teaching staff that it is possible to include into the mainstream, children who are at present educated in special schools?

Further reading

In order to get a grip on the current debate about educational and social inclusion the three following journals are almost compulsory for background reading. Your school's Special Educational Needs Co-ordinator (SENCO) should have back copies.

Support for Learning – *British Journal of Learning Support*, published by the National Association of Special Educational Needs (NASEN). Details can be found on http://www.nasen.org.uk.

British Journal of Special Education – also published by NASEN.

Special Children – Published by Questions Publishing; Birmingham, UK.

Also worth subscribing to is 'senit'. This is a mailing list run by British Education Communications and Technology Agency (BECTA) for those with a particular interest in using IT for SEN solutions. Contact BECTA via their website http://www.becta.org.uk.

References

Banes, D. and Walter, R. (1997) 'The Internet: a new frontier for pupils with severe learning difficulties', *British Journal for Special Education*, Vol. 24, No. 1.
Fine, B. (1998) 'Miracle or myth, special children', *Questions Publishing*, January.
Gates, A.I. (1930) *Interest and Ability in Reading*, London: Macmillan.
Hopkins, C. (1998) 'The role of information and communication technology in providing access for all support for learning', *NASEN*, Vol. 13, No. 4, November.
Lunzer, E. and Gardner, K. (1981) *The Effective Use of Reading*, London: Heinemann.
McKeown, S. (1997) 'Spinning the Discs', *Special Magazine NASEN*, Spring.
Rahamin, L. (1997) 'Talking with computers', *Special Magazine, National Association for Educational Needs*, Autumn.

Rooms, M. (1997) 'Fast forward', *Special Children*, Questions Publishing.

Stanton, D., Doreman, N. and Wilson, P. (1997) 'Virtually there', *Special Children*, Questions Publishing, April.

Wedell, K. *et al.* (1997) 'SENCOs sharing questions and solutions: How to make a more convenient phone call', *British Journal for Special Education*, Vol. **24**, No. 4.

9   Videoconferencing across the curriculum

Lawrence Williams

Introduction

Until fairly recently, the use of videoconferencing equipment has been seen largely as the province of the Modern Foreign Languages Departments in schools, for example, for the fine tuning of French or German accents. Generally, this work is carried out on a one to one basis (see Leask and Pachler (1999) Chapter 6: Video-conferencing) and as such the equipment has proved to be a very useful learning tool. However, at Holy Cross School we have been exploring the use across the curriculum – across the range of secondary school subjects. What follows here is an outline of some of the projects we are developing using video-conferencing equipment, our vision and plans for the future, and finally, some general guidelines for using it creatively, based on our own practical experience.

Videoconferencing: is it just an expensive gimmick?

To answer this question directly, and briefly, 'Yes, videoconferencing is expensive,' but, 'No, it is not a gimmick.' Like all information and communication technology tools, videoconferencing is completely neutral. That is, it rests with the user whether or not any value can be gained from its use. With a hammer, for example, you can choose to smash windows, or build the Taj Mahal; with a word-processor you can waste your life copy-typing, or use it as a creative tool to develop writing skills; with email you can send endless and useless 'How's the Budgie?' messages, or use it to create international drama activities; with a CD Rom you can click and print out mindless acres of text and pictures, or you can integrate it into schemes of work involving increasingly complex searching skills. The tool itself has the potential both for good and ill, and teachers must learn how to explore and to exploit this potential effectively.

Costs, as with all new technology, are reducing almost daily, and what is at the time of writing somewhat expensive will soon become relatively cheap. PC based systems will eventually become a cheap daily method for many pupils to contact their friends, just as email does presently. The question to ask, then, when confronted by any new technology is very simple: What can it actually do? Subsequent questions are: At what cost? How complicated is it? Does it enable my pupils to do things better than before? 'Better' here can mean quicker, more easily, or with more attractive results: seldom does an ICT tool allow anything completely new to be undertaken. One is reminded of T.S. Eliot's famous statement that anything entirely new is entirely bad.

So, what does videoconferencing allow us to do? The answer is simply that it is a technology which enables us to communicate directly, both in sound and in vision, with other pupils and teachers, who may well be on the other side of the world. With ISDN cabling running at 128K, good quality audio, and reasonable quality video can be exchanged in real time. At Holy Cross School, we have been very excited about the potential of this ISDN based equipment, and accordingly we have set about exploring those new aspects of learning which it enables us to develop, using a little imagination. The immediacy of the feed-back from partner schools which the equipment makes possible is a vital ingredient in any such exploration, and there is obvious potential for the use of this equipment, for example in music, through shared creative workshops, comparison and actual teaching of dance steps, collaborative art and drama work, the exchange and comparison of scientific and geographical data, and so on.

At Holy Cross, we are working with Ikeda Junior High School, Osaka, and are engaged in a series of videoconferencing links, one of which we have called the 'Kabuki Project'. This is a multi-layered, international collaboration between the UK and Japan, working under the 'Konet Plan' which is currently being developed by Nippon Telegraph and Telecommunications (NTT) – the Japanese equivalent of BT (previously British Telecom) – and supported by the Japanese Ministry of Education. Holy Cross School, New Malden, Surrey, was invited to become a leadership or 'hub' school in the 'International Exchange Project' of this plan, and to collaborate with the Japanese in exploring together the exciting educational possibilities presented by the new ICT technologies – email, email attachments, image files, General Midi music files, the web, twinned sites, the National Grid for Learning, document exchange technology and videoconferencing. As part of this project, Holy Cross has signed a 'sister school agreement' committing us to work with Ikeda Attached Junior High School, a mixed school in Osaka. ('Attached' here means 'attached to Osaka Kyoiku University'. 'Kyoiku' means 'Education'.) The head teacher, or principal, of the school is a university professor of education, and the school is run by the deputy principal. This arrangement results in very close links between the school itself and the teacher training courses undertaken at the university. There is more about this educational arrangement in Chapter 4.

Three videoconferencing projects

Project 1: 'Kabuki Gift'

'Kabuki Gift' is a short play, (a love story), set in Japan and written in English by the American playwright, Douglas Love. Parts of the play were translated into Japanese by the Ikeda pupils, so that by using videoconferencing technology the two schools were able to undertake a performance of the same text 'live' in the two countries (UK and Japan), on two school stages (in Osaka and New Malden), in two different styles (traditional and modern), and in two languages (English and Japanese). The Japanese school, Ikeda, opted to do their scenes in a style which incorporated some elements of traditional Kabuki. By way of contrast, Holy Cross chose to perform their scenes in modern contemporary English style, with modern music added, several dances, and a finale which included the beautiful love song from the film 'Titanic'. The pupils in both countries used email to develop the planning of the performance itself, so that, for example, the first scenes were performed by Holy Cross girls in English, and the next scenes, shown on the video screen live from Japan, were performed by the Ikeda pupils, in Japanese. Then Holy Cross performed a scene in Japanese, and Ikeda performed a scene in English, and so on. A 29 inch colour monitor enabled a good number of visitors to see the play, though the relatively small screen size was clearly an aspect for us to develop further. We have now moved up to a 55 inch screen for the next series of conferences, with financial help from Peter Hand of the Great Britain Sasakawa Foundation, an organisation which kindly supports Anglo-Japanese initiatives.

A special introductory scene was added to the play (see pp. 56–8) both to introduce a humorous element into the production itself, and also to save writing lengthy explanatory programme notes for the audience to plough through prior to the performance. Designs for part of the UK costumes were based on ideas sent by Naomi, an artistically gifted Japanese pupil from Ikeda, the English girls were taught how to write the word 'Kabuki' in Japanese calligraphy live from Japan using the videoconferencing equipment, and the Ikeda pupils taught the English girls how to speak Japanese properly! This was done both as a part of the preparation sessions live over the video-conference link, and through the exchange of letters and audio tapes sent by 'snail mail', the new term for air mail . . .

Learning outcomes were amazing, in both countries. As with any school drama production, the pupils learned to work together as a team, but this time with an international dimension:

- they memorised their lines of text in two languages;
- shared ideas about costumes;
- designed and made those costumes;
- designed and painted the sets;
- used their new calligraphy skills;
- wrote background music;
- created dance steps;
- rehearsed and sang songs;
- prepared make-up;
- sent email messages to help them plan the various stages of the production;
- learnt how to use audio equipment;
- learnt how to operate video cameras;
- worked with pupils across the year groups;
- stage managed, planned and developed the production itself;

- designed and made the programme notes and advertising posters;
- learned to meet deadlines;
- negotiated changes in the performance;
- became close friends with their partners in Osaka; and above all,
- made learning fun.

All of this integrated their language, artistic, technological, physical and collaborative skills extremely effectively. As a senior representative from the Japanese Embassy, Hiroshi Minami-san put it, 'We have witnessed an excellent mix of dance, drama and music, with new technology, which has helped to further the close liaison between our two countries. I have been very impressed by what I have seen. It is important for young people to build up a good basis for mutual understanding'. When Michael Spencer from the London Symphony Orchestra's 'Discovery' team heard of this work, through the Japanese Embassy, it was time for us to join forces in a new venture.

Project 2: Festival of Enlightenment

This festival also formed part of the continuing educational collaboration between Holy Cross School, New Malden, Surrey, and Ikeda Junior High School, Osaka, under the NTT's 'Konet Plan'.

Participants:

In the UK

Holy Cross School pupils (100)
Members of the London Symphony Orchestra, directed by Michael Spencer

In Japan

Ikeda Junior High School pupils
Members of the Japan Philharmonic Orchestra, directed by Kuma Harada
Local musicians

The aim of this project was 'a sharing' of creative musical experience over ISDN cabling and videoconferencing equipment. Both schools invited professional orchestral musicians to assist in the creation of practical music workshops in the two countries, with the results being shared through a final performance. Accordingly, the LSO team under the direction of Michael Spencer, spent a day with the Holy Cross School Orchestra, working with the girls on developing musical improvisations on the theme of 'Auld Lang Syne'. This music was chosen because it is well known in both countries, and therefore any variations on the theme would be easily recognised both by the pupils and by the audience. Meanwhile, in Japan, members of the Japan Philharmonic Orchestra travelled from Tokyo to Osaka specially to participate in this workshop, where under the direction of Kuma Harada, they, too, worked out improvisations on the same musical theme. (See the following table).

Planning details for the musical aspects of the Festival of Enlightenment (*with the London Symphony Orchestra's 'Discovery' team, under the direction of Michael Spencer*)

(More information about the LSO's Discovery programme can be obtained from: London Symphony Orchestra Limited, Barbican Centre, London EC2Y 8DS, email: discovery@lso.co.uk)

Aims

To stimulate the pupils at both locations to produce an *original performable composition* based on selected material, and to *share the results of their exploration via the videoconferencing link*.

To utilise the skills of two major arts institutions to underpin, and exploit artistically, the technological advances developed in association with Holy Cross and Ikeda Schools.

Content

The project took the form of a practical musical exploration of 'theme and variation', based on 'Auld Lang Syne'. The use of this traditional melody, common in both countries, provides an opportunity to compare similarities and differences in its usage in both Japan and the UK. The melody of 'Auld Lang Syne' is taught in Japanese schools, but with different words applied (see below). The use of the pentatonic scale is a feature of both Western and Japanese traditional music. However, the scale used is only one of four different forms of pentatonic scale to be found in Japan. In the UK, the song is used to mark the closing of the year: in Japan, it is a graduation song which marks the end of the pupil's school life. In both instances, the songs were composed and have become 'traditional', rather than emerging from the anonymous melting pot of folk tradition. Robert Burns wrote the original text, and the Japanese Ministry of Education added the Japanese words when the education system was restructured and made open to foreign influences at the start of the Meiji Era.

Structure and method

One of the most important aims in working in this way is to stimulate and enhance the music-making that takes place within the classroom. It may be helpful if the players have a knowledge of how Benjamin Britten uses the arpeggio presented at the start of 'A Young Person's Guide to the Orchestra', in forming his material for most of the piece. 'Auld Lang Syne' can be fragmented in a similar way.

There are many ways to start such a project. However, I would recommend a preliminary 'high energy' game, like the 'Zip Bop', '2's and 3's' or the 'Name Game'. The second game is one way in which the use of the pentatonic scale can be introduced using the traditional Japanese game of Jankenpoi.

Jankenpoi (Stone, paper and scissors game)

Ask the pupils to find a partner, and have them devise a musical equivalent to this game (e.g. using three different notes). The non-tuned percussion players can take a short rhythmical element from 'Auld Lang Syne', but find three different sounds instead.

Compare some of the results.

Get half of the group to take the three notes (D, F natural, and G) and have them repeat the exercise. Have the other half repeat the pattern, but starting on A (that is, A, C natural, and D)

Show that when these are placed together they produce a pentatonic scale.

Get the pupils to make up a partnership with a person from a different group in order to produce a whole scale between them, and see if they can find any tunes which can be made from these notes.

Play the tunes!

Use accompaniments of pentatonic swirls, ostinati or drones.

Fragment the tune and build a new piece around it.

Make a rhythmical variation.

Find a vocal accompaniment.

Turn the melody backwards.

Find a way to finish effectively.

Hotari No Hikari (Japanese words for the tune of 'Auld Lang Syne')

Hotari no hikari, mado no yuki
Fumiyamu tsuki hi, kasane tsutsu
Itsu shika toshi mo suginoto o
Aketezokesa wa, wakare yuku

Translation

Oh, fireflies, oh white snow, how fast my school days fly,
Full of youth and memories burning in grandest flames,
Let's sing our parting songs so that they reach the sky.
This is the day of parting, oh, let's shout 'Farewell' to you!

For the conference itself, in both countries, pupils were nominated as chairpersons for the festival. In the UK, two Year 7 pupils, Naomi and Harriet (both aged eleven) held the Holy Cross end together, and in Japan this function was very ably performed by Miho. The event began with the usual testing of equipment for sound balance and vision, then Naomi and Harriet played a hand game 'Scissors, paper and stone', in Japanese. First they played each other, then they played Miho. They explained how they had used this game as a basis for the musical ideas of their performance. Holy Cross then played the full orchestral version of their 'Fantasia on the Auld Lang Syne theme'. Ikeda responded with their own version of the same theme, and a lively discussion ensued with demonstrations of the various instruments, and musical ideas which had just been exchanged.

In the second section, both schools sang choral music to each other, on the theme of 'Enlightenment', and after a drama item introduced by Mrs Sedgwick, there was a most amazing piano solo from Ikeda, a personal composition based on the pupil's experience of seeing the aftermath of the Kobe earthquake. It was a stunning composition and performance by Risa, a very able young pianist, and the Holy Cross pupils, teachers and our visitors watched absolutely transfixed. Then, after another lively discussion, the pupils in both countries joined hands to sing a final rendition of Auld Lang Syne, with the English girls singing in Japanese, and the Japanese team singing in English. Many of the participants were deeply moved, such was the emotion of the event. As the Japanese teachers put it in an email message – 'We can't express our impression by using words. Our pupils were moved to tears when they finished singing the last song.' The idea of 'Friendship Technology' was being born (see Chapter 4).

Such events are not possible without some support, however, and we were grateful for the help of:

- Michael Spencer (LSO's 'Discovery' team) for ably developing the musical content of the event, and for arranging for the Japan Philharmonic Orchestra members to visit Ikeda;
- Becky Shaftoe;
- Nigel Broadbent;
- Robert Turner;
  musicians and administrators of the LSO, for their professional help and encouragement;
- Kuma Harada (Barefoot Cultural Exchange Initiative) for inspiring the Ikeda pupils and directing the musical activities in Japan; and
- Chris Everett of the Daiwa Foundation, for assistance with funding, and for his enthusiatic encouragement

Michael Spencer summed up his own reaction to the project as follows:

The initial concept of exploring the same musical material (Auld Lang Syne/Hotari no Hokari) and using the results as the basis for original group creative work to take place simultaneously in the UK and Japan produced some extremely stimulating and worthwhile results. In particular, this method of working proved particularly appropriate for videoconferencing, where similarities and contrasts could be observed, compared and discussed immediately. We all felt that the project demonstrated the value of this form of communication as a resource for creating global partnerships that are not restricted to the world of commerce alone, but have considerable educational applications. We are keen to repeat and extend the experience.

We are now extending this work to plan a music festival with an American school. Figure 9.1 shows an 11 year old pupil planning this with her American counterpart. Being able to see the other person as well as talk is an important factor in developing intercultural relationships and collaborative work.

Figure 9.1 Planning a UK–USA Music Festival

The spreading of these ideas – and a new science conference

Anglia Television approached the school about filming this work. It is important to us as a school that when we are asked to recreate our work (for the BBC, for example, or for NHK – Japanese Television) we co-operate as best we can, but we also try at the same time to add a new dimension to the work, so that the pupils' learning outcomes are extended and developed. We do not wish our pupils to stagnate, even when they are performing on television. Accordingly, we decided to add a new science element to link the Japan work with the science work.

Project 3: Channel 4 visit to Holy Cross

At 9.30 UK time (17.30 Osaka time), two Holy Cross girls, Charlotte and Sarah from Year 8 as chairpersons; the Holy Cross School choir; a Year 10 science group with their teacher Mrs Michell; and a group of Irish dancers, all assembled in the Kells Library to wait for the 'Incoming Call' signal from Japan. Holy Cross pupils were particularly excited because, as well as performing for the television film crew, they could all see their Japanese partners much more clearly on the 55 inch colour monitor (with a ten speaker sound system!) which had arrived only a couple of days earlier.

The conference began with four Year 10 Holy Cross pupils showing Ikeda some of their work in GCSE science, including a 'live' chemistry experiment, which they described and discussed. The purpose of this was to explore in what ways it might be possible to share scientific knowledge and understanding through the use of the new videoconferencing technology. Having carried out a chemistry experiment, a second, document camera was then used to show Ikeda some of the computer calculations which the girls had made and had printed out as part of the recording of their science work for GCSE coursework assessment.

The Japanese contribution began with a 'surprise' item, when two Ikeda science teachers gave us a fascinating chemistry experiment, in reply to the Year 10 contribution. There is excitement both in Japan and the UK about how this work can be extended in the future. We learned, for example, that it is easily possible to demonstrate a scientific experiment in this way, and that if a second document camera is connected to the same system, then detailed statistical information can be read and discussed by the pupils in both countries. The potential of this is enormous, although a great deal of careful planning will be necessary to ensure effective learning outcomes in both countries.

Next, the Ikeda pupils presented a lovely series of dances and songs, which they had either researched or composed, as part of their own musical studies in the school. There were many beautiful, colourful costumes on display, and many musical instruments were played, with audiotape recordings also used to accompany this musical feast. We were fascinated to learn that the Japanese children's songs, which were also danced to, were similar in many ways to the songs and dances of English children, such as our own 'Oranges and Lemons'. The results of the Ikeda pupils' research into their musical heritage were very clearly seen on the huge projection television. Then the Holy Cross choir, now a regular feature of our conferences, sang two songs, in two part harmony accompanied by guitar, and this was interspersed with some stunning Irish dancing. Incidentally, the dancers had earlier used the new TV as a video tool to view their dance rehearsals, and found this to be a valuable new use of the large TV monitor and camera system. By looking at their own images on the large 55 inch monitor as they rehearsed their Irish dance steps, they were able to make careful and detailed corrections to their positioning relative to the camera. The conference ended with Claire, a Holy Cross pupil, teaching a group of Ikeda pupils some of the dance steps which she had previously performed as part of her dance routine This was an important day in the life of the two schools, who share a common vision of how teaching and learning styles must change in the new millennium.

Future development – the need to combine the technologies

The new ICT tools – email, email attachments, the internet and video-conferencing – are powerful in different ways. The next task for our two schools, therefore, is to explore in what ways these tools can be successful when used in combination with each other: our own videoconferences are always planned, developed and evaluated by email, for example. We feel very strongly, however, there are potentially many more powerful ways of working than this. As our next step, therefore, we are setting out to see how a new project, called The Banner Project and involving product development in textiles, can lead us to harness the combined power of some of these new tools.

The Banner Project

The objective of this next project is for Holy Cross to design and make a series of decorative banners for our partner school, Ikeda, in time to be displayed during their Open Day, when many important visitors will arrive from all over Japan. We therefore have a clear and fixed deadline to meet. As part of their Year 9 Japan studies, the pupils will set about creating a series of colourful fabric designs, using CAD software, for later manufacture into banners which will be sent to Japan. The preliminary designs for these banners will be emailed to Osaka, where the Japanese pupils will be encouraged to ask for suitable adjustments to be made to the colour, shape, material, or size of the products. Artistic ideas from Osaka may also be incorporated into these designs. The new specifications will then be emailed back to London, for further development by the Holy Cross pupils. These final design specifications will then be made up into the banners, and posted by 'snail mail' to Osaka.

It will be possible for us to move the videoconferencing equipment from its present location in the library into a computer room, so that the pupils can see each other, and talk about various aspects of the project, while they are actually working on the designs. There is also the powerful document camera coupled up to the videoconferencing equipment which can be incorporated into the system to show, in excellent close-up, details such as stitching, or intricate design points. By switching between these different tools, we hope to develop the final banners to very precise design specifications, as indeed is the case with actual industrial practice. The problem of teaching what is otherwise a quite theoretical aspect of the school's textiles course in technology is thereby imaginatively resolved, and our partners will have the pleasure of displaying to their visitors the banners which the Japanese pupils have themselves helped to design. The whole process can then be published on the websites of the two schools, for others to see and develop further.

Some students' reactions to the videoconferencing work

The views of the pupils about using this new equipment are varied, but very positive:

> I loved being shown how to create origami animal figures by the Japanese pupil. It was incredible – much better than from a book. You can't ask a book questions.

> I like art, and so learning how to use a special Shodo brush to create Japanese characters was really exciting. A drawing lesson, live from Japan! I liked it best when I could ask the teacher to show me how to write my own name in Japanese.

> I can see how videoconferencing could be very useful in business when I am older, and working.

> Funny things are interesting, like the Japanese pupils asking us why we wore safety glasses when we showed them our science experiment. I didn't expect that.

> It was really lovely to work with the LSO musicians, and then to see what the Ikeda pupils had done with the same music. I suppose we could have just sent them a videotape, but we couldn't then have talked about things.

> I am sure that the Ikeda pupils were as nervous as we were about performing the play together, but we all learnt to keep our feelings under control, for their sake as well as ours, so that the performance would be successful.

> It's fun doing new things with the technology.

Guidelines for using videoconferencing equipment

- As with any communication between pupils, the most important single factor in ensuring the success of a conference is that both groups should have an equal commitment to the topic or project at hand. If this is a drama, a dance, a music festival or workshop, then such commitment is automatically ensured. Students like to share their talents in music, and are eager to see how others perform, too.
- A clear, previously agreed agenda helps all participants to find their way through any discussion, and it is important that pupils have a part in the planning of this aspect of a conference.

- Sound quality and good lighting need to be checked carefully, and often, a short introductory practice session can usefully resolve any difficulties in these areas. Audio-feedback is avoided by placing the microphones well away from the main monitor's speaker system, for example. Failure to do this can result in a most amazing echo effect, as voices are beamed back across the world!

- Fast movements can cause difficulty for the camera, an especially difficult aspect when dealing with dance and drama. However, creative solutions can easily be found. For example, the dance like that to the music of 'Titanic' during the 'Kabuki Gift', was resolved by creating dances in the the two countries which worked to circular, fluid patterns of movement, so that a precise musical beat was unnecessary, (to allow for the unavoidable second's time delay), and a more graceful dance response was thereby created.

- One surprising problem arises when handing over discussion from one pupil to another within the conference. When the pupils come from varied cultural backgrounds (e.g. UK and Japan), there can be a delay while body cues are read and appropriate responses made, especially when everyone is trying so hard to be polite! Experience is the only solution here.

- It is important to ensure that each pupil has a clearly defined role in each session, such as make-up artist, sound recordist, camera operator, actor, singer, dancer, choir or orchestral member, and that he or she has some chance to rehearse any difficult tasks. Since running costs are still quite high, much of this work needs to be done separately in the two countries, and then put together fairly rapidly. Our experience shows, however, that no matter what demands you make on pupils, they will always rise effectively to a challenge, and exceed the wildest optimism of their teachers. The best example of this was when two Holy Cross girls had only a week in which to prepare an entire scene in Japanese (they had both been away from school on various educational visits) yet were able to impress their Japanese counterparts with the excellence of their Japanese pronunciation.

- In dealing with pupils from another country, two complementary strategies have emerged:

  (a) to use the target language very deliberately, for example by our UK pupils acting some of the drama scenes in Japanese, and
  (b) to use musical language and mime so that these language-free elements are easily shared, without a communication problem arising.

  This was particularly appreciated by the music and drama teachers at Ikeda, who could easily see the value of producing a play with music and dance, as many participants could be involved without the need for advanced language skills, while other pupils could develop their English in a very real context.

- The effect of working in English was, for the Japanese, an immense spur in learning to use the English language. In an email evaluation they remarked that the pupils 'also started studying English harder, because they felt it was necessary to do so'.

- We are often asked about the difficulty of working with a school where there is a significant time difference. (Japan is 8 or 9 hours ahead of the UK depending on Summer Time, whereas the USA is 6 hours behind us.) There is, indeed, a problem arising about times, but it is not what you might expect. We have experienced more problems over the matching of holiday dates than about differences in the hour of the day. Ikeda pupils were always more than willing to stay after school to work on the collaboration with us but then they, or we, had to break for half term, Easter, activity weeks, and so on. Plan the year carefully: holidays are a greater problem than time differences!
- The motivation of pupils is always high during videoconferencing projects, especially when this work is tied effectively in with other cross-curricular ICT project work, for which Holy Cross is now well-known (see Williams in Leask and Pachler, 1999). In the case of our Year 9 pupils, this is the geography-based cross-curricular study of Japan, its economy and culture, which takes up a good part of the September to Christmas term.
- The Japanese were most keen to allow the pupils in both countries to exchange their personal feelings about culture. They considered this to be of paramount importance, over-shadowing anything possible by way of email, valuable though this is as a planning tool. The Japanese pupils' interest in English culture was greatly deepened by the video-conferences, but interestingly, so too was their interest in their own culture. If you have to share your understanding with others, you have first to understand it yourself.
- Finally, actual discussion is probably best kept to a minimum, hence our own emphasis on creative music, dance and drama events. Discussion is best for face-to-face evaluation sessions, with email providing a better vehicle for the exchange of detailed factual information. If general midi music files and JPEG images are also added to email messages, then much information can be exchanged before and after the actual conference.

We have serious doubts about hoping to maintain the interest and commitment of large numbers of pupils through lengthy discussion sessions. In fact, the worst thing you can actually do with videoconferencing equipment, it seems to us, is to hold an actual conference!

Conclusions

Having seen some of the projects through which Holy Cross School has explored new uses of videoconferencing equipment in music, dance, drama, science and textiles, you may wish to consider what ways you think that regular access to teachers and pupils from another country could enhance learning outcomes in your own subject area.

Questions

1 Think about the differences there might be in:

    a. working through videoconferencing with an English speaking school in, for example, the USA, Canada, Australia or New Zealand, and

    b. working with a school where the first language is not English.

2 What are the main likely difficulties you might experience, and what are the benefits in terms of learning outcomes?

3 How might you link your videoconferencing work with that of colleagues in other subjects across the curriculum?

Further reading

Leask, M. and Pachler, N. (1999) *Learning to Teach Using ICT in the Secondary School*, London: Routledge. See especially Chapter 4, 'Using the Internet as a teaching and learning tool', and Chapter 12 'Whole school approaches: Integrating ICT across the curriculum', for some practical ideas on using email and the internet for supporting the development of creative frameworks for learning.

Milosovevic, L. (ed.) (1999) *School improvement in the UK*, British Council, 10 Spring Gardens, London SW1. Chapter 20 contains background information on the UK/Japan school linking project.

References

Leask, M. and Pachler, N. (1999) *Learning to Teach Using ICT in the Secondary School*, London: Routledge.

10 Creating and maintaining the school website

Meaningless task or educational activity – luxury or necessity?

Alastair Wells

Introduction

More and more schools are developing their own websites, sometimes co-ordinated by a local education authority or Internet Service Provider (ISP), sometimes by enthusiastic individuals or by a team within a school who have identified a specific need. There is no doubt that many schools are producing excellent websites but what is meant by excellent? Why are these schools developing websites and what guidelines are they following?

A suitable ICT infrastructure must be established before launching or being distracted into creating a school website as appropriate and effective websites evolve from good classroom practice. Creating a website at too early a stage may mean a lot of energy is wasted in having to redesign the site to meet the higher demands of large volumes of traffic and content development that are usually associated with the more popular school websites.

Establishing a good infrastructure means establishing good communications, networking, classroom access, intranet and internet and appropriate hardware and software facilities to deliver the Information Communication and Technology (ICT) needs of a school.

A good school website will reflect the development of ICT within the curriculum and support the school's ICT activities and policies. This is by no means the primary goal, which will differ significantly between schools and types of school. However, it is usually the ICT department or skilled ICT teachers that will have responsibility for creating and editing, adding and maintaining the school website so it is important that they are aware of the need and time involved in such a project.

Types of website

School websites can be grouped into a number of categories:

- Non-existent
- Passive
- Active
- Interactive
- Dynamic

- *Non-existent* websites are simply absent, the school probably hasn't considered creating a website or if they have there are no plans being put into operation. However, there may be a degree of awareness and, with time, such schools often develop a passive website.

- *Passive* websites are little more than a collection of information pages. They describe the school, how to contact the school by phone and fax and sometimes email. There may be a map of where to find the school and some information about courses and the life of the school. These sites are limited but they are a start, and the school does at least have a web presence and the potential to do more web-based activities given time, resources and an identified need. Passive websites are rarely updated although once a year is the minimum requirement to check the existing information is still relevant.

- *Active* websites take the passive website one stage further. A lot more information is provided for the visitor and there is generally a page for all departments in the school. The school prospectus is available and details of all courses together with additional information such as syllabuses, exam results, the life of the school, clubs and activities. New pages, features and updates, appear on a fairly regular basis. Active websites are refreshed on a termly basis or at regular intervals during a term but there is no regular maintenance of the website.

- An *interactive* site has a wide ranging collection of information about the school, courses and pupil guidance together with department home pages that support classwork and homework. The website is regularly updated and because there is a large amount of information the website is supported by search facilities and easy navigation aids. An interactive website will also meet some of the interests of the users and consider an audience, so that information is provided for pupils and parents and there is a feedback mechanism to the school. School work may be publicised on the website, such as a local history study complete with interviews of local residents. A bank of questions and answers builds up over time and new readers offer additional information for the project. Pictures and sound accompany the materials, creating an incentive to return and explore the site in greater detail. An interactive site is updated on at least a weekly basis and usually by a team of dedicated staff and pupils.

- A *dynamic* website is very exciting and not only encourages the visitor to interact with the site, but the website is capable of interacting with the user. There is a wealth of information, easy navigation and a wide range of sections to explore. A dynamic website will document the interaction with its wider community and build resources that will be a first port of call for the pupil wanting to find information to support their studies. The website needs to be tailored to the needs of the pupils and focused on the school curriculum, but even so this remains of immense benefit to many other pupils throughout the world. There will be interactive sections such as multiple choice questions and answers that give the pupil revision opportunities and a test score and there may well be on-line conferencing facilities. Visitors to a dynamic website will find multimedia materials, resources such as data files and programs to download, worksheets and spreadsheet data to support their studies and examples of good pupil work to stimulate their own studies and provide an incentive for achieving high grades. A dynamic website is also a fast track to good learning resources, often having tailor-made links to other good websites identified by teachers in the school.

Dynamic websites also offer pupils the opportunity to have on-line mentoring or conferencing with friends in a year group or particular class, so that on-line homework and homework support is a reality. A dynamic website demands high levels of maintenance, almost on a daily basis. As the website increases in complexity it usually goes beyond the generation of simple HTML pages, by incorporating the likes of cgi and java scripts. This in turn usually demands the skills of a webmaster to coordinate the work/efforts of a well organised team which passes on large volumes of materials to be authored and added to the website. Certainly for schools supporting on-line homework and interactive resources, the presence of a full time webmaster is essential. Also vital is extra free non-teaching time for a member of staff to co-ordinate the activities within the school and manage the webmaster.

There is no perfect model – indeed much depends on a school's resources and approach to ICT as well as its needs and priorities. The type of school plays a big part in the decision making process as does the whole school development plan for ICT. However, as more and more families acquire internet connections at home they are beginning to look at the role of the school within the on-line learning community and the school can be very much the focus of such a community – provided it has a web presence and provided it is willing to evolve and meet the challenge of an increasingly on-line society.

What is needed from the website?

Ask one question and many more follow, all relating to important school management issues. In some cases the answers involve a considerable cost to the school. The following table contains a few questions for you to consider, whether you are embarking on the first steps to creating a website or whether you want to reflect on materials already created and in need of updating or extending:

Questions for you to consider in drawing up website plans

What hardware and software is required to establish an effective school website?

Are the headteacher and governing body involved with strategic planning of the school website?

Who is authoring the content?

Who is responsible for maintaining the website?

What is the purpose of the school website?

What is the intended audience?

How easy is your website to navigate?

What is the structure of your website and does it cater for the whole school?

What is the value to the school of the website?

How many people are involved with monitoring and adding content?

Does the school need an internet connection?

What is the cost of connecting existing school computers to the internet?

Will I need to buy in new hardware and software to make use of the internet?

What will be the true cost of running an internet site?

Will the school need to staff the website in terms of authoring and developing content?

Have you considered what you really want or why you need a website and have you planned for the future to ensure the website delivers the business of the school?

What is needed and what is the role of the school website – is it a luxury or a necessity?

How can a school website be used effectively within a school as well as in the extended community around the school?

How does the website differ from other on-line resources and who manages the authoring and quality control of the site?

Does the school have a network?

Can the network be connected to the internet?

How will schools be able to manage active websites?

Are they simply marketing tools or can they support the education of pupils in the school and provide interactive learning materials?

Can a website help to raise standards through on-line learning and how can all pupils have equal access?

All these are important issues (with no easy answers!) that need careful discussion and planning within a school and preferably by a team which includes the headteacher, senior management, governors and teachers. Strategic planning is essential for the effective use of a school website as is an investigation of the need by the school for a website. The need for a website should not replace the higher priority of good ICT facilities in the school, but once these have been established, a website can certainly help ICT to grow within the school community and the area that it serves.

Competence and capacity

Competence and capacity plays a very important role in this respect. If we were to look back a couple of years and consider the type of ICT being carried out in a school we could look at the types of skills that were at the core of ICT teaching and training. The focus was very much on keyboard skills, the ability to use appropriate computer assisted learning software and disc handling and filing skills. Although these skills remain important, pupils have progressed to a higher level, at a younger age, and communicating and handling information, modelling, measurement and control, multimedia authoring skills and the use of peripheral devices are everyday skills being displayed by more and more pupils.

Today pupils are much more comfortable with the use of data logging equipment, control technology, multimedia materials, simulations, spreadsheets, databases, computer graphics and desk top publishing as everyday tools to meet their curriculum requirements.

Even more apparent is the increased use by pupils of Interactive Learning Systems, email and the World Wide Web. Staff are also increasing their use of desk top computers, pocketbooks and laptops for record keeping, classroom assessment and departmental administration. There is a clear pattern of better access to information technology from pupils, teachers and parents, and schools are increasingly facing the problem of how to meet this growth in demand.

All ICT co-ordinators will know that they have a certain capacity and competence to deliver ICT. By competence I mean their ability to co-ordinate, to teach ICT, to plan, to effectively control a limited budget, to be aware of technical specifications and developments and to keep up to date with developments and adjust their action plans in the light of ever changing uses and demand. By capacity I mean the number of computers in the school, the size of the network, peripherals etc. that can be monitored and effectively controlled and kept in use by an ICT co-ordinator.

All schools have a ceiling for their use of ICT and this depends on staffing, time allocation, technical support and funding. Schools of the same size may well have different ceilings because there is a certain degree of competence that dictates the capacity of ICT for that school. To increase the capacity, management issues, school plans and action plans need to be initiated to improve competence.

A successful school may well have already reached very high levels of capacity and competence and there will still be increased demand for the use of ICT, so how can the increase be brought about without an internal collapse in the system through exhaustion or a dispersal to departments that proves so wide that the internal cohesion of ICT co-ordination is lost, together with effective management and progression of ICT developments within a school?

Co-ordinating ICT

IT co-ordination demands a tremendous amount of energy and diversity of skills. The skills of an effective ICT co-ordinator are seldom recognised and job descriptions in advertisements for new posts tend to show how badly understood this important role is. The very nature of the ICT industry means constant change and ICT co-ordinators have to be aware of trends, upgrades, new technologies and user skills and immerse themselves in what is happening to ensure they can provide good advice to colleagues as they become more computer literate. If an ICT co-ordinator is successful, he or she will have developed the curriculum, provided an effective infrastructure, be building resources, providing access to computers in network rooms, departments, libraries and other open areas. They will have implemented a school ICT policy and an investment scheme for the future to replace ageing hardware. As resources grow they will have taken on appropriate technician support, network management and servicing contracts whilst also helping to deliver appropriate content to staff and pupil users via the stand alone, intranet and internet facilities. Few schools will have reached such dizzy heights but the value of the internet and a school website must not be overlooked in this important scenario.

Eventually, ICT co-ordinators will realise that adding hardware to their inventory may not be the answer to delivering an effective ICT curriculum. If their capacity for handling computers in the school is 100 and 20 new computers are purchased, are they able to manage 120 or do they ignore the oldest 20 computers and maintain a serviceable 100? If the increase is accompanied by extra curriculum management time, extra network management time or technician time, then capacity can be increased but this is seldom the case in most schools. It may also be that all environments have been saturated with computers: available classrooms have been converted into network rooms, smaller areas have been turned into clusters of computers, the libraries are equipped with computers, departments have stand alone and network computers. What options are then available if demand continues to rise for access to IT?

In my own school we have faced this very problem and with 1500 pupils wanting to access their email at lunchtimes, they have approximately 2.45 seconds each to logon, read their mail, send a message and log-off. Email is very popular and important but it must not distract from more important curriculum activities using computers, such as coursework and research. Where, when and how should pupils use email and how can the school direct the focus of email to effective learning rather than banal electronic conversations with friends? The school website can be a creative medium for effective use of email at school and at home providing a 'safe' environment for internet chat and forums, without having to be involved with people you don't know outside the school community.

One effective strategy for using email is to involve some of the wonderful skills that parents have to offer via the internet. Many parents are employed as experts in their field and if asked to contribute to the life of the school, via email, often prove more than willing to answer questions from pupils. If the school is acting as a 'go between' and access to private email addresses is through teaching staff at the school, parents can play a very active role. Questions and answers to experts can be displayed on the school website and links created from the answers to good learning materials on the web. My own school has experts on fields such as astronomy, geology, education, religion, science, computing, mathematics and engineering.

Yet another effective use of email and the school website is for on-line work experience. Many pupils have excellent work experience placements and they thoroughly enjoy the opportunity of exploring the world of work. However, having established contacts in career areas it would be good for them to keep in touch with people they have met who can also help them with exam courses that will lead to success in the career area of interest. Support can be on-going once the pupil has returned to school and the expert can offer advice on projects and courses, particularly if they are recently qualified in their own area. Questions and answers to on-line experts can also be posted on the school website, building a career centre that the careers advisers can make use of as an additional resource in their school.

Finally email and the website can be used for mentoring pupils, on-line conferencing and internet relay chat. With web-based management tools ICT co-ordinators can establish conferencing and mentoring groups via the internet so only specifically listed users join the groups. This means that the user's email address can be used for departments to hold virtual department meetings, management can email important notices and documents, by-passing the need for printed copy and pupils can interact with each other in homework clubs or ask questions and receive on-line support through mentoring – probably with their classroom teacher. The latter is likely to stimulate pupils to ask questions that they would not normally ask in the classroom, due to shyness or nervousness, in the same way that word-processing encourages some pupils to write because of spell checkers and improved quality of output.

The school website is now providing a mechanism to increase ICT capacity within the most well-equipped schools and helps deliver higher levels of competence by involving more staff, while also reaching a wider audience and involving pupils and parents in the business of the school.

An effective communication mechanism is therefore essential and in order for an ICT co-ordinator to manage this within their school they must have effective software tools at their disposal, not a range of disparate tools or complicated managed services but an integrated suite of flexible resources that caters for a mix and match approach for the way in which different schools operate. Without appropriate tools and technology the time involved in setting up and delivering web-based activities is well out of reach of even the most dedicated staff and the school will never get beyond the passive website status.

Teachers and the website

Given the right opportunities and resources, many teachers will use ICT very effectively in school and at home. Some do not understand some of the very basics of the computer systems they use but if they are effective users of the technology, good facilitators and can deliver a good lesson in their own subject area using ICT, then they are making progress.

Teachers are natural multimedia authors and prepare worksheets, slide shows, videos, experiments, illustrations, tape recordings and anecdotes in advance of every lesson. Where technology can help and there is a need, teachers will integrate ICT in their classroom. If the lesson can be documented and referred to, then pupils who were absent or pupils who would like to repeat the lesson could use the materials to improve their learning and understanding of a topic. The school's website provides a mechanism by which this is possible and there are ICT tools that make the preparation of such lessons relatively straightforward for the teacher.

Schemes of work and details of syllabuses and reading lists also help to provide parents with the information they need at home to support their child's education and so in turn the school website is a tool to raise standards of education.

Given a good infrastructure within the school and good access to computers teachers can make effective use of ICT with their classes. When departments also know that resources and weblinks can be added quickly and easily to their own department homepage, demand for web-based materials increases as does the imagination of teachers on how to use the internet in their teaching. A web visit to a Picasso exhibition encourages pupils to paint in the style of Picasso and the website provides a school-based exhibition for the world and, more importantly, for parents who seldom get to see the work of the school. Virtual fieldtrips are possible to the Amazon Rainforest or Antarctica, and the chemistry department can fly to Venus and research the properties of the atmosphere in order to test metals in the laboratory suitable for a spaceship flight. The results of such activities can be recorded and stored on the website for all to enjoy, but more importantly as a stimulus or revision site for pupils as an aid to their learning. Good projects established in one school can be shared with others and a wide range of examples can develop.

This is also a good way of sharing limited resources between schools, particularly those in remote areas. Small schools may have excellent teaching in a number of subject areas such as art and science but weaknesses in languages. Another school within the same area may be strong in languages and weak in art. Some schools have already addressed such problems and through the internet, and the school website, teachers have been able to share expertise and exchange resources and schemes of work and raise standards in their own schools through effective partnerships.

Focus of the school website

The home–school community therefore becomes intertwined and the school becomes the focus of a large community through its website. The secondary school can encompass Primary Link schools and provide on-line materials for other schools and their communities and address the concerns of pupils moving up to the 'big school'. Likewise the Primary Link schools can offer on-line information and support to their parents who often have a strong interest and involvement in the early years of education which tends to tail away as their children move to the secondary school. The parents remain very interested in their child's education at secondary level but 'street-credibility' of the child comes into play with peers, if parents are seen to become too involved with the school. The school website provides an excellent discreet way for parents of older children to become involved in the life of the school.

The website also gives a school a sense of place and identity not only within the local community but the wider world as well. Contacts with other schools and parent groups throughout the world can be immensely beneficial and the school website allows a wide audience to read of the activities of smaller groups of teachers, pupils and parents who have established contacts. In my own school we have an art exchange of pictures drawn by pupils with a school in the Czech Republic. Few colleagues, pupils or parents would get to know what was happening without the materials appearing on the website.

The school website is a superb communication tool for pupils, staff and senior managers. In some ways school websites can be likened to airports. The passive website is one where there is a small hangar and airstrip and once a month you may be lucky to see an aeroplane take off. A interactive website is like a national airport with lots of inbound and outbound traffic and the need for air traffic control and plenty of public information and services. A busy airport is an exciting place to visit and if you are passing through there is the magic of wondering what the destination will be like and the peace of mind in getting back safely. Communicating with other schools, staff and pupils throughout the world is tremendously exciting and leads to excellent curriculum use of the internet and ICT by departments. Pupils can exchange emails, pictures, datafiles, music, conference on-line, develop languages skills and much more. The school website can be used as an archive of materials but also a management tool where different time zones affect communications. The website becomes a postbox of materials in the two way exchange but also a drop in cyber-school for any other visitors from around the world to watch and even join in with the activities.

The same activities can of course operate between classes in the school and between school and home, between homes and involve the local community. Some pupils are already busy creating their own websites at home and exchange electronic resources so the school has an important role in helping to ensure that pupils' skills are directed and utilised for learning in this dynamic environment.

Financial aspects

Senior managers can make use of the website for advertising and communicating all kinds of information about the life and ethos of the school, syllabuses, schemes of work, exam results, extracurricular activities, announcements and regular news bulletins. In some ways it is a more efficient means of communication than paper, in that not all newsletters, and similar materials, arrive home with the pupils and if and when they are passed on they may be quickly read, put aside for careful reading later and then get lost. The same materials are permanent records on the website and can be archived easily. Potentially, and quite likely in the near future, all news and communications can be sent by email to parents as well as being archived on the school website. This will save a lot of time and money in preparing and distributing the paper-based materials.

There are other financial aspects related to a school website. Most of these relate to staffing, particularly the funding of a webmaster as demand for web-based resources increases. Initially, increasing publicity through a website, whilst maintaining the reproduction of paper-based materials, will cause costs to rise. In time it is possible to switch to an all electronic system and the balance of ancillary staffing will change, as will job descriptions and the nature of their work. In order to fund the interim extra staffing through such an evolutionary period, sponsorship may be required. This can come in many forms and some schools are happy with advertising revenue, others are not. It isn't the only form of fund raising, however, and the school website can be used to host webpages for the companies of parents, many of whom would not have considered a web presence. Local electricians, plumbers, builders, accountants, advisers, hairdressers and shop owners of all kinds interact with the same local community as the school and although recommendations can be passed on by word of mouth many companies would be happy to sponsor the school and become registered on the school's equivalent of yellow pages.

The website can also be used as an exchange and mart facility within the community in the same way as parents advertise in a newsagent's window. A single fee or weekly rate is paid to the school to advertise everything from school kit, to textbooks, fridges and even cars. This may seem extreme but is just the right sort of activity to encourage users to pop into the website and view the latest adverts whilst at the same time looking for homework support, guidance and subject testing. Variety makes the website interesting and it has to provide very relevant curriculum support or keep changing the content of some pages to keep users visiting the site.

Pupils and the website

Pupils have a major role to play in the development of a good website and can offer good original ideas and energy in collating and authoring materials. A well organised cohort of pupils can produce excellent source materials and if given a responsibility, perhaps attached to certain departments, they can develop management, assessment and design skills that belie their age. Pupils involved with collaborative website activities also develop web-authoring skills and business skills and an appreciation and knowledge of ICT that goes way beyond the demands of the National Curriculum.

Pupils are the ideal test bed to assess the design of the school website and any new web pages to be created. They also have many gifts from art and graphics skills, to music, html authoring, reporting and group co-ordination that are brought to the fore simply being a part of the school website authoring team.

Legal aspects and the website

The legal aspects associated with creating a school website need careful consideration. What are the Intellectual Property Rights of teachers, staff and pupils who have authored materials that become available for others to use via the website? How do you ensure that copyright is not being breached through your site? Copyright can potentially be breached through the website. For example, staff and pupils may produce some wonderful artwork which is downloaded elsewhere and used in a publication without the authors' permission. Alternatively a pupil may submit materials to be published on the school website which have been taken from elsewhere, exposing the school, or local education authority, to court action. A school therefore needs to be provided with information, control, monitoring and also legal protection and insurance against such problems.

Networking

Networking is a critical aspect of delivering good ICT resources throughout the school and although many school buildings do not lend themselves to effective networking there are usually solutions to this or the potential to network certain areas. Networking allows ICT to flourish in a school and also allows resources to be shared and management time and costs to be reduced.

Clearly certain computers and types of software and peripherals are better at delivering certain types of ICT use within the school. Administration and accountancy packages within the office are not always the best systems to use within departments. Weather satellite receiving stations vary as does the hardware and software required for music composition or computer controlled sewing machines. Most ICT needs can be served by a particular hardware manufacturer but the performance can often vary enormously, as can the cost. In effect the ICT coordinator is becoming a system analyst but also needs to be aware of how different computers can be integrated (if at all) with the existing network. The network manager is always facing pressures for increased speed of access, increased performance and reliability and greater flexibility in the use of the network e.g. individual disc space and shared resources, user friendly front ends and bigger, better more efficient back-up routines. They also have to cope with demands for internet and intranet access. Although the internet looks after itself, the school based materials need managing and pupils and parents need educating into the types of materials available from the school via the internet.

There is then the question of whether you provide open access to the internet or whether you only 'allow' access to certain sites. If you go for open access you will definitely need to install on the webserver software that prevents access to undesirable sites. Parents, staff and pupils need to be aware of the school's internet policy and even sign an Internet User Agreement if they intend to use the school's network to gain access to the internet.

If you are running your own website from computers in the school then security becomes very important as resources grow and more expensive computers are almost certainly being installed. Good effective backup must be in place and a weekly, if not daily routine, established to secure data. Backing up is not difficult, but good backup systems do cost money and if a wide range of computers need backing up, the time involved can be significant for a member of staff.

Conclusion

There is no doubt that the internet is here to stay and that more and more pupils and staff will have internet connections in the very near future. A school needs to cater for pupils and provide access for those who cannot afford the internet at home as well as providing good access for all pupils for curriculum based activities. A good ICT infrastructure clearly needs to be in place and the school website becomes very much a part of the home, school and wider community environment.

Whether you view a school website as a luxury or a necessity depends more on the school's current ICT status in terms of development plans and management. It is a luxury if an appropriate infrastructure is not in place but essential once the investment has been made. In the classroom it becomes a necessity for pupils and staff who have developed good ICT skills and know that motivation, performance and learning is enhanced through the use of ICT. The school website can back this up by providing a wide range of support for the pupil's learning both at school and in the home.

Questions

1   What makes a successful website? What do you need a website for?
2   How will the website be managed and maintained? How will the website evolve and meet curriculum needs? What links will you provide to other sites? Are there suitable categories of links?
3   How will the website integrate with the school intranet? Do you need firewall protection?
4   Who will do the authoring of the website? What software will you require for authoring and managing the website? Where will the website be hosted? What staff and pupil involvement will there be with the website?

Further reading

The texts which follow provide ideas related to school improvement, developing a policy for ICT in the school and website design.

Abbott, C. (1998) *Making the web Special; A Guide for Special Schools and PRUs*, Kings College, London.

Ainscow, M., Hopkins, D., Southworth, G. and West, M. (1994) *Creating the Conditions for School Improvement: A Handbook of Staff Development Activities*, London: David Fulton Publishers.

DfEE (1997) *Connecting the Learning Society: A Consultative Document*, London: HMSO.

Frost, D. (1997) *Reflective Action Planning for Teachers: A Guide to Teacher-led Professional and School Development*, London: David Fulton Publishers.

Harrison M. (1998) *Co-ordinating Information and Communications Technology across the Primary School*, London: Falmer Press.

Leask, M. and Terrell, I. (1997) *Development Planning and School Improvement for Middle Managers*, London: Kogan Page.

Poole, P. and Capstick, N. (1995) *Managing IT: A Guide for Senior Managers*, Coventry: NCET.

Tagg, B.(1995) *Developing a Whole School ICT Policy*, London: Pitman Publishing.

11 Key Skills and the post 16 curriculum

An innovative approach

Phil Langshaw with Richard Millwood

With the new emphasis on the National Specifications for Key Skills (live from September 2000), schools are looking for innovative and relevant approaches to their inclusion within the post 16 curriculum. The experience of Plume School offers such an exciting and innovative solution, avoiding piecemeal, ad hoc delivery.

Introduction

During the summer of 1999, Plume School Art and Design Department joined forces with ULTRALAB,[1] the Learning Technology Research Centre at Anglia Polytechnic University Chelmsford, to work on a project with sixth-form students using the latest cutting edge digital technologies.

The impetus for the art department to involve itself in such a project stemmed from a number of issues which were beginning to well into a strong and undeniable confluence, stirred directly by pupil need. The first was a realisation that in the last few years there has been a renaissance of art and design fuelled by the development of multimedia technologies. This was reflected in the fact that increasing numbers of our students were stimulated by, and were entering into, multimedia degree courses, or if entering into so called ' art courses' were required to have a wide ranging knowledge of the digital technologies if they were to have an advantage, not just at college, but also in the employment market itself. In recent years we have thus had students entering into courses on multimedia, film video and animation, photography and digital media, special effects and model making for film and television, advertising, marketing and magazine work.

Digital media had already been a priority within the Plume School art department, in that we had already worked with professional animators using the latest digital technology, producing PSE related material, and we possessed a dedicated graphic design studio, including industry standard Applemac computers, scanners, digital cameras, and a separate photographic studio. However, it was clear that we needed to extend our brief, such that students were aware of website design/ CD Rom production, and the potential to bring together many of their skills through a multimedia project. Central to this was a desire not abandon traditional skills, but to develop and integrate them into a cutting edge multimedia project.

What has certainly been made clear is that with the shifts in the employment market and the mirrored shifts in the structure of art courses, for art and design students (or indeed any creative area) with skills in the new digital media technologies, there has never been a more exciting time for their future employment prospects.

A recent government advisory committee report on Creative and Cultural Education under the subheading 'The Challenge for Education' states:

> Digital media, the industry responsible for designing and creating content for the internet and other digital formats, such as CD Roms, could create up to 80,000 jobs over the next eight years. Some 20,750 people in the UK are employed in digital media, a sector that barely existed a decade ago, according to a study commissioned by the Digital Media Alliance, a consortium of companies involved with the industry. There are 2,750 digital media companies in the UK with combined annual revenue of £687.5m. Roughly 2,000 freelances, mustering combined annual income of £50m, work in the digital media sector. The study estimates that 500 specialist digital subsidiaries of traditional media groups produce annual turnover of about £187.5m. The work of these companies and individuals has given the UK an international reputation as having recognised indigenous talent for creative ideas and cultural innovation. The UK's digital media industry has the potential to grow by at least 20 per cent per year over the next decade, more than double the rate of traditional creative sectors, such as film and advertising. It could then employ 100,000 people and generate annual revenues of £5bn by 2007. The education system needs to be restructured to train the type of skilled employees that the industry needs and eradicate its present skill shortages.
>
> (The National Advisory Committee on Creative and Cultural Education 1999: 221)

College courses reflect this demand, and in one prospectus for multimedia, it is stated:

> Ultimately, working, learning, leisure and entertainment will be affected by this technology. However, there is a shortage of multi-skilled professionals who know how to use it effectively ... being a new discipline, the fast emerging field of multi-media offers excellent career prospects.

In essence, the above reflects the fact that the future focus in education is moving towards the development of transferable competences to meet an ever changing and flexible employment market (not a body of knowledge) in that the economy will need multi-skilled professionals who are computer and business literate, team players, creative, innovative, and with good communication and presentation skills for whatever area of endeavour they may find themselves in.

This is because in the future, through technologies such as the internet, facts and information will be readily available. It will be the ability to analyse, process, creatively develop and apply such information, which will be the prized skill of the millennium – whether such information is written, visual, or aural (see also Chapters 14 and 16).

It has been pointed out that in distant history, wealth stemmed initially from the ownership of land, then with the industrial revolution the possession of the means of production and of goods gained the high ground, and alongside developed the oil barons. It is now, only in relatively recent history, that wealth is now being built upon knowledge (and the purveyors, and gatekeepers of knowledge) through the digital media revolution – hence Bill Gates' status as the world's wealthiest man.

ICT, creativity and the arts

The emphasis on digital media has also run parallel with an emphasis upon creativity, and this has placed the creative subjects at centre stage once more, and made the development of creativity a major imperative. Hence the title of the May 1999 Government report 'The National Advisory Committee on Creative and Cultural Education' (May 1999).

In the most successful businesses, the development of a well motivated, creative, and innovative work force with realistic vision, has become the major concern to be addressed, as corporate Britain realises that their very economic survival depends upon it. Going are the team building, white water rafting, white knuckle rides in Wales. Businesses are now just as likely to programme a management training course around the theme of creative development, as anything else.

In August 1999 *The Sunday Times* reported how the Cranfield School of Management's Praxis Centre and the Globe Theatre in London, were running courses for corporate managers at the theatre itself, exploring Shakespeare's *Henry V* for insights on the art of leadership. Management books which proliferate e.g. *Shakespeare on Management* by Paul Corigan (Corigan 1997) seem to reflect the fact that the natural home for the nurturing of creativity is within the traditional arts.

This is not to argue that the development of creativity is the sole preserve of the arts, but that through the arts, creative skills can be developed which are transferable to all spheres, including business management. The arts are not simply about self-expression, but also the development of critical, technical and problem solving skills, therefore, this is an argument against philosophies which pose dichotomies between science and the arts, or vocational education and the arts. Drama, for example, in this context, becomes important because in schools it is through such a subject that students learn self confidence, and how to develop presentation skills in front of a critical audience – surely key life skills that everyone needs (see Chapters 4 and 9). The necessity for the development of such life skills for post 16 students is also reflected in the new stand alone National Specifications for Key Skills 'which went live, in part, in September 2000 – not only do they specify Communication; Application of Number and ICT, but also Working with others; Problem Solving (for which should be read "Creativity") and "Improving own Learning and Performance".

The excitement for the arts within the new digital media revolution is that there is this clear emphasis upon creativity, such that the gentle revolution undertaken by the creatives within the fields of graphic design, film video and advertising, (armed with their trusty Macs), has turned into a total repositioning of the status of the Geek – with the new digital technology revolution, size does not matter – it's what you can do with it that counts! (Although they do say that a good internet business requires a Geek, a suit and a hippy for success).

In November 1999, *The Daily Mail* reported that a major computer company was establishing a partnership with 100 secondary schools to counter a lack of skilled workers in the ICT Industry, and there was not a 'Geek in site' (spelling meant). The paper quoted the company's head of group:

> This is about building a working partnership between industry and education . . . companies think you have to have graduates, but some of these 14 year olds are already doing amazing things with web technology . . . this project is going to allow us to pick up people with a *lot of artistic flair*, rather than just the intellectual capability you get with graduates (my emphasis).
>
> (*Daily Mail* 30 November 1999)

We are very proud that the joint Plume School/ULTRALAB digital media project, marks an enthusiastic and determined attempt to address such imperatives. I am also justifiably proud of our students' level of effort, determination and commitment in the execution of their multimedia presentation – because in all my past teaching experience, I cannot think of another project which has engendered such commitment, excitement and creativity as this.

The multimedia project between ULTRALAB and Plume School

The aim of our project was for the students to produce a multimedia website presentation, linked to the promotion of the Plume School sixth form. A multimedia CD Rom was also to be written in HTML, which allowed for cross platform browsing, with hyperlinks to specific internet based sites including our own, and those within the community. The CD Rom was also to act as a promotional CD Rom within our sixth form prospectus for the year 2000.

This project integrated a number of multimedia technologies including video, still video, animation, website authoring, and all the more traditional skills of a graphic designer/creative artist, while the work produced would also be examined for sixth form coursework, and provide a foundation for continuity and progression into further and higher education for the students concerned.

Plume School art students have been involved in leading ICT developments within the arts for a number of years, but it was apparent that we needed to address the new technologies, particularly multimedia, as events were beginning to overtake us as an art department. Students were gaining a fascination for, and interest in, the new technologies, and it was clear that when returning from interview there had been a fundamental change in the structure of many art courses, and course requirements had changed as a result. Moreover, ex-students employed in the field of graphic design were also reporting that their career prospects were limited if they had not developed skills in multimedia alongside their traditional graphics skills.

Thus the ULTRALAB project:

- introduced students to the new multimedia technologies through the execution of a 'live' project linked to promoting our sixth form courses;
- acted as INSET for department staff in the use of the new technologies for teaching and learning in school;
- through hands on experience enabled art staff to identify our needs with regard to the upgrading of art department hardware and software for future purposes, and concomitantly, identify INSET needs;
- acted as a pilot project for ULTRALAB to evaluate the teaching and learning potential of the new technologies within a school context at sixth form level – including its creative use and pupils' general depth of understanding;
- established links between a school and a university which would be of mutual benefit to students on both sites through a process of pupil mentoring, and which could act as possible coursework for the student mentors at APU; and
- developed APU student mentors' own understanding of their subject through the mentoring of younger students two steps behind themselves on their career journey.

The interactive CD Rom itself, also addressed the fundamental fact that while many school students have access to a computer, not all have access to the internet. Thus at the present time, a school website will not reach a wide audience for a school wishing to promote itself. A CD Rom written in HTML which can be used with a web browser, would address this issue, and prove a more exciting presentation vehicle to Year 11 students than a simple sixth form prospectus. Those with internet, could still access the school and other sites from the CD Rom through hyperlinks. The actual cost of writing to CD is relatively inexpensive, and so it would not be prohibitive to include a CD Rom in every sixth form prospectus – if the school so desired.

Project management and structure

The main players included: Richard Millwood, Reader at ULTRALAB at APU Chelmsford, Phil Langshaw, Head of Art and Design at Plume School, Maldon, nine GNVQ Level 3 art and design students, and five undergraduate student mentors from the Multimedia Department at APU. (GNVQ is a vocational two year A-Level equivalent course).

The original structure for the project was for a 14 week period, with one day of each week spent at ULTRALAB with the five student mentors, and the rest of the time spent on the project in the art department back at school. An on-line

Community was established for mentors, staff and students to communicate to one another, to share thoughts, and to keep a day to day diary. Meanwhile, Plume School was to upgrade ICT hardware and software facilities – including establishing an internet link in the art department – to support the project, and to meet the cost of the student mentors.

The reality was that while the one day a week at ULTRALAB continued for the full 10 weeks, delays with regard to the delivery of new hardware and software, and incompatibility problems between systems, meant that the technology was not in place in time for the start of the project, and was eventually in place two weeks before the project was due to finish. A 14 week project was thus reduced to twenty working days – ten at ULTRALAB, and ten in school with the relevant technology. Unfortunately, this software and hardware was essential to establish the on-line Community, and to run the web/animation software, which existing equipment would not cope with and this had a dramatic effect on what could actually be achieved in the time with regard to end product, i.e. a comprehensive sixth form online prospectus, and Interactive CD Rom. Thus a less ambitious site was created, but one that given the time, was a credit to the students. Importantly however, in terms of process, students enjoyed a rich learning experience and developed fundamental and transferable key skills which I describe in more detail below.

The website and CD Rom were to promote our sixth form courses, and so including information about life in the sixth form and courses on offer was going to be important. However, to absorb our art students in the project and to make their interest immediate, we began with them building their own art gallery/ web page with personal statements. This got the project off to a good start, as they were excited about seeing their own work on the net. It also allowed for students to experiment with different approaches, and to compare ideas.

The development of a critical approach to the new technologies was encouraged, including a critique of their constraining and enabling possibilities. Students were finding ways of exhibiting traditional art media and technologies, through a different and new medium, and noting how this new medium affected their work, and raised new problems to be solved.

> The scans of my silk paintings look duller than my original pieces – and we spent a long time getting them to look right – colour balance problems – they look pretty different on the actual screen, but the original pieces all feel and look better.
>
> (Dana GNVQ Level 3 pupil)

Thus a loose approach was encouraged at the start of the project without overrestrictive planning and design work. This was important in that it allowed students to explore and experiment with both the enabling and constraining nature of the technologies, and until this was understood by the students more formal design work would not work effectively. The mentors played a key role in this by making students aware of what was possible and what was not, but this realisation could only come from this initial experimentation with unfamiliar technologies. This initial period of experimentation with such web software, also gave more meaning to discussions and critiques of other websites with the mentors at a later date.

At this stage we had a number of students working on their own disparate parts, but it was becoming clear that the site by necessity did require at least two students to take charge of overseeing the whole site, and this fell naturally to two boys who were developing high levels of expertise and who tried to maintain the design integrity of the site as a whole, and adding a corporate identity. Both boys also undertook the task of creating links and stitching the parts into a whole. They also acted as mentors to other students and set a pace by giving other students deadlines for work to be ready for they themselves to work on.

It was clear that we had to move from very individual pieces of work and start to give students a wider vision of the project as a whole. Therefore simple diagrammatic plans of the site were developed by the group, and this helped students to identify more general areas of the site that they wished to work on after they had completed their personal on-line gallery. Thus some students decided to work on the introduction to the whole site, while others concentrated on other background material linked to life in the sixth form and the courses on offer etc. One pupil took charge of producing the 360 degree panoramas of the school's new Learning Information and Technology Centre, and another the installation of a digital animation that had been produced earlier in the year.

Difficulties

The first difficulty that the project encountered related to its size. Students were not used to working on such a large project as a team effort, nor were they used to handling and saving such a vast amount of data, and as such, good housekeeping with regard to filing and saving files, was not ideal. Files were labelled differently by all students and were often saved in the wrong place, and this meant that it was difficult to find specific files when the site was stitched together near the end of the project. Certainly for future projects we would give more attention to this fundamental aspect. At the planning stage, standardised file names should have been established to be used by each student. Likewise, more emphasis should also have been given to the correct labelling of .JPEG and .GIF files, as we found that some files had been saved in TIFF, and not converted, and some had been converted to .JPEG and .GIF files, but had not been labelled as such, and so did not get recognised by the web browser (.GIF and .JPEG are the file types that work on the internet).

The file sizes of images on the internet by definition have to be small, so that download times are fast, and this was another area that we should have spent more time on with students. While techniques for reducing file sizes was discussed, once again this could have been given more emphasis as was clear when the two students, who were overseeing things, fine tuned the site and found some very large files which militated against fast downloads.

Technology

The complex nature of the project meant that it certainly helped that students were well versed in the use of Applemacs and in particular the use of Adobe Photoshop. It became clear at the beginning that it was important to build upon students' strengths, and Photoshop was therefore used as the starting point at ULTRALAB. This gave students confidence through using a technology they knew.

Adobe Photoshop also became the key software used at school while we were waiting for the delivery of Dreamweaver, and Fireworks. Students had to assess how far Photoshop could be pushed as a technology in order to be adapted back at ULTRALAB for the website. Students experimented by creating a series of changing images in Photoshop which when linked together with other software resulted in some very ingenious animated sequences, which worked on a small scale within Photoshop itself. Pagemill was the introductory web design tool, but students soon outgrew this and moved to Macromedia's Dreamweaver web design package.

Incompatibilities at school between new software and old operating systems meant that software could not be placed on all computers. The iMac's, when they arrived, were invaluable in terms of speed and memory, and we would not have finished the project without them.

The technologies certainly gave students another vehicle through which to express their creativity, and we were very impressed with some of the ingenious approaches to the technology, and the thought that went into each individual student's web page. It was felt that that students used the technology to realise an idea, and did not let the technology dictate the outcome. In the main this worked, as art students are taught to begin with a design idea and then try to realise it. Where the technology could not realise the idea, most students adapted the idea to match the capability of the technology. However, this adaptation of ideas to meet the constraints of the technology was not learnt by all, and did mean that one pupil found technical difficulties in trying to make the technology realise the idea – no matter what – and this led to frustrations with the technology, and a less than satisfactory part of the site.

The mind set of trying to make the technology realise the idea, was helped by the fact the students already had the art work they wished to use and digitise, and which was the result of traditional art skills and techniques. It is certainly true that when students produce art work using computer technologies only, then it is easy for ideas to be technology led, and the results bland and predictable. The use of existing art work enlivened and enriched the visual impact of the site.

Student skills

Despite the final time restrictions on the project, in terms of process, and competences learnt, here the project was a great success.

The learning curve for the students and staff was steep. Problem solving and the development of transferable competences were the key outcomes. Students had not worked on a major project as a team, and the level of group discussion and task allocation was something that they were not used to, but something they soon mastered. Planning of the whole site was crucial, particularly presenting it in diagrammatical form, and the site plan formed the basis of most planning decisions and task allocations.

Yes, there were inevitable frustrations and fall outs typical of that age of student, but what excited me was that the fall outs were over the website itself, and students feeling that they had been let down by others not meeting deadlines, frustrations with the technology, or lack of it, and the general stress of completing a major project in such a small space of time. This in itself was a valuable learning experience for the students, and made them realise that frustrations and disappointments are part of the deal. This all maintained a pace and a momentum to the project, which we might otherwise have lost. This pace and momentum was certainly witnessed at ULTRALAB on the launch day where I felt the sense of teamwork was at its height.

The aim to produce an on-line sixth form prospectus and Interactive CD Rom provided a good focus for the development of further personal skills. Students had to interview other students, and senior staff, obtain information about courses and check the validity of such information. They had to think about the presentation of their own page, and how they would describe themselves. Much thought went into the target audience – Year 11 pupils – and how the site could be made exciting and attractive to such a group, and something that was also easy to navigate.

Linked to the above was the development of the critical faculties of the students, and how soon they dismissed many sites for being bland and uninspiring, and how important they thought it was to communicate the excitement of the art courses they had gone through in their website.

The end product also gave students a purpose to what they were undertaking and all the basic technical understanding of web design, which they will value at college. They also all have an on-line CV for future interviews, and so from this point of view the original objectives were fulfilled.

Students involved

Originally nine GNVQ and five 'A' Level students were involved. The flexibility offered by using GNVQ students was a major contribution to the success of the project because they are full time art students which meant that they could be at ULTRALAB for the whole day, and dedicate the majority of the term to the project, without having to concern themselves with other subjects. 'A' Level students, because of their other timetable commitments, found it difficult to involve themselves, and so this group withdrew at an early stage.

Staff skills

One further objective was to improve art staff expertise in the use of the new technologies. While staff have learnt much inevitably, due to teaching commitments, staff could not attend every session at ULTRALAB and thus colleagues feel that there is still a need to establish a mentoring programme for staff so that they may be taken through the basics and be given one-to-one attention which was not possible during the project itself.

Time

Undoubtedly, the reduction in the time left to complete the project at school was a crucial factor in what could finally be achieved in terms of the comprehensive nature of the end product and led to the most frustrations. Thus one lesson is not to underestimate delivery times and technical difficulties when setting up brand new equipment, and making it work with older systems. We also happened to order Apple iMac's when there was a waiting list due to their popularity!

Reducing such an ambitious project to a relatively small period of time meant that students, in order to complete the tasks in time for their examination assessment, had to work overtime, and this was also good discipline. It led to some students coming into school at weekends, working in the art department until 9.00 pm, and all students giving up a day's holiday in order to meet the dead-line. This was to their credit and, more positively, the time constraint did lend an immediacy and pace to the project that we might have lost. It also gave students a flavour of the real world, where the pace of work is more than pedestrian. The down side was that as the final deadline approached, tempers and nerves were understandably frayed!

Costs

Schools benefit from working with colleges because they can take advantage of the input of high end skills from some very competent university students indeed, while at the same time keeping within extremely tight budgets, which most schools have to operate within. As a department we benefited from the school's financial support of the project. Mentors were paid by the day, which meant budgeting for five mentors per day for ten days.

The on-line community

An enclosed on-line community was established for students to share ideas between themselves and with their mentors. This was an excellent idea, but was not used comprehensively by the students, due to problems of access, both in school and at home. When it was used, its success was in that students used it as a vehicle to talk openly about their true thoughts and feelings about the project. Thus we found that the on-line community allowed access to frank views that would perhaps not have been communicated to us otherwise. If repeating the project, we would make far more use of this facility, the potential of which we were only just beginning to develop.

Symbiosis

Mentors

The success of the collaboration between Plume School and ULTRALAB was because it was symbiotic. This was particularly true with regard to the use of mentors from APU's multimedia department.

Richard Millwood, Reader at ULTRALAB, summed up this symbiosis well:

> We involved students from the multimedia department at APU for two reasons. Really one is that the students coming here benefit from a relationship with people who are a bit further down their career path than they are themselves. There is a purely practical part of course, you act as tutor to them, and develop their skills because you can do a 'just in time learning' to help them with problems they are solving which are clear and direct to them, and this provides a really nice learning environment. But there is a second reason which is to do with the students at the University being tutors – to articulate how something works, and to show how it works – and all teachers know this – you are obliged then to really make sense of it, it does not matter whether you can do it or not, you probably cannot do it, but to talk about it probably means that you know it as well as can do it.

We certainly experienced a rich variety of personalities and approaches within the group of mentors, and as a group they worked well together, giving a rich and wide range of opinions and views which was healthy for the students.

Some minor problems stemmed from how mentors defined their role. This was no fault of theirs, but some saw the role as solely a supportive one and tended to follow the students. Others took a more hands on approach, and set a pace. Some didn't sense an imperative to realise a final outcome, while others saw this as a key imperative. Some were critical of students' work, but some students felt they did not follow up the criticism with practical ideas and help. Others took part of the website home to work on when time was tight. All of this was inevitable, and it made me appreciate what a craft teaching is – enabling, encouraging, cajoling, mentoring, planning, teaching, pacing, assuring an outcome etc., etc. With hindsight I think more attention is needed in helping mentors identify their roles more clearly, but this apart, the mentors were the key to the success of the project, and allowed students to interact with young adults who were closer to their own ages, and who could also talk to our students about the next stage of their educational career.

ULTRALAB

Ultralab is the Learning Technology Research Centre at APU, and for them the project addressed a number of their needs:

The primary purpose for Ultralab is to benefit from observing, in this case, sixth formers, engaging in the new technology. It helps us in formal and informal ways, but informally, we learn: what can they cope with? What difficulties do they come up against? . . .

. . . when we design educational software for on-line communities, the more we have in mind about how children react to technology, the better we will make those designs . . .

. . . It is a great place to have students working in the lab on a regular basis. The pleasure is also because I am a former school teacher, as many of us are in Ultralab, and to get back to some kind of 'schooly' relationships is just fun. Every time I explain things, I learn – great fun.

(Richard Millwood, June 1999, Plume Website Video)

Conclusion

The Plume School's art and design department's website and CD Rom was produced by 9 art students in just over 20 working days. It was an experimental vehicle, and thus, more about process than end product, allowing students to confront and understand the new technologies – to problem solve, to work within a team, to experiment, and to push the new media technologies to their limits – and, as such, we tried to develop a wide range of ideas, styles, and approaches. We were not pursuing a bland homogeneous slick site – this was not our aim – we set out to excite our own and future students to the potential of the new technologies, and to give them a life chance in a very new and exciting, brave new world!

Thus, given the practical constraints already mentioned, we all felt that the project was a great success. Restrictions on time meant that we had a less comprehensive end product, but end product is only one success indicator, and for us, not the main one. Most if not all the objectives of the project were fulfilled, and the students confronted the imperatives, problems, frustrations and disappointments that they will find in the real world of work. They all went away with fundamental transferable skills that they will find invaluable at college, and a virtual on-line CV of their work.

Content was certainly enhanced through the use of traditional art work, which lends a richness to our website as against one that is solely computer generated. Improvements for a similar project would obviously revolve around saving and labelling of files; reducing file sizes; etc.

Students all matured emotionally as the project progressed, and they have more confidence in what they can now do, and value what they have achieved. It was good to see certain students with the confidence to undertake a presentation at the launch of the website at ULTRALAB in the presence of many distinguished guests, including the Director of Learning Services for Essex – something they previously would have avoided.

At the conclusion of the project, it was clear that the students were genuinely proud of what they had achieved, and were very keen to demonstrate their achievements to their friends and family. It also established the benefits of working with local colleges, departments and students on a project which has mutual benefits for all concerned.

Many colleges are establishing Schools Liaison Officer posts, because they are keen to attract the right calibre of pupil to their courses, and to support colleagues in school in delivering a curriculum which maintains continuity and progression between the respective institutions. The onus lies with schools to consolidate such initiatives for the benefit of their students and themselves – for such projects concomitantly develop the expertise of staff alongside that of the students involved.

We hope this review of our efforts will prove inspirational to other colleagues planning similar projects, as it is possible to bring together a number of diverse needs simultaneously in one quite exciting package. The project addressed the needs of our students as they enter into college, university and the job market, together with staff INSET, mentoring experience for undergraduates, and for ULTRALAB, valuable insights into the use by students of the new media. It was also a lot of fun for all those involved!

The National Specifications for Key Skills went live in September 2000, covering Application of Number; ICT; Communication; Working with Others; Problem Solving; and Improving own Learning and Performance. Schools will be looking for innovative and worthwhile vehicles to deliver such skills, therefore what better way than through a multimedia project which has relevance for every subject, and which provides students with the life skills that they will need in whatever field they may later find themselves?

Notes

1 Ultralab are the prime movers behind the TescoNet 2000 project, support for the Learning Zone in the Greenwich Dome, and the government impetus to place all school pupils on-line with their own learning community and email address through the Oracle Millennium Project – Think.com

Questions

1   Key Skills managers are often asked to decide in which courses Key Skills will be developed alongside i.e. A Levels, GNVQs or as free standing. Undoubtedly, the most ideal delivery of Key Skills is through their integration into the main provision of GNVQs or A Levels. Thus, the suggestion here is for a far more flexible approach which could, with careful mapping, be a combination of all of these. The combinations are endless: a sixth form digital media/technology course within the arts could run as part of a wider ICT based course, or as a fully fledged independent multimedia course, but delivered through the arts, and all could feed into a separate media/journalism course. Subject specialist areas could also pick up key elements of delivery alongside

this. The curriculum 2000 for A Level also means that existing courses at A/S Level could be used for delivery with no major additional timetable/resource implications. What combination is a possible option at your school?

2   Could a Compact arrangement with your local university, allow for prior accreditation of your students for some HE courses?

3   Ideally, for Key Skills to have relevance, there needs to be natural vocational opportunities for their delivery and assessment. This can be through more obvious vocational subject programme delivery, and/or for an academic subject programme, through a curriculum informed by the real world of work, and work placements. Has the school strong business/school links that it can draw on, not simply for student placement, but for guest business professionals/trainers to work with students in school?

4   How will student progress in key skills be assessed and monitored where the curriculum delivery is over a wide range of subject areas ? (Some schools are allowing students to log their own progress using carefully developed log books which are monitored/assessed by the Key Skills co-ordinator and certain subject staff, and/or Key Skills specialists).

References

Visit our efforts at www.ultralab.ac.uk/projects/plumev2/default.html
Visit ULTRALAB at www.ultralab.anglia.ac.uk
Corigan, P. (1997) *Shakespeare on Management*. London: Kogan Page.
The Daily Mail (1999) 'Headhunters in class' article by Tony Halpin, 30 November 1999.
The National Advisory Committee on Creative and Cultural Education (May 1999) *The Challenge for Education*, London: DfEE, See full report at www.dfee.gov.uk.
R. Millwood (1999) Plume Website Video, Chelmsford: Anglia Polytechnic.

Further reading

The following documents, websites and texts provide details about key skills across the curriculum:

DfEE (May 1999) *The National Advisory Committee Report on Creative and Cultural Education*, London: Department of Education and Employment.
http://www.dfee.gov.uk

Corigan P. (1997) *Shakespeare on Management*, London: Kogan Page.

FEDA (2000) *Key Skills in GNVQ Programmes*, London: Further Education Development Agency.
This provides an overview and organisational checklist for managers of Key Skills programmes. http://www.feda.ac.uk/gnvq

QCA (2000) *Introduction to Key Skills*, London: Qualifications and Curriculum Authority.
This gives an overview of the National Specifications for Key Skills.
http://www.qca.org.uk

City and Guilds (2000) *The Key to Learning*, London: City and Guilds.
This covers the issue of delivering Key Skills alongside A Level and NVQ provision – principles and good practice http://www.city-and-guilds.co.uk

City and Guilds (2000) *Forging Links that Last*, London: City and Guilds.
City and Guilds have produced a guide to approaching external organisations for support in GNVQ and other learning programmes.

12 Making and using multimedia

A critical examination of learning opportunities

Steve Bruntlett

Introduction to multimedia

Despite its proliferation in the media and home computing, multimedia has only been in common use in schools, in its most recent form, since the mid-nineties. The early forms of multimedia in the late seventies comprised training or learning materials based on computer controlled videotape and videodisc. It is perhaps indicative of the state of the use of CD Roms in schools that one of the first commercial CD Roms, Art Gallery, published by Microsoft, based on the in-house multimedia guide to the National Gallery and produced in the mid-nineties, is at the time of writing still in use in many schools. The number of educational CD Roms available has grown over the last few years, although the medium seems now to be in decline since the rapid development of the world wide web. The main use of CD Rom now seems to be for software delivery. Some good quality educational CD Roms continue to be released but most are for the home entertainment market rather than for education. An increasingly common form of multimedia is that found on the internet in the form of web resources accessed through web browsers such as Internet Explorer, Netscape Navigator or NeoPlanet.

When the world wide web was developed in the mid-nineties it comprised hyper-linked documents containing text and still images. It now includes sound, animation, video, and live video streaming, some of which is useful, such as that from volcano-cams, and some that is not. The web provides a resource-rich multimedia environment with which, in many ways, conventional publishing and information dissemination cannot compete. The technology is developing to such an extent that the way in which an increasing number of us access information is changing relatively rapidly. It may, for example, completely change the way we shop, communicate with each other, book holidays, buy and listen to music or watch television.

The web may also be set to change the way we educate our children. Much of our curriculum is still set in the nineteenth century. Multimedia, however, is firmly set in the twenty-first century and its use is increasing exponentially to the extent that many children are learning much of what interests them from the web rather than from school. Children learn by pursuing those things that interest them rather than by what is laid down in a curriculum. They also need to learn different things at different times. This, the web can cope with, as that is how it is designed. Whether school in its present form can cope in a similar way remains to be seen. In *Diversity in Learning* (Papert 2000), the author talks about the new technology being a learner's technology, not a teacher's technology. He describes it as, 'a technology that can be appropriated, taken over by young people, who clearly use it to feel the power of their own individual intellectual personalities'. However, multimedia is a set of tools that can be used by both teachers and pupils. At the moment there are a few teachers designing for multimedia though in the long run it will be pupils who are the main users of multimedia in representing and communicating their beliefs, values and understandings of the ways in which they live.

Forms of multimedia in education

This chapter examines the two forms of multimedia currently being used in general society and in schools. The use of multimedia has increased significantly in schools and colleges since the introduction of the National Grid for Learning and other government information and communications technology (ICT) initiatives. The two current forms of multimedia, CD Rom and web-based, have elements in common but are used very differently in the classroom, home, workplace or library. CD Rom is regarded by some as an outdated technology since the increased use and provision of very powerful forms of browser-based multimedia to be found on the web. However, full-screen computer, disc or CD Rom based multimedia still has uses in supporting existing, or providing new, forms of learning opportunities. It is instantly accessible, takes no time to download, can provide exceptionally high quality resources and can be used where no access to the internet is available.

One use of multimedia is in providing solutions to problems occurring in formal education. It may be being used to deliver parts of the curriculum that otherwise cannot be delivered or are difficult to deliver because of constraints in educational funding rather than to provide new forms of learning. Using the new technologies, as a fix for elements of formal education that are failing pupils, is arguably not its best use. Rather, multimedia should be used to help provide new learning systems in which teachers and pupils can play a part but which also allows others to play a significant role. However, this significantly changes the teacher to pupil relationship. The introduction of multimedia needs to be carefully considered as it may fundamentally affect the way pupils learn and the way in which teachers teach. In *Vision for Education – The Caperton-Papert Platform* (Papert and Caperton 1997), the authors argue that whatever the forms of technology being used, the educational discussion should be about 'developing and choosing between visions of how this immensely powerful technology can support the invention of powerful new forms of learning to serve levels of expectations higher than anyone imagined in the past'. Changes to the curriculum need to be based on educational thinking rather than on technological expediency. Multimedia has clearly come a long way in its first few years, especially in its new web form, but it may be only the first manifestation of new technologies that may change schools forever.

Research in interactive educational multimedia

A critical examination of these forms of multimedia in relation to learning opportunities is provided here by means of three case studies based on postgraduate educational research carried out in the Centre for Postgraduate Teacher Education at De Montfort University on the MA (Art and Design Education) course. This is supported by research at a national level and the work of agencies such as BECTA, which is charged with the development of learning opportunities through the use of information and communications technology (ICT). While the research is primarily based in art and design education, the principles of the production of multimedia and its pedagogical framework in supporting the development of learning opportunities for pupils and students clearly applies to other subjects in the curriculum. The issues relating to the development of new, or support of existing, pupil-learning opportunities include design, production, pedagogy, classroom use, inclusion and integration. The case studies also address the impact that the forms of multimedia may have on classroom based teaching and learning strategies.

The first case study critically examines some of the ways in which practising teachers could work with outside agencies such as museums and galleries in using external resources to develop and enhance school-based work within a larger community. It addresses issues of professional production, liaison with external agencies and guidelines and procedures for developing community based work. It also addresses the issue of support for practising teachers wishing to develop and enhance teaching and learning who may not have the technical skills necessary to design and produce full-screen or web-based multimedia materials.

The second case study critically examines the practicalities of a teacher producing multimedia materials to enhance and develop an already resource-rich teaching style. The case study examines the issues facing classroom teachers who want to develop their own multimedia materials in preference to using commercially produced multimedia or web-based materials.

The third case study critically examines the uses made of multimedia and the web by students as an assignment support and study resource in comparison with conventional resources such as books, videos, journals and magazines available in libraries. The case study examines the ways in which students choose and use multimedia and web resources to support self-study and project-based learning experiences and the possible opportunities they have to do so.

The development of interactive educational multimedia

The best interactive educational multimedia products and applications currently available have increased in sophistication and developed out of all recognition since the beginning of multimedia as computer-controlled videotapes and videodiscs in the early eighties and its subsequent development into the hypertext and hypermedia systems of the late eighties. The early pioneers at the Media Lab at MIT saw hypermedia as a means of accessing and purposefully navigating massive amounts of multiple media, i.e. digital text, images and video resources, as a basis for new forms of teaching and learning. Most of these resources were stored on laser-disc, a technology that was used considerably more in the United States than in the United Kingdom. In terms of technology, the LaserVision videodisc was introduced in 1977, the CD Rom in 1986 and CD-I and CDTV in 1991 (Looms 1993). Of these, only CD Rom is still used in classrooms for teaching and learning as this medium has taken over the attributes of the other technologies to provide interactive multimedia learning opportunities through the use of increasingly sophisticated multimedia authoring tools. A clear account of the history of multimedia can be found in *Understanding Hypermedia* (Cotton and Oliver 1993). By the time *Understanding Hypermedia* was published, multimedia was the more commonly used term for integrated and interactive multiple-media.

Hypertext can be described as a series of interlinked and cross-referenced digital texts such as an interactive book with hyperlinks to associated parts of the text. If a user clicks on an author's name in an English text, for example, he or she may be presented with a biography of the author from whence could be accessed the original text or resources, leading to other lines of enquiry. Working with multiple, rather than single, texts clearly presents enhanced and arguably completely new learning opportunities. Hypermedia can be described as text, animation, video, sound and images presented as high quality digital resources in a holistic and integrated learning environment.

Apple funded the pioneers of hypermedia at the Media Lab. They developed the first hypertext and hypermedia systems and produced the first commercial programme, HyperCard. In HyperCard, the first commonly available multimedia authoring program, text, images and video were linked to each other forming the basis of interactivity – although they were only available in black and white due to the displays of the early computers being used. Companies other than Apple began to develop software packages to take advantage of higher resolution colour monitors and included the software control of the complete range of digital media at that time. Multimedia as a term began to be used as the description of this new set of design and communication tools in the early nineties. However, multimedia has been for many years, and still is, a term associated with art and design practice and was also a term used for broadcast foreign language courses in the early eighties (Looms 1993). HyperCard enabled teachers and researchers to develop new teaching and learning strategies, materials, and resources, by controlling laser-disc based text, images and video to provide what we now understand as multimedia. Science experiments, which were unsafe or could not be carried out in most schools or colleges, could be carried out using sections of video to simulate what would happen as a result of the decisions made through the course of the experiment. The early forms of what we now understand as virtual experiments were being developed by educationalists who were concerned to give pupils as near to first-hand experience as possible in order to maximise their learning opportunities.

In the United Kingdom, in the early eighties, several laser discs were produced and controlled by a computer. The most notable of these was the Domesday

Project videodisc produced for the nine-hundredth anniversary of the Domesday Book in 1986. Over a million volunteers in over ten thousand schools gathered information about their local communities to produce an extensive national database of life in Britain in the eighties (Looms 1993). Such use of computer-controlled videodiscs was a major development in the way some schools used technology to support and develop, at that time, revolutionary pupil learning opportunities. Le Ville was an early form of virtual reality in which a pupil could tour a French village and ask questions at the Boulangerie and other shops and buildings to practise speaking and understanding French. Tesco ran their Schoolnet 2000 project on a similar basis to the Domesday Project for the millennium.

However there were other early pioneers of multimedia in England such as the researchers working at the Exploratorium at the then Anglia Polytechnic headed by Professor Stephen Heppell. They produced interactive multimedia representations of Shakespeare's work based on developing forms of pedagogy associated with the new technologies (Heppell 1993). This piece of multimedia gave pupils the opportunity to access the work of Shakespeare in completely new ways compared to those presented in paper and video based forms. The ULTRALAB, based at Anglia Polytechnic University, is one of the leaders in the field in educational multimedia development. It acts in a consultancy role to the government and is playing a major part in the ways in which new information and communications technology is impacting school provision of a range of new and enhanced learning opportunities for pupils and pupils through a range of prestige projects (ULTRALAB 1999).

ICT pedagogy

While the technology was developing at MIT and providing new ways of representing the world, the educationalists working as part of the Epistemology and Learning Group at MIT (MIT 1998) were developing new forms of pedagogy. Most notable of these was Seymour Papert, who wrote and developed the LOGO programming language we now see used in floor turtles and roamers or on-screen turtles. Mitchell Resnick, Associate Professor of Learning Research at MIT, and others have developed ideas about the way in which we understand the world through newly applied theories such as Constructionism that are based in part of Levi Strauss's thinking on bricolage (Kafai and Resnick, 1996).

It is interesting to note that Seymour Papert's seminal book, *Mindstorms* (Papert 1980), is now used by Lego as the title for their new robotics invention system, 'Mindstorms'. This is no surprise as Papert is Lego Professor of Robotics at MIT. The Media Lab at MIT developed the RCX code, a simple but powerful programming language, in association with Lego to provide a powerful robotics system that closely matched elements of Constructionism learning theory. The Lego group and MIT share a common philosophy about how children learn best. 'You can't just give children knowledge. We believe that children learn best when they build their own theories of how the world works – and try them out by building their own inventions.' (Lego 1998). If you visit Toys'r'Us you'll see that LOGO has clearly come a long way since those early software versions on the first mainstream computers to be used in schools as part of the BBC Literacy Project back in the early eighties. Howard Rheingold's seminal book, *Tools for Thought* examines issues related to the use of machines in learning to think and a more recent book, *The Virtual Community*, examines the uses we make of technology in developing new forms of communities. If we are to develop appropriate learning communities through the use of multimedia and ICT then we need to take careful note of what writers and thinkers such as Papert and Rheingold have to say.

Information and communications technology in schools

Clearly there are implications for the increasing use of new information and communications technologies in schools. If learning is taking place on the web then pupils can have access to a wide range of teaching and learning resources in their local library, community centre, Cyber café and many other places. Students have always had access to forms of expertise other than their teachers but now younger pupils are rapidly becoming powerful users of the web, sometimes for trivial uses, but often finding extremely useful information to support projects or schoolwork often to the embarrassment of their teacher. They may also be producing their own websites when, at the same time, their teachers have still not made any significant use of the web for teaching purposes, if they are using computers at all. Teachers need to engage with the forms of multimedia found on computers or on the web as soon as possible, otherwise pupils will be directing their own learning or being directed by commercial providers which may make life extremely difficult for less ICT literate teachers. We have to embrace these new technologies, examine their potential and critically determine what part they play in existing or new forms of education, schooling and teaching. Given instantaneous access to unlimited information and resources for all curriculum areas, what may now be described as the role of the teacher?

Many teachers are embracing new technologies and have been doing so for many years, often from personal interest, but much of the time through in-service training , continuing professional development courses or through higher academic study. Teachers are concerned with what and how their pupils learn. They are concerned with education rather than technology. They are not concerned with how technology improves learning but in how to improve learning through the effective and appropriate use of technology. They need to be concerned with the nature of learning rather than the nature of technology. The established curriculum is dictated by 'the pre-twentieth century technology of writing, printing and calculating. The real offer of digital technology is liberation from the consequences of having been restricted by these primitive tools.' (Papert 1998).

The teachers whose work is represented here as a means of examining the potential of multimedia as a learning opportunity and a means of breaking away from older restrictive technologies, are all working classroom teachers with concerns for how they deliver teaching and enable pupil learning while making use of new technologies. Two of the case studies presented here focus on the development of self-contained multimedia such as is found on CD Roms, and the other on the use of the web made by her pupils in comparison with traditional library resources.

Case study one – multimedia museum

An experienced Portuguese teacher, Silvestre Pestana, while studying on the MA (Art and Design Education) course in the Centre for Postgraduate Teacher Education at De Montfort University: Leicester, produced a complex and professional piece of multimedia comprising an interactive multimedia guide to a local museum, the Casa Museu Teixeira Lopes in Vila Nova de Gaia, Portugal. This was formerly the house of one of the foremost Portuguese sculptors, Teixeira Lopes, and now houses many of his works. Pupils at local schools visit the museum from time to time for a range of projects across their school's curriculum in history, art and culture. Teachers who have little knowledge of the sculptor, his work, his life or his times usually arrange these visits. Pupils visiting the museum would typically make drawings from the collection for a project on portraiture or make notes from cultural displays for history or humanities projects. Pestana felt that the teacher and pupils were making a minimal amount of connection with the collection and gaining superficial understanding of its local and national importance. The piece of multimedia he produced presented a range of enhanced, extended and, in some cases, completely new learning opportunities.

Illustrated introductory information was produced for pupils to use in advance of the visit, written for their level of understanding and related to their particular curriculum as opposed to the limited available material which was essentially academic, text-based and written at an adult level. An illustrated map of the museum complete with video clips was provided as part of the multimedia application so that pupils could see in advance what it looked like, where the rooms were and what they contained. Not only were clear guides to each room produced, which could seem a bit boring to a twelve year old, but also several of them included time-based or hidden animation. When pupils were studying the ballroom and clicked on a particular part of the screen or waited a few seconds, instead of quickly moving to the next screen, a ghostly pair of dancers appeared in an overlaid animation accompanied by wistful Portuguese music bringing to life a seemingly dead room. Such multimodal learning opportunities clearly engage pupils in examination of such multimedia materials, as one of the first places pupils wanted to visit when they arrived at the museum was the ballroom to see if the dancers were still there (Figure 12.1).

A typical way of visiting a museum for an increasing number of teachers is to make a preliminary visit and plan the route and the activities, but many just book a visit and turn up on the day and make the most of what they find by intuition. This piece of multimedia not only allowed the teachers to develop particular curriculum materials and plan an appropriate strategy for the visit, but also much more importantly, gave pupils ownership of the visit. By the time they arrived at

Figure 12.1 Sala 1 – Ballroom – Artist's House – Animated Dancers

the museum after viewing the multimedia in class prior to the visit, they had lists of images and sculptures they wanted to see for particular aspects of their projects and knew exactly where to find the images and sculptures thus making effective use of limited visiting time.

Pupil use of computers outside school is beginning to change the way in which they use computers inside school. Rather than designing multimedia to supplement school-based learning, it is beginning to be designed to replace or directly challenge such methods of learning. Clearly the multimedia produced by a teacher here was for use in a public place by pupils or adults. Pupils construct their own reality and they increasingly do so using multimedia and from quite a young age too.

A gallery of work produced by pupils on previous visits formed part of the multimedia so that pupils planning for the current visit could see how other pupils had addressed some of the same issues they were being asked to consider by their teachers. The intention is to add this gallery to the multimedia application on an annual basis so that a wider range of responses can be viewed and used by successive groups of pupils and teachers in gaining the most from a single and often expensive visit. It would also be useful to add teacher responses to a web-based version of the materials.

The multimedia application included a series of screens showing the sculptor's work in relation to that of pupils' responses to the primary experience of the visit.

Not only were pupils able to see the sculptor's work in detail before the visit, they could also refer to the multimedia application when working on their projects back at school. The work was categorised into furniture, costume, sculpture and design so that pupils could understand the range of art forms which the sculptor practised and was involved with. Visiting the museum and reading an academic text would not have given them this understanding, but the multimedia application could and did so very successfully. Other learning opportunities provided in this section of the multimedia were a breakdown of the processes employed by the sculptor with reference to proportion, facial expression and lighting. A series of tutorial exercises based on the work of the sculptor was provided, but within the context of the school curriculum. The tutorial exercises include life drawing, the elements of art and design, modelling, shading and collage. These tutorials all made connection with the school's curriculum and were illustrated by pupil work from previous projects or by specially commissioned artwork from Celeste Cerqueira. The text was spoken as well as written in case any pupils or adults had reading difficulties.

The learning opportunities provided by this form of multimedia tutorial are clear. Pupils can work at their own speed, they don't need to feel embarrassed about bothering a teacher with a trivial question and can revisit any part of the tutorial as and when necessary throughout the course of the project, subject to computer access. There was also opportunity in the multimedia to refer to definitions of terms and explanations of why the sculptor worked in particular ways at that particular time. The tutorials also gave clear guidance on image production that supported the teachers who may not have been trained in this curriculum area (Figure 12.2).

Clearly, the learning opportunities in such a piece of multimedia are enabled by having access to a range of experts i.e. curator, historian, teacher, graphic artist, researcher. Their expertise can combine in a single piece of interactive educational multimedia to provide resources and teaching materials that are well researched, produced, presented and highly motivating for the teacher as well as the pupils. If all schools in the area used such multimedia resources then the quality of work produced as a result would be greatly improved as the research in this case demonstrated. If pupils know a wider audience will see their work then in most cases they'll rise to the challenge and produce their best work as they did in this case. Pupils had their work shown in the piece of multimedia being developed for all level 2 and 3 schools in and around Porto when it was put on public display in the museum over the summer period of the research on the researcher's own computer system. The multimedia was installed in the museum in a kiosk to test its efficiency as an information provider as part of the research. Parents saw their children's work on public display and were justifiably proud of their children's achievement. In typical circumstances pupils often see the production of work as an exercise in itself which is sometimes displayed and sometimes not. When they were working as part of this multimedia project they knew some of their work would be seen in public with a resulting increase in levels of motivation and enthusiasm.

Figure 12.2 Cabeça – Portuguese Graphic Design Tool – Shading

In using a powerful combination of such an integrated range of informed information and relevant educational experiences, multimedia really can be said to be a 'killer application'. It certainly made the museum curator and teachers think long and hard about their role in the community and the way in which they communicated with, and served that community.

Case study two – multimedia textiles materials

An experienced head of design technology working in an English high school, Anne Bruntlett, while studying on the MA (Art and Design Education) Course in the Centre for Postgraduate Teacher Education at De Montfort University: Leicester, produced a multimedia teaching resource for use in a Key Stage 3 multicultural textiles project. The multimedia application was developed for a single stand-alone computer to be used by the whole class on a rotation basis to complement the research being undertaken using postcard and book-based resources to support a multicultural textiles project. The multimedia application was developed to extend and enhance the teacher's extensive use of high quality resources and was designed to make use of her pupils' enthusiasm for working on computers. In developing learning opportunities for her pupils, the multimedia application cut across barriers of race and gender that can be problematic in some textiles activities. The production of professional quality multimedia materials gave them a validity that was difficult for pupils to challenge in comparison with some materials developed by some educational publishers. The multimedia resources had validity and an element of street credibility that engaged and encouraged pupils in its use. However, despite all the attractions of the teaching medium, the multimedia resources, as well as printed resources, were poor substitutes for access to physical artefacts. Durbin, Morris and Wilkinson (1993) found that any picture-based resources would not allow the following areas to be studied accurately:

- detail;
- exact colouring;
- sensations of smell, awe, location, etc. associated with the object;
- size, scale, weight, mass;
- tactile evidence of textures, temperatures, shape, manufacture;
- the three-dimensional design of an object; and
- 'feeling of age' compared to the newness of a reproduction; the concept of an original.

Bearing the above in mind, the teacher based her multimedia on real artefacts and ensured accuracy of reproduction to keep as much of the look and feel of the original as possible by using high quality Kodak Photo CD images of the artefacts. In designing the multimedia application, the teacher built on Heppel in Latchem's (1993) theory that the 'learner is self motivated and self directed, searches for meanings within the task, personalises the task, integrates it into the whole, and tries to theorise about the task and form a hypothesis' (Figure 12.3).

In designing the multimedia application, the researcher also made use of the work of Preece who identified four components of human–computer interaction. These relate to:

- the learners; in terms of memory load, perception, attention, previous experience of multimedia systems and previously acquired knowledge of the learning domain;
- the learning tasks in terms of the goals of the users in relation to finding answers, gaining a sense of scope for information, exploring concepts and collecting and tailoring information;
- the characteristics of the environment in which the learning is taking place, i.e. physical conditions; and
- the technical limitations of the hardware and software used in the development and delivery of the multimedia.

(Preece, Latchem, Williamson and Henderson-Lancett Lexie
1993: 138–141)

While the multimedia resources were not intended to enable learning opportunities in relation to information technology teaching, nevertheless, her pupils gained IT skills more easily and in more depth due to the subject relevance and application of IT skills compared to an arguably more theoretical and less

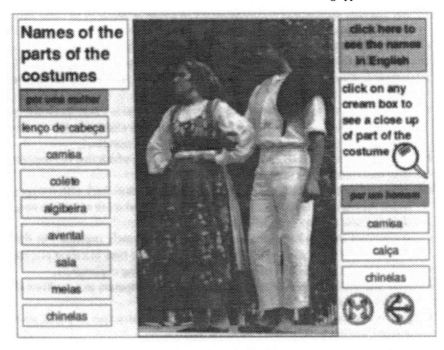

Figure 12.3 Namescost – Page from Multimedia Textiles Materials – Names of costume items

pupil relevant approach to IT teaching. There are a number of specific learning outcomes that came from the development and class use of the multimedia resource materials.

The multimedia resources:

- encouraged group work through which pupils were required to share experiences and support each other's learning,
- brought out the innate knowledge of pupils and supported them in discovering new forms and areas of knowledge,
- provided an excellent way of focusing pupils' minds on the task in hand with less distraction than usual, and without constant teacher intervention,
- provided a structured system for pupil research through a series of structured on-screen tasks which were tied into the particular teaching style of the teacher and acted as an extension to her expertise,
- occupied a group of pupils purposefully while the teacher worked to support other pupils with more individual and more time-consuming needs and develop more detailed learning opportunities for them in the process, such as working with pupils engaged in potentially hazardous activities with sewing machines and wax kettles,
- were highly motivating, engrossing. Pupils were observed to be 'lost in a virtual world' despite the close attention of the video camera being used to record

the research project and the usual melee of pupils working in an open plan area across food, art and textiles,

- encouraged on-target talking through the use of closely focused questions by means of which pupils linked their own experience to that being shown on screen as they perhaps do when watching television, another authoritative medium,
- tackled controversial aspects of multicultural education in a non-threatening way, i.e. clothing, which often polarises opinion in a classroom, but in this case was overcome by the perceived neutrality of the computer,
- showed traditional and contemporary clothing in ways which may not happen with traditional forms of resources,
- supported weaker and less able pupils by enabling them to work with stronger pupils on reading and comprehension. They were also more secure in using the computer in pairs or small groups,
- encouraged the teacher designing them to be extremely organised in the timetabling of work, making maximum use of available time in a short project and taking up any slack in lessons to maximise learning opportunity,
- were inspirational because of the unusual use of computers in a traditional textiles department,
- gave the subject an edge, a credibility, which was attractive to pupils who thought textiles to be a 'girls" subject,
- played an important part in breaking down gender bias and racial stereotyping,
- were a poor substitute for real artefacts but at the same time provided access to a much wider range than otherwise possible,
- provided access to good quality secondary resources which can often be of poor quality and quite minimal for Key Stage 2,
- provided accessible information compared to the over-complex information to be found in books aimed at an adult market,
- allowed the teacher to differentiate the material for individual year groups and within each year group explaining terms and processes in appropriate language,
- allowed the teacher to fine-tune and add to the material as it was used using her own experience and research rather than working with fixed content resources,
- encouraged the skill of looking at pictures and reading the content, in turn providing skills that could be used elsewhere in the curriculum,
- provided contextual information and constructional detail of the textile being viewed enabling it to be better understood, unpacked or deconstructed and assimilated.

The teacher found the development of the materials a long, but not necessarily complex, process. She was proficient in the basic use of the computer for word-processing and desktop publishing but had to learn to use a multimedia-authoring package. This is not necessarily an over-complex proposition for someone who has a reasonable working knowledge of desktop publishing. Any teacher with such basic skills could attempt multimedia design. Such multimedia resource development would be better accessible if designed for the web so that it could be used and added to or developed by other teachers working in similar situations. This could provide a bank of well-designed and appropriate multimedia resources to enhance subject teaching and provide learning opportunities for pupils who would not otherwise have access to such stimulating forms of subject teaching and learning (Figure 12.4).

According to Papert's interview in Zine Zone with Dan Schwartz, (2000: 1) 'the computer's true power as an educational medium lies – in the ability to facilitate and extend children's awesome natural ability and drive to construct, hypothesise, explore, experiment, evaluate, draw conclusions – in short to learn – all by themselves'. If teachers are to produce relevant and appropriate multimedia for their pupils then they need to be aware of that power and of the impact of multimedia on teaching and learning.

Case study three – multimedia approaches to graphic design

A teacher in an FE college and freelance graphic designer, Annabelle Holland, while studying on the MA (Art and Design Education) Course in the Centre for Postgraduate Teacher Education at De Montfort University: Leicester, ran a small scale research project to examine the use made of web resources by her A level,

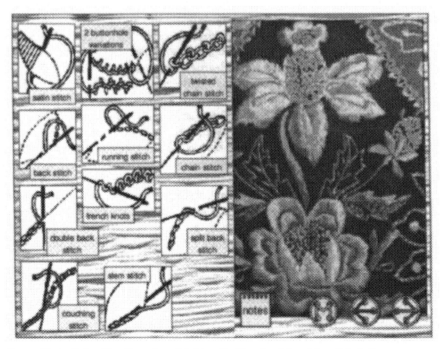

Figure 12.4 Colete2b – Page from Multimedia Textiles Materials – Stitch Spotter

BTEC and HND Graphics students in comparison with that of conventional library based resources. She found that although there were variations among her target teaching groups in their use of web or library resources, her main research finding was that students didn't have a sufficiently sophisticated search strategy to enable them to find resources relevant to set projects or support ongoing work. Library searching by students seemed to be just as random as web searching. Despite a library induction that dealt with the use of an on-line library catalogue (OPAC) and an introduction to search procedures on the web, students were still looking for both forms of resources intuitively rather than systematically. When they needed information on a particular graphic artist, such as Eric Gill, or on an area of graphics design, such as Propaganda Posters of the Second World War, they tended to look on shelves where they might expect to find such resources or just run a general search on the web rather than using more sophisticated search techniques and processes.

Internet and CD Rom-based multimedia resources

Clearly, if students at all levels of education are to make the most of resource-rich web or CD Rom based multimedia materials then they need to learn how to purposefully search and navigate increasingly massive resource databases or catalogues to find particularly relevant resources rather than becoming frustrated because they have difficulty finding appropriate resources or give up in frustration because they're trying to find a needle in an ever increasing haystack using intuitive or random searching.

Teachers and lecturers need to be increasingly aware of the types and forms of resources that are increasingly available for research, preparation for teaching, support for learning and extension of learning opportunities. They need to be aware of sophisticated forms of searching and the possibilities of refining searches using commonly available tools provided with web browsers such as Netscape Navigator, Internet Explorer and NeoPlanet and powerful search engines such as AltaVista (AltaVista 1999). They also need to be aware of the ready made collations of useful and appropriate web sites such as Yahoo (Yahoo 1999) put together by operators of search engines who have a general interest in providing such lists of sites under particular topics for commercial reasons. These are often good starting points for real-world exploration of multimedia web sites that can provide much useful and useable information to support student research and learning. There are libraries of web resources such as the WWW Virtual Library that should be explored (WWW Virtual Library 1999). The BBC On-line site is also a good starting point for educational multimedia resources (BBC 1999).

Information and communications technology supporting curriculum development

Agencies such as the Virtual Teacher Centres in England (VTC), Scotland (SVTC), Northern Ireland (NIVTC) and Wales (WVTC), provide a valuable starting point for investigation, selection and use of web based multimedia resources. News media such as the TES and the Electronic Telegraph, but also British universities, academics, subject organisations and subject specialists often direct teachers, lectures, pupils or students to educational resources related to the National Curriculum, GCSE or A level and post 19 education, or to resources less relevant but nevertheless useful. Similar agencies and organisations in other countries often relate their lists of web resources to their own form of educational curriculum, which may be worth comparing with our national curricula for a variety of reasons. It is important to remember that there were other forms of curricula before the introduction of the National Curriculum and that there are others forms of curricula beyond the National Curriculum which teachers need to be aware of lest their teaching become over-prescriptive and limited by current curriculum models.

There are also commercial educational providers of dedicated educational resources targeted on British forms of national curricula. Although these often charge a subscription for their services and resource provision, they are, nevertheless, worth investigating. The most well established commercial providers, such as Anglia Interactive, (Anglia Interactive 1999 p. 178) which draw upon years of experience in educational television and publishing, often have the depth, breadth and quality of resources with which teachers may be familiar and may find useful in extending and enhancing their pupils' learning opportunities. Such commercial providers often provide access to areas of their multimedia resources for trial purposes. An example of this is the ArtEducation website (ArtEducation 1999) that comprises extensive amounts of teaching resources for art and design education and is supported by the National Society for Education in Art and Design, NSEAD. Some commercial educational providers also issue their site on CD Rom from time to time so that resources may be used on a school network or intranet off-line, or on computers without Internet capability, thus saving telephone charges.

What is important in using web resources, just as it is in using printed or otherwise published resources, is that they are evaluated, carefully selected and their use monitored so that pupils have access to the best resources to support their learning opportunities. Just as there are evaluation criteria for the selection of conventionally published resources so there are well-established evaluation criteria supported by long-term research and the work of BECTA who publish criteria for both CD Rom and web-based multimedia. (BECTA, 1998).

Evaluation of multimedia resources

CD Roms have been evaluated by Curriculum Information Technology Support (CITS) subject groups as well as by BECTA generally. The CD Roms reviewed by BECTA over the last few years now amount to more than 600 (BECTA 1998). These can be found in the Multimedia for Portables section of the VTC. There are also a number of independent documents from the Curriculum Information Technology Support groups for national curriculum subjects including art,

(Choosing and Using CD Roms for Art and Design 1998), history, science, design and technology and geography. Some of these are on-line in the Professional Development section of the VTC. Some are also available from BECTA as paper-based documents though their real power is in their interactivity. The work of the CITS groups has now been taken over by Curriculum Consultation Groups for National Curriculum subjects. These comprise expertise at a range of levels throughout the educational system whose task it is to consolidate, develop and exemplify the use of ICT through individual subjects which now include PE, RE and ICT. The work of these groups is developing to include a subject on-line discussion forum so that there is wide access to the strategies, materials and training being developed in order to enhance and develop learning opportunities as well as to the issues underpinning the thinking and direction of the groups.

Many forms of teaching and learning can be supported, enhanced and developed through the use of ready-made multimedia resources. The most interesting aspect of the way we use multimedia comes from the ways in which practising teachers have not been able to use ready-made resources because they don't fit with their perceived teaching style. The ways in which they use resources to support particular aspects of their subject are not supported by commonly available commercial multimedia materials. Such teachers have decided to produce their own forms of multimedia, with and through which, to support their particular ways of teaching and pupil learning. These are not radically different to the way most other teachers work but when teaching in a resource-rich environment, some teachers want to work with resources from particular cultures or to make the connection with the outside world on their own terms rather than being dictated to or constrained by commercial products.

Issues for teachers as multimedia designers

From the case studies it may be seen that the main concerns of teachers as multimedia designers are that the materials they produce:

- are professionally presented;
- are attractive to pupils;
- are well founded in accurate background research;
- are presented in ways which teachers would typically use;
- communicate the intended information clearly and concisely at an appropriate language level and medium;
- engage pupils in the learning process resulting in higher standards of work;
- enable pupils to learn in multimodal ways using a range of multiple intelligences;
- enable pupils to have access to a wider, and more up to date, range of resources at an appropriate level than can be found in libraries;
- enable pupil learning to take account of learning opportunities away from school;
- can be used by others, rewritten for other purposes and augmented to form

larger sets of resources that can be used by a number of schools or across a group of schools either locally or internationally;

- enable new forms of teaching and learning that are stimulating not only for pupils but their teacher.

Conclusions: ways forward

As educators we seem to have two choices. We can make substantial and critical use of existing multimedia materials and develop ways of integrating these resources into the way we work with our students or we can develop our own materials for particular purposes where ready made materials are neither appropriate nor adequate. The third way is to produce re-authored materials for classroom use from resources gathered from the web, though subject to copyright. At least then we use such resources on our terms and in line with student needs or abilities. Often resources cannot be used live and direct from the web as the language level, structure or form is inappropriate. We need to be able to access resources from the web and use them in appropriate ways. The potential to develop such multimedia materials and access them from a school intranet is enormous. Even if teachers do not produce materials from scratch, there is much potential in teachers from groups of schools working on materials for similar projects and sharing them through new communication technologies. Resources can be produced using desktop publishing packages in either printed or web form. The convergence of these two technologies is such that either paper based or web based materials can be produced, lessening the learning curve for teachers and promoting integration of the two forms of resource based teaching and learning.

Another way forward is to consider ways of learning that are web based rather than merely using web based materials to support existing curriculum strategies. The work of Tom March through ozline.com (ozline.com 2000) is worthy of examination. He has been writing about the interaction between the web and education since 1995 and has developed strategies for pupil use of the web including WebQuests. These were developed with Professor Bernie Dodge at San Diego State University in 1995 to help teachers integrate the power of the web with student learning. There are now variations on the theme of WebQuests being produced by teachers. Some are harnessing the rich resources of the web to produce Treasure Hunts that develop printed worksheets that integrate often out of date school library resources with interactive web-based worksheets that make use of up to date contextual information from world-wide sources. These are not complex multimedia materials but simple educational strategies that make use of the powerful range of resources of the web. They can be produced by anyone with basic word-processing skills and access to the web (Bruntlett 2000).

The range and number of multimedia resources to support the development of pupil learning opportunity is developing rapidly. As educators we need to examine such resources critically, determine whether they help us teach and pupils learn, and decide when we should develop our own multimedia materials to either fill gaps or explore new subject teaching territory. There are trial materials available to support the development of multimedia and web sites. Software to develop such multimedia resources is becoming increasingly easy to use though perhaps forcing us into set patterns of output through the use of 'wizards'. In the UK we need to make the most of training being offered through local education authorities (LEAs), universities, commercial agencies, National Grid for Learning training or government-funded training through the New Opportunities Fund (NOF).

Now is the time to get started. We have the computers, the software and the training. There are no longer any excuses. What we need is the vision to enter the brave new world of web-based multimedia and use the newly available technologies to develop new forms of teaching and learning that transcend old curricula to the benefit of pupils. Such ways of working were unthinkable in the mid-nineties. Now we have them within our grasp.

Questions

1 As a teacher, why would you use web- or computer-based multimedia rather than other media such as print or video and for what purposes would you use such multimedia? What advantages and disadvantages do the varying forms of multimedia have over other media for educators and learners?
2 What skills and support do teachers need to develop and be provided with in order to produce good quality multimedia and who might provide such training and support? What kind of equipment and software base do teachers need access to in order to produce good quality multimedia?
3 What cognitive mapping of subject knowledge and processes do teachers need to undertake before in-house multimedia is planned, developed and produced? What might be the impact of twenty-first century interactive multimedia technology on a print-based nineteenth century curriculum?
4 What learning and development of knowledge and understanding is to take place as a result of teacher or pupil use of educational multimedia and how is it to be integrated with forms of knowledge and understanding related to the use of other forms of media?
5 What purpose does teacher developed multimedia serve: is it for simulation, stimulation, directed or structured learning or for use as a resource? How might teachers use multimedia to extend their own subject experience and that of students?

Further reading

The following books, journals and magazines extend the ideas in this chapter.

Books

Bruntlett, S. (2000) *Producing High Quality Multimedia Resources and Presentations – NOF Module 6 Reader*, Midlands South-East Consortium, De Montfort University, Bedford.
Giudice, M. and Dennis, A. (1999) *Professional Studio Techniques: Web Design Essentials*, Peachpit Press: New York.

Honeywell, P. (1999) *Visual Language for the World Wide Web*, Intellect Books: Exeter.
Sefton-Green, Julian (ed.) (1999) *Young People, Creativity and the New Technologies*, Routledge: London.
Wise, R. (with Steemers, J.) (1999) *Multimedia: A Critical Introduction*, Routledge: London.

Journals

Outline (*LTSN Journal*) University of Brighton ArDeCo
JITTE (*Journal of IT for Teacher Education*) – Triangle Journals Ltd

Magazines

Web Pages Made Easy – Paragon Publishing Ltd
net – Future Publishing
Steve Bruntlett – *Questions* – 23 June 2000

References

BECTA	http://www.becta.org.uk
NGfL	http://www.ngfl.gov.uk
NIVTC	http://www.deni.gov.uk
SVTC	http://www.scotland.gov.uk
VTC	http://www.vtc.ngfl.gov.uk
WVTC	http://www.cymru.gov.uk

Bibliography

AltaVista (1999) – http://www.altavista.com
Anglia Interactive (1999) – http://www.angliainteractive.com/
Art Education – http://arteducation.co.uk
BBC Education (1999) – http://www.bbc.co.uk
BECTA (1998) *Multimedia Authoring for Schools*, Coventry: BECTA
BECTA (1998) *CD Rom – Compact Disc Read Only Memory*,
    http://www.becta.org.uk/technology/infosheets/html/cdroms.html
Bruntlett, A. (1997) *An Action Research Approach to Designing Multimedia Curriculum Materials for Textiles on a Multicultural Theme*, De Montfort University, Leicester: Unpublished MA Dissertation.
Bruntlett, A. (2000) *Adinkra Scavenger Hunt*,
    http://gideon.mk.dmu.ac.uk/NGfl/AdinkraWebExercise5.htm
Bruntlett, S. (1998) *Choosing and Using CD Roms for Art and Design*, BECTA: Coventry.
Caperton, G. and Papert, S. (1997) *Vision for Education – The Caperton-Papert Platform*,
    http://www.mamamedia.com/areas/grownups/new/21_learning/home_alt.html?whicharticle=papert_caperton
Cotton, B. and Oliver, R. (1993) *Understanding Hypermedia: From Multimedia to Virtual Reality*, London: Phaidon.
Durbin, G., Morris, S. and Wilkinson, S. (1993) *A Teacher's Guide to Learning from Objects*. England: English Heritage.
Harel, I. and Papert, S. eds. (1991) *Constructionism*, Norwood, NJ: Ablex.

Heppell, S. (1993) 'Interactive multimedia in education' in Latchem, C., Williamson, J. and Henderson-Lancett, Lexie (1993) *Interactive Multimedia,* London: Kogan Page.

Holland, A. (1999) *The Use of the Internet as an Information Source for Graphic Design Students,* De Montfort University: Leicester, Unpublished MA Dissertation.

Kafai, Y. and Resnick, Mitchell (eds) (1996) *Constructionism in Practice: Design, Thinking and Learning in a Digital World,* Mahwah, NJ: Lawrence Erlbaum.

Latchem, C., Williamson, J. and Henderson-Lancett, L. (1993) *Interactive Multimedia,* London: Kogan Page.

Lego Mindstorms (1998) *What is Lego Mindstorms.* http://www.legomindstorms.com/

Looms, P. O. (1993) 'Interactive multimedia in education' in Latchem, C., Williamson, J. and Henderson-Lancett, L. (1993) *Interactive Multimedia.* London: Kogan Page.

MIT Epistemology and Learning Group Papers (1998) http://el.www.media.mit.edu/elpapers.html

NCET (1996) *Multimedia Authoring in Schools,* Coventry: NCET.

NCET (1996) *Evaluating CD Rom Titles,* Coventry: NCET.

NCET (1996) *Making Multimedia,* Coventry: NCET.

ozline.com (2000) http://www.ozline.com

Papert, S. (1980) *Mindstorms; Children, Computers and Powerful Ideas,* New York: Basic Books.

Papert, S. (1993) *The Children's Machine: Rethinking School in the Age of the Computer,* New York: Basic Books.

Papert, S. (1996) *The Connected Family: Bridging the Digital Generation Gap (includes CD Rom and web-site links),* Atlanta, Georgia: Longstreet Press.

Papert, S. (1998) 'Let's Tie the Digital Knot', in *Technos Quarterly,* Vol. 7, No. 4, http://www.technos.net/journal/volume7/4papert.htm

Papert, S. (2000) *Diversity in Learning: A Vision for the New Millennium,* http://www.papert.com/articles/diversity/DiversityinLearningPart1.html

Pestana, S. (1998) *Multimedia as a Resource for Museum-based Art and Design Teaching,* De Montfort University: Leicester. Unpublished MA Dissertation.

Preece, J. Latchem, C., Williamson, J. and Henderson-Lancett, Lexie (1993) *Interactive Multimedia,* London, Kogan Page.

Rheingold, H. (1985) *Tools for Thought,* http://www.rheingold.com/texts/tft/

Rheingold, H. (1986) *The Virtual Community,* http://www.rheingold.com/vc/book//

Schwartz, D. (2000) *Ghost in the Machine,*

Tesco Schoolnet 2000 – http://tesco.schoolnet2000.com/

ULTRALAB – http://www.ultralab.ac.uk/

WWW Virtual Library – http://www.vlib.org/

Yahoo – http://www.yahoo.comhttp://www.zinezone.com/zones/digital/software/papert/interview.html

Part III

Wider issues for the educational community

13 Intranets

Developing a learning community

Darren Leafe

Introduction: new technologies and raising standards

Teachers are expected not only to cope with, but to also implement change on a grand scale. In the UK we have witnessed the introduction and review of the National Curriculum and the implementation of the literacy and numeracy strategies. In addition, schools, pupils and teachers have been involved in a technological change. A change that not only involves 'connecting the learning community', but also involves developing a range of strategies for 'learning within a connected community'.

It is argued that this degree of change is in the name of 'raising standards'.

> The National Grid for Learning will also send a clear message, both here and internationally, that the UK intends to be among the world leaders to harness new technologies to raise educational standards . . .
>
> (DfEE 1997: 3)

We could argue, however, that standards of teaching and learning will only be raised if the various elements of change are implemented effectively at school, local and national levels. The implementation of the National Grid for Learning can not improve standards alone. The successful integration of Information and Communications Technology (ICT) into the curriculum will, however, have a definite impact. To achieve this, schools need to be well organised and planned. Teachers need to develop the ability to identify opportunities for ICT and develop the concept of using the technology as a tool for learning, particularly within the literacy and numeracy framework. However, can teachers, pupils and schools effectively deal with this degree of change?

We could argue about the answers to this question for some time. One way in which to reduce individual burdens is to further develop collaboration on a number of different levels. The cry that is often heard is that 'we shouldn't be reinventing the wheel'. If a school has developed a range of resources based on a particular theme, then there may be many opportunities for that content to be shared with other schools. The same notion of sharing resources applies to individual teachers and local and national institutions and this is perhaps one area where new technologies can assist the raising of standards to a great extent. If the technology can assist with the sharing or resources, then it becomes a tool through which teachers and schools can develop and build upon their existing practice by using the experiences of their colleagues. Pupils too, would be able to share their learning experiences in whatever format or style.

A criticism of many educational websites is that there is never enough content. In a recent interview, Stephen Heppell of Ultralab, Anglia Polytechnic University, stated that:

> Teachers have traditionally selected content and done their annotation, whether it be photocopy lesson plans, reading lists or whatever. We should be doing the same with ICT content. There will never be enough content for every school, so we panic and try to develop even more commercial content. What we should do is encourage schools to develop their own content and share it with others . . . . . . We should be filling our servers up with opportunities rather than just content.
>
> (Heppell 1999: 12)

We could argue that there is enough content but that we are not particularly good at sharing it. New technologies can be used to help teachers and schools share materials that have a proven record in the classroom. Shared content should be evaluated by others and developed to integrate successfully into another school's curriculum thus, on a very simplistic level, raise standards. We need to develop a sharing culture as not only are there changes within the curriculum, but also within the culture in which schools work. This is not a dramatic change for some schools, however others will need to move away from the 'closed door' policy where curriculum plans and resources are closely guarded secrets and only accessible to others at a cost.

New technologies have a major role to play in developing opportunities, and facilitating the sharing of resources and content. An intranet provides a platform on which collaboration in various ways can take place. The technology can provide a set of tools that enable teachers, pupils and schools to raise standards through collaboration and communication. An on-line 'learning community' is a phrase often used to describe a community of learners who use new technologies as tools through which to develop professional practice and learning.

An educational intranet (web or network based system open to approved users) can be developed on a number of different levels, therefore, existing networks can often be utilised to provide a technically simple intranet. With investment, more complex intranets can be developed where specific tools can be developed to encourage and facilitate collaboration, but whatever the scale of the intranet to be developed, key decisions have to be made in relation to how the technology is to be used and in relation to the nature of learning that the intranet will support. A balance needs to be found between the type of learning community to be supported and the technologies that are available. We discuss these issues below.

Learning in a networked society

When developing an educational intranet, whether for a school, a school and its local community or an LEA, it is important to consider the type of learning that the design of the system will promote. Some decisions will be restricted by the type of technology available to develop the system, while other decisions will reflect how content materials will be accessed, interacted with and developed. What will be the aims for users of the intranet as learners? When a user approaches the intranet, what type of activity will they be involved in? Who will be involved in developing the community? What tools will they be given?

We could argue that when a user approaches an intranet they can do one of three things; browse pages of information, interact with pages of content or collaborate with other users. A user may be involved in any number of these tasks during one session (Fig. 13.1).

Browse – A user uses the technology to gain information. The activity requires the user to read information presented on the screen and take away from the information a degree of knowledge. This activity relies on the learner being able to interpret the information effectively and to be able to draw relevant conclusions.

Interact – On this occasion, the information is developed and shaped by the user. The information retrieval process relies on the interaction of the user with the system. Key questions may be asked of the user and choices made or communicated using on-line forms. This activity involves the user directly in the learning process and requires the user to interact with the information to enable relevant conclusions to be made.

Collaborate – The learning activity relies on the user collaborating with other users, sharing information and knowledge. When a user approaches the system

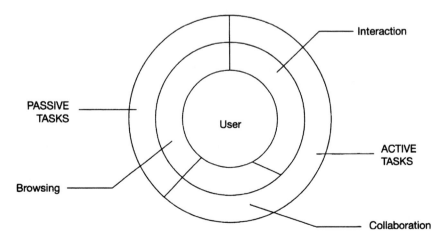

Figure 13.1 Ways of using an intranet

they are actively involved in the activity, which can only take place when users interact. Information is provided by other users. This activity involves the user directly in the learning process.

We could take this concept even further. If we take each activity and evaluate the type of activity that is being promoted via the technology, we could argue that the *browse* activity is essentially a *passive task*, where learning gains are dependent entirely on the effective interpretation by the learner of the information presented. We could also argue that the last two activities encourage *active tasks* where the technology encourages the involvement of the user. This is in many ways a crude model as it presumes that all of the activities are solitary tasks, where the learner is on their own using the system. This is perhaps one of the best ways in which to approach the development of content if assumptions have to be made regarding the effect a particular material has on learning. When developing content for an intranet, the type of content presented to learners is therefore critical if the technology is to have an impact on learning and on raising standards.

These concepts have implications for the type of community that will develop. Will users be encouraged to interact with the technology and with each other or will they be encouraged to take from the system relevant knowledge? If we imagine our intranet to be a large room, we need to consider how the room is set out and what type of content is displayed, where it is displayed and how to encourage learning to take place. An intranet that encourages users to browse for information and knowledge will encourage a relationship to develop between the user and the technology that ignores other users on the system to a great extent. Our room would have no furniture, but the walls would be covered with 'posters' of information. There would be many entrances and the room would be full of people searching for relevant information and looking at the 'posters' to gain further understanding and knowledge. Even though the room may be full of people, it is silent as no one is encouraged to communicate with another.

An intranet that encourages users to communicate and collaborate would be similar to the room described above, but, this time, there would be areas of the room set aside for people to meet. When searching for relevant information, someone may guide you to a particular resource. When looking at a 'poster' of information on the wall, users will be encouraged to turn to the person next to them and discuss the content and they may need to interact with the 'poster' to gain a full understanding of its meaning.

We could well argue that the latter example describes an active learning community where users are encouraged to use the relevant technological tools to develop a range of skills, concepts and understandings. Learning becomes a collaborative, shared experience as advocated by Vygotsky.

The concept of a collaborative learning community is sometimes difficult to communicate fully to all users. Many users, who may wish to use the technology to share resources, often think in terms of digitising materials that already exist in paper format. While there is an obvious place for this type of content within an intranet, if the whole intranet contained materials of this nature, we would be discouraging collaboration and encouraging the concept of a browsing intranet. Furthermore, the intranet becomes an information dissemination service to those in authority and the quality of that information provided is only as good as the group that have control over the content to be distributed. Therefore, we should encourage contributions from the many, with an integrated quality control mechanism, that facilitates communication and collaboration between users of all types.

Opportunities within the classroom

One key question is how can learning opportunities be extended into and from the classroom? There are many ways in which intranets can add to the overall learning experience within a school (see Leafe 2000). A local intranet can give many users access to the same materials at the same time and enable knowledge, concepts and understandings to be communicated between many users. A teacher can display content as many times as there are machines available, enabling many pupils to access a single resource without huge photocopying costs. Content can be immediately updated, with updates available to all users.

Projects between classes and school have been established on a local, national and international level, building upon information available to the pupils via the intranet, on a daily basis. Email between users becomes a standard form of communication. Some schools have used an internal email facility to broadcast messages related to the smooth running of the school (see the table below).

What can we do with the technology that cannot be achieved any other way?

A KS5 CAD/CAM example

Our year 12 pupils designed a range of products using a vacuum forming machine and designed various moulds using CAD/CAM (computer aided design and computer aided manufacture). They worked with our link school in France for a number of weeks using email as the main form of communication. The idea was that the product could be manufactured in France as well as the UK. If this proved to be successful, then other European countries could be involved.

Our pupils emailed all the relevant files and construction information to their French colleagues. This led on to a great deal of communication, ensuring the documents were clear and that the software would produce an identical match.

What I found really exciting about this project was the way in which the pupils had to use a wide variety of skills from our curriculum. As staff, we decided that our pupils had to communicate in French and that they had to also communicate with the staff at the French school. There were obvious links within the Design Technology and Modern Foreign Languages courses that the pupils were studying, and the Information Technology department became heavily involved, helping the pupils solve various technical issues.

For just over a month, the project pulled people and departments together, our link school were eventually able to produce the products and digital images of the products were shared and evaluated.

Key Stage 5 Teacher

Schools, teachers and pupils need to also know when to and when not to use the technology and be able to identify the appropriate opportunities. One question that relates to the type of content developed is what can we do with the technology that can not be achieved any other way?

The extent to which an intranet can be developed within an institution will depend to a great extent on the availability of appropriate resources. We can describe these issues as the 'physical boundaries'. These physical boundaries can be restrictive, but the concept of an intranet that a school or other organisation may be working towards is only limited by theoretical boundaries. A school may not be able to fully implement its vision for intranet learning because it lacks the appropriate resources, yet it can still be working towards it.

Developing content for an intranet: whose values? Whose knowledge?

We have already discussed the type of content that may be developed, and in addition to this we need to consider the values attached to content provided via an intranet. Whose values are represented? How can quality be assured? Whose curriculum is catered for?

The curriculum is value based (Morrison and Ridley 1988: 2), therefore we could argue that all content, whether it be on the internet or intranet, is representative of the author's own values. This has important implications for the development of content for an educational intranet as a balance of resources and values would be required. The technology gives users the opportunity to question others' values.

If content is only developed by a small group and disseminated to all other users, the accuracy and quality of that content will be a reflection of that group's knowledge, skills, attitudes and experience. The intranet should enable and encourage contributions from the many, representing the values of the whole community. Within the structure of the intranet, two opposing value items of content could sit next to each other and users be given the opportunity to make their own professional decisions and use or interact with the most appropriate resource. A balance between content that is developed by a small group and that which is developed by the whole community should be encouraged and facilitated through the intranet.

Quality control

The technology can be used to provide an element of quality control, and, on the majority of occasions, there will be two distinct levels of quality control; High Level Quality Control and Low Level Quality Control. The high level content is often referred to as the content that has been stamped with the approval of a governing 'expert body'. This level of content is often 'commissioned' by a set group of users who have identified a particular need. The low level quality controlled content reflects the collaborative nature of the intranet. This area includes the capacity for users to add to an on-line discussion and to submit content materials. This type of interaction is difficult to monitor, so a submitted item of content should not be placed in a 'live' state on the intranet until it is released by an expert in that particular area of the curriculum.

The needs of schools, teachers and pupils will influence the type and subject nature of material available on the intranet together with national strategies and priorities. The question to be addressed here is how the development of content is prioritised. If content is developed by many schools and teachers and not a single group, then the development of resources will reflect users' priorities. If a group of users commissioned content then that content would reflect their priorities to a great extent. The two can co-exist, where a number of priorities determine when and how content is developed.

Making the most of available technology

The National Grid for Learning initiative in the UK has given many schools new equipment, software and access to the internet. The ratio of computers to pupils varies greatly throughout the country with some schools having one machine with access to the internet, while others may have a whole network linked to multimedia projections or electronic whiteboards. This has an enormous impact on the type of community that can develop.

The school with a single computer with access to the internet via a modem and telephone line can still develop a limited intranet on the one computer. Internet pages are identified and saved to the local hard drive and pupils access these resources by using an index page designed by their teacher. An institution with a network where only one machine has internet access can develop the same type of intranet by saving files onto a shared drive of the server which allows any machine on the network to access the downloaded resources. The type of intranet content that is available is limited to materials that do not involve a large amount of interaction and internal email. If the network has internet access, then link pages can be developed that link local content, held on the local server, and web-based content available on the internet. Resources can be accessed that have a full level of interactivity and the use of email is not restricted to the physical boundaries of the institution.

Developing this further, a regional intranet, linking the whole educational community of an area can and should be developed. Schools connect to other schools, central resources, local museums, libraries, universities and other relevant services. Information is shared and passed between each organisation as required. The boundaries of each organisation are increasingly blurred around the edges and users of the system are given the opportunities to communicate and collaborate using the direct connections made available. It is this type of intranet facility that will have the greatest impact on learning within the classroom; a concept that can only be achieved by using new technologies.

This raises the issue of how a user will interact with this type of intranet.

- How will users navigate, organise and best use their time on the intranet?
- What opportunities will be provided to enable schools, teachers and pupils to communicate?

The regional intranet will need to cope with the many demands of the many users. Screens should provide opportunities to submit content to the system, edit existing content, participate in discussions, find other users and locate relevant, useful resources. One of the most important issues is that of ownership. Users should be given, wherever possible, the opportunity to personalise their screen. Pupils could be allowed to decide what colours they want to use, and which subjects they want to receive the latest news about. An A Level pupil's view of the intranet will be different from a primary school pupil's and a teacher's viewpoint. At this level, programmers will need to be involved to write small web-based applications that meet the needs of all users.

Access to the intranet need not be restricted to schools and there is enormous potential for the traditional boundaries of the school being stretched further. The number of pupils who have access to the internet from home is increasing at an unprecedented rate, therefore we now have the opportunity for schools not to finish at 3:30. Teachers and pupils should be given secure access to the intranet from their normal internet connection and access should eventually be extended to the wider community, enabling Life Long Learning to be enhanced.

Conclusions

We have discussed a range of issues related to developing educational intranets. We have discussed the type of activity that can be promoted and how intranets can have an impact on learning within the classroom. We have also briefly looked at the issues related to developing content and how the resources available to institutions govern the type of community that can develop.

Intranets can, and do, make an impact in the classroom and have enormous potential for helping to raise standards in schools. For this potential to be realised, we need to further develop a 'sharing culture', where the local educational intranet is one of the first points of call, for relevant resources and collaborative opportunities, for teachers and pupils.

Questions

1   What different types of materials will teachers want to share and how will colleagues and pupils interact with these resources?
2   How can an educational intranet contribute to the raising of standards within the classroom?
3   What strategies can be developed to ensure 'equality of access' to an intranet?

Further reading

DfEE (1997) *Connecting the Learning Society*, London: HMSO.
This document sets the scene and provides a degree of background information in regard to the development of the NGfL initiative.

Heppell, S. (1999) 'Tripping the light fantastic *in* on-line', – Computers in Education, *Times Educational Supplement.*
Heppell raises a number of important issues in relation to the concept of Content Development.

Leafe, D. (2000) 'Managing curriculum projects using ICT' in Leask, M. and Meadows, J. *Teaching and Learning with ICT in the Primary School*, London: Routledge.
This chapter offers practical advice on implementing an ICT curriculum project and includes example projects supported by a number of different agencies including the Central Bureau of the British Council.

Morrison, K. and Ridley, K. (1988) *Curriculum Planning and the Primary School*, London: Paul Chapman Publishing.
Morrison and Ridley discuss in depth the complexities of the primary curriculum. Whilst not based on ICT, there are important curriculum issues raised as to the implementation of ICT across the curriculum.

References

DfEE (1997) *Connecting the Learning Society*, London: HMSO.
Heppell, S. (1999) 'Tripping the light fantastic *in* on-line', Computers in Education, *Times Educational Supplement.*
Leafe, D. (2000) 'Managing curriculum projects using ICT' in Leask, M. and Meadows, J. *Teaching and Learning with ICT in the Primary School*, London: Routledge.
Morrison, K. and Ridley, K. (1988) *Curriculum Planning and the Primary School*, London: Paul Chapman Publishing.

14 Lifelong learning in the electronic age

Christina Preston

Preamble

I spent the Easter weekend 1999 with my Czech friends. In their fifties, this university couple were dissidents during the Russian occupation having lived through the Second World War and previous occupations by the Austrians and the Germans. They have lived in nine different countries, although they have never left Prague. This kind of political instability and change is unknown territory for us British. I learn so much from their perspectives, particularly on matters I had entirely taken for granted.

Tired of modern urban life in London and Prague, we drove off in pursuit of traditional religious and pagan traditions still practised in the remote Moravian village that we had found on the internet. We appeared to be the first on safari and our dreams of a rural idyll were realised. An 82 year old woman came into view riding to church on her bicycle in full traditional costume: a short colourful skirt over full net petticoats, a lace bodice and a white silk headscarf: against the biting wind an embroidered wool cape.

The old ladies in their bright short skirts invited us in to see the flowers they had laid against the feet of their Lady and to admire the clean and neat church that they kept in her honour. The Catholic congregation wreathed in the smoke of incense knelt respectfully before the scarlet clad priest and his young male assistants who had pony tails: multi-sensory pageant of colour, ritual and song in a life that can be physically hard and visually drab.

In the simplicity of the small community of the Czech Brethren church, the congregation sit in a circle around the altar. The dates on the leather bound prayer books laid out for us by one of the families were 1908, 1903 and 1873. The print had sometimes worn away but the pages were always the same. Since the traditional service had been going for so long we imagined they knew it by heart. When our friend was 12 her father had been advised not to go to church again if he wanted to remain a teacher. This was the first time she had returned.

We saw only two people under 30 in the congregation and most were over 50. Congregations have dwindled since the Wall came down. During the occupation going to church was a protest against the regime and preserving religious traditions, songs and customs was paramount when the Czechs were not allowed to celebrate in the streets. Now, say our friends, money is the first consideration in an economy that limps on the new rules of capitalist markets. There is no time to luxuriate in long family breaks and to sing protest songs long into the night. 'We're in the rat race now.'

We were invited to sup in a sixteenth century wine cellar with the extended family who preserve this tradition, courtesy of UNESCO. The wine made from the family vineyard is being undercut by the price of supermarket bottles. Most who continue the traditions do so as a business. The owner, who is also a trouble-shooting consultant for several major computer companies, asked us to put our photographs on the internet for him to download.

On the Slovak border, we found a village mayor in the pub. He recommended ensuite accommodation in the next village that cost about four dollars. Although the landlady had had to redistribute some small children to accommodate us, we were given a spotless room with a state of the art shower and radio. They did not serve meals officially, but for two dollars they rustled up pork, sauerkraut and dumplings and begged some salad from a neighbour. Because it was Easter they did not charge us for the exquisite home-made cakes which would have cost about six dollars each in London.

The local headmaster arrived with his Yamaha to accompany the dance. Tickets were 20 cents. In our honour he sang 'Greensleeves' in English and played a melody of the Beatles, Elvis, several rock tunes of the sixties, traditional polkas, the twist and punk rock. In his late 50s he used to have a band but since the changes people would not play for so little money so he was accompanied by the electric organ which he programmed using his computer. He had also used a software package to learn English in which he conversed creditably with a clear Oxford accent. He also spoke excellent Slovakian, Russian and German.

The dancers' footwear ranged from mountaineering boots to slippers. From 60 to 6, they made a good stab at the complicated steps until none of us much cared whether we were heading in the right direction or not.

I drank too much of one of the Moravian family wines. Normally I drink one glass of wine and get an additive headache. This wine was so pure that even after half a litre, I was bright and fresh in the morning at seven o'clock when we went in search of young men. Traditionally they hunt in packs on Easter Monday morning, carrying woven willow canes to whip their favourite women. They whip to hurt I discovered, but poppy seed cake and slipovic and melodious singing was a good cure.

Some homes receive nearly a hundred small boys who call for eggs, to pacify them on Easter Monday morning. We saw them struggling home at midday with plastic bags bulging with booty. Mother is presumably studying egg recipes. Only the older men still sing the old songs of love and wear the costumes, but the tradition survives vibrantly amongst the young, since the gains are clear for the participants. I should have been better advised and sought out the region where the women beat the men!

At home our friend's young son was nervous and pale studying for his final exams to be a doctor. He is a well educated, delightful, sensitive and imaginative young man, a vegetarian who speaks several languages and takes photographs like a professional. With other students he stood on the tanks and spent three days 'talking out' the Russian soldiers occupying Wenceslas Square in 1987. He felt sorry for them. Many of them illiterate peasants, they did not know which country they were in nor why they were there.

This young man is afraid. Despite a string of A grades, he could fail this exam. His professors can ask anything they like from the last six years' work. Yesterday their medical guru told the class they were all stupid. Why could they not remember what they did six years ago? I asked if anyone had tested his compassion or his ability to relate to people in the last six years. You know the answer. He quoted one enlightened French doctor who said that studying medicine was like putting to sea without any water in sight. His partner who graduated last year earns four dollars a month for long hours in a local hospital. She is lucky to have a job. He does not yet have one to go to. They are planning to emigrate to America.

So much to learn, so much to adapt to, so much to communicate to survive in the Third Millennium. How will the global teaching profession cope with the changes that are taking place in the world with them, or without them?

Will teachers lead the revolution?

One interpretation of 'literacy' is being able to communicate within the medium of your culture (Wagner 1995). A culture can be defined as a particular stage in the intellectual development of a civilisation or a society. Literacy, therefore, is integral to the aims and ideals of the society that defines the concept.

Pressure on education to be the agent of change is common across the world, because most societies and governments believe that education can make a difference to the cohesive culture of a nation. But when they are seriously evaluated, many of the major attempts at innovation through education since the sixties have failed to take root. Teachers are accused of rejecting reform. Fullan and Stiegelbauer (1991) suggests the problem is not rejection, but the fact that teachers at the chalk face have not been guided in the management of change.

Wisdom is now accumulating amongst the policy makers and industrialists around the world about the multifarious complexities unleashed in the change process. For example, it is clear that the agreement, understanding and cooperation of the social partners must be sought: government, industry and education as well as reference to the church or other influential groups.

But even now, despite considerable international wisdom, teachers are being set up as the leading agents of social reform, rather than being partners in a social movement. Teachers are then caught in the cross-fire, because the society that supports them is in conflict about values and aims. The irony is that in asking teachers to lead the revolution in teaching and learning, society is asking them to preside over the demise of the traditional professional role. Globalisation and internationalisation of education challenges the tradition of teachers as authoritarian distributors of knowledge, of classrooms rooted in locations and governed by time and fixed terms for learning ending with maturity. Worst of all, the skills required for living in the future do not seem to depend on what has been done in the past. Futurology now demands an imaginative leap into the unknown.

Despite his analysis of the failure of educational reform in the last quarter of the twentieth century and the continuing opportunities to squander effort, Fullan thinks that education has never been in a better position to make a difference. But he is convinced that effective change will only come about through the development of the shared meaning in the full social setting. 'Systems do not change by themselves. People change systems by their actions. It is time to change the way we change'. (Fullan and Stiegelbauer 1991: 352).

Teachers need to make changes to survive. It is up to the profession to find the strategies.

What is the future of lifelong education?

Beare and Slaughter (1994) are enthusiastic about the role of new technologies believing that when a right relationship is established between people, culture and technology a new world of options emerges. They agree that powerful new technologies are not intrinsically threatening. If they were linked to, and directed by a higher-order ethical commitment, they could be deployed in life affirming ways.

The electronic network is likely to be the main facilitator of learning and teaching in new modes. Already electronic networks have had a profound effect on the lifestyles of those who use them in homes, in companies and in universities: the opportunity to contribute to a global village culture alongside the diversity of established cultures has been established, precipitately confusing notions of national culture and identity. In the spirit of post modernism, people can subscribe to more than one culture without compromising their identity or integrity, as long as they can handle quantities of information, the scope for choice and conflicting loyalties. These attitudes are immensely threatening to those who subscribe to a monoculture and to many who have currently isolated power in their own hands. For example, nation states in Europe did not exist in medieval times and the concept of citizenship came from the French revolution only 200 years ago. Intensifying regionalism and the development of supra-national structures suggest that nation states may be a transitory stage in the evolution of human societies.

The impact of advanced technology on teaching and learning has hastened changes. Electronic mediums of communication are the vehicle for powerful messages and for authoritative, public debate. Therefore, to make computers the catalyst for change in an educational project makes sense. There are dangers of imbalanced input, however, if the education team consists of technically trained educators. In this context too much is expected of the mere presence of hardware and software without a full understanding or commitment to the human processes involved in the creation of new mind sets and new paradigms. Generally middle-aged, many would-be innovators in educational software do not have the skills, knowledge or appropriate talents to specify world class education products: convergent and linear thinkers cannot envisage what the future requires. If the education design team is intensely reading and writing centric they will not be able to envisage the multimedia options that today's learners expect.

Educators with a background in educational software usually fight against commercial involvement on the grounds that companies will not respect the special needs of education. Because of their lack of experience of the kind of network products that are being designed for multinationals, educators involved in education specification can hold up the process rather than facilitate it.

In partnership with governments they have tended to oversee products and projects that have limited applications and serve education badly. As an example of investment at too low a level, the UK National Council for Education Technology set up a four million pound research project to follow the trials of US education integrated learning software over three years. This comparatively large resource was invested in poorly designed, culturally inappropriate software based on the traditional and outdated learning model, mainly drill and practice. The software was already four years old when the research began and remained unchanged throughout the period. By the time the report was out the CD Roms were eight years old. There was no way in which the evaluation could be formative because the companies had no intention of completing a 'finished' product. As the software was not industry standard, transferability and opportunities for global dissemination were missed, although there was more than one multinational training product on the market that would have merited investment. The schools market is small and fragmented. Quality cannot be maintained at this level.

Long term learning networks cannot be sustained without the prospect of a global, lifelong learning market. Since multinational technology can offer multilingual translation, good educational specification can still maintain cultural and linguistic diversity. Educators have to find a means of identifying companies with 'cathedral building' cultures (Handy 1994) rather than trying to preserve the educational software industry in its present form (Harris and Preston 1993).

There is much to be gained by working with the best technical experts in the world. Technological advancements have reached a stage where the non-technical user is empowered to develop their own creative paths and even to author high quality software products. Power may well end back in the hands of the teachers who can change. In fact most of the needs of education like privacy, confidentiality, censorship and avoidance of overt advertising have already been considered on scaleable multinational sites.

For example, Think.com, a web-based environment is costing the software company, Oracle, more than 14 million pounds to develop, pilot and evaluate in a three year cycle. This software is being tested by more than 10,000 educational users and will be given free to the community and will be without advertising. The evaluation is formative which means that teachers and pupils are feeding back their needs to the developers whilst they use the software. New features related to learning need are under debate by the Early Adopters. In these circumstances, educators can be involved in software development as well as being able to customise the software for their community and author the content.

A very different situation from buying an eight year old CD Rom with unalterable content designed for a different cultural situation. Oracle have used all their knowledge about security to create a safe environment for young learners. Governments could not hope to invest so much in a software project of this kind.

The decrease of state funding for education and the rise of the market means that educators are dependent on their multinational partners to develop the kind of scaleable network infrastructure that are required for lifelong learning. If they do not utilise these opportunities lifelong learning opportunities and access to the best possible learning tools will decrease.

The historical development of literacy

Looking at history can throw some light on the current research and pedagogy partners education chooses today. There is no record of the invisible process of mind on mind communication used by the close knit communities of the Dark Ages, except in terms of extant drawings and illuminated illustrations. The populace did not require reading or writing skills but sensitivities of quite a different kind. Oral relay was the dominant literacy whether in speech, story or song. Effective speakers with the ability to entertain had great power. There is, of course, no record of effective oral literacy. Nor the power of human memory which our civilisation does not train, although we are still in awe of Shakespeare's players who held his scripts in their heads long after his death.

Anthropologists and historians understand some of these techniques, because existing indigenous peoples of the world still practise them. In Chile, for example, two centuries of Mapuche resistance to the Spanish invaders was attributed to lack of written messages which could be intercepted and decoded. The fierce united defiance of these indigenous people was impenetrable. Right into the nineteenth century, the Mapuche communication methods triumphed over European military processes. In fact, the Mapuche were never conquered, but finally negotiated a treaty for peace.

What is important about the time before reading and writing is the quality of thinking and communication which was different, but not necessarily inferior, from that which is common today. In fact, many small communities in inner cities and villages, who rarely depend on reading and writing, run in these time honoured ways, but the techniques are unsung or distrusted by the book literate.

Chandler and Marcus (1985) identified three main developments of literacy as it relates to the decoding of print. The book culture has been 400 years in the making. Readers and writers have been in control: the tyranny of the literate (Meek 1995).

In the early print culture the church and the state were the main partners with the community rulers. The individual had no chance of publishing widely. Collaborative authorship was controlled by the church who were also the agents of communication and in control of education. Illustration in biblical tracts and in icons indicates an ability to convey time, locations and abstractions which is close to film imagery. Those who could scribe and read were rare and powerful.

Those who were international policy makers, traders and churchmen spoke fluent Latin as well as their own dialect.

Since the invention of the Gutenberg Press, the growth of literacy has been focused on linear thinking recorded in printed form on paper. The problems and expense of illustrating text stunted the visual aspect of the mind for communication for at least two centuries. The growth of reading and writing importance created new gatekeepers and new conventions of individual authorship. The complexity of coding and decoding written symbols made the long term education of professions a necessity. Concepts that grew up with the dominance of the book worked against collaboration and public communication. Concepts of copyright, cheating, definitive texts and national languages developed and the gatekeepers became those who had the power, the money and the influence to publish.

There are fierce storms taking place in the British teacup about reading and writing and the status of English as a national language. Intermittent evidence that some school leavers are illiterate or underperforming in English attracts particular outrage from the Right in Britain. Prince Charles has complained publicly that his secretaries cannot use Queen's English correctly. Teachers must therefore be failing in their duty to develop literacy. A Campaign for Back to Basics in schools was quickly abandoned, but teachers were advised by Tory ministers to discourage any community language or dialect other than Queen's English in the classroom and even the playground: except for Welsh, an exception which is apparently alone as a 'source of cultural and social diversity'. In state schools, children share as many as seventy community languages between them. British parents with multicultural roots as well as the indigenous population resent the low literacy standards in English that can result. These parents believe that basic reading and writing skill are crucial, as jobs become scarcer and more demanding of white collar skills. Are they right?

The British do not enthuse about language teaching at a young age. Although the National Curriculum advises one other foreign language, the education minister has refused to follow the latest European Union recommendation for at least two other languages to be studied by sixteen. The compulsory Literacy Hour in the UK reinforces the belief that reading and writing are of overriding importance. Surprisingly the launch of the National Grid for Learning has not yet impacted on the literacy or the numeracy programmes.

On the other hand the networked society era that we are entering in the run up to the twenty-first century appears to be abandoning this reading and writing emphasis. Professor Gunther Kress (Kress 1996) discusses the shift in communication towards visual forms, which he sees as a fundamental challenge to the hitherto unchallenged centrality of written language. For example, when images were used in 'A' Level science text books in the thirties, they were illustrations of the text. Progressively images have come to communicate in their own right, not dependent on written commentary and often adding another idea.

This study is textbook based but one of the new literacies that Gunther Kress highlights is the icon revolution which is a manifestation of the electronic age. Experiments with icons are connected with an increasing awareness about the problems of communication through language alone in a heterogeneous and multicultural society. The use of icons is also related to the problems presented when language is used as a medium of authority in an international context (Kress 1996).

Children and learning

Eighty per cent of children do not find traditional reading and writing technologies easy. Schools have to coach them intensively in the formative years. Many of those who jumped the education barrier despite their severe reading and writing handicaps came from homes that could afford to deal with the problem or had conveyed to their offspring what to expect from education (Gardner 1993). Well known names like Einstein, Churchill, Edison, Faraday and Yeats are cited by Thomas West who maintains that new developments in computer technology herald a significant shift towards the increased use of visual approaches to information analysis throughout the economy. These changes will, in time, affect the fundamental nature of both education and work. It may even be that creative visual thinkers, aided by computers, will be at the forefront of innovation in a dramatically changing society (West 1991).

New technologies reverse the concepts of experience, continuity and progression in teaching and learning, further challenging the teacher's traditional role. Heppell reports that children are probably better at using and benefiting from technology than parents, teachers and society previously believed. Multitasking and making hypertext connections came as second nature to those who were already active participants in interpreting the multimedia message from computers and television.

CD Roms on factual subjects are more challenging and than books. Most factual information is better understood in the form of animated models, sound, graphics and high resolution colour photographs than in written text alone. Interaction is also important in children's learning (Spenser 1996). A CD Rom has defined limits. Multimedia surfing, in contrast, demands a clear understanding that there is no single path through the infinite jungle of data and good navigation techniques are essential, especially as the terrain may well have changed completely when the traveller tries to return.

Stephen Heppell's team at Ultralab, Anglia Polytechnic University has studied what children are actually doing with the new technologies. His team has pioneered the evolutionary stage for CAL (Computer Assisted Learning). The first CD Rom and games software were linear in their design and execution. At the second stage navigational, investigation and exploration features created participation. In the third stage of resources, that is still being explored, participation moves to interactivity state and ever closer to the twenty-first century vision of virtual reality. This concept coupled with the findings within Artificial Intelligence (AI) and linked to traditional CAL provides intelligent tutoring systems and intelligent computer aided instruction (ICAL). Current integrated learning systems are a long way from this vision (Heppell 1995). Professor Stephen Heppell is one of the authors of the Stevenson Report which first promoted the idea of the National Grid for Learning. His research has clarified the size of the operation he recommends and the need to work with industry partners (Stevenson 1996).

It is significant that Heppell is the designer who has been working jointly with Oracle to develop Think.com. His research into children's learning shows that children, unconstrained by the linearity of the education system as we have known it, seem to be able not only to retrieve information stored in a multimedia form, but also to create it. For example, one of the top prizes in the 1995 NCET National Educational Multimedia Awards (NEMA) was won by a team of Scottish 6 year olds from Inverkeithing Primary School. They were able to offer their audience a variety of routes through the narrative and hot links to more information if the user chose to dig deeper. They had used multimedia as a way of describing concepts that are hard to handle in words. The key to success was the integral use of graphics and pictures as narrative. Overall the 6 year olds had an intuitive understanding of the hypermedia connections that characterise the best multimedia compositions – connections that more closely resemble the free flow of human ideas than books do.

Multimedia is challenging the role of reading and writing in culture. See, for example, the Mapuche Indians in Chile who have no written language and who have jumped 400 years of book culture. The children have been using multimedia resources to communicate the essence of their culture to the outside world. The Mapuche teachers have been closely involved in these developments and the children's self esteem has risen while their failure in the conventional system has been arrested. The improvement in the national language of education, Spanish, has been measurable. The importance of this example is the value given to verbal, musical, storytelling and other non lingual forms of 'knowing' which are not well covered in conventional schools (Preston 1995a).

New pedagogies

'Knowledge workers' of the future will be able to handle unprecedented volumes of multimedia data while coping with extensive choices and balancing conflicting loyalties. The jury is still out on how much reading and writing competence will be required by these high flyers who will be in demand all over the world, but exponential developments in computer storage and broadcasting power suggest that reliance on remote face-to-face and iconic contact will increase.

In *The Unschooled Mind*, Gardner insists that pedagogy should be developing to embrace the new knowledge about thinking and to reflect children's' multiple intelligences that flower throughout life: spatial, visual, oral, textual. These intelligences colour the individual approach each child has to learning. Only a narrow subset of the brain is developed and tested in conventional education, and schools, as they are currently organised, cannot provide the variety of learning styles that a class requires.

Technology should make it possible for schools to deliberately collect and make available resources – human and technological – that fit comfortably with disparate learning styles and cultural backgrounds that exist in any learning body. Different entry points will attract one child more than another and cause different kinds of confusion about the concepts that are being taught.

Gardner suggests approaches like traditional apprenticeships and the use of children's museum techniques. He calls for a revitalising of the teaching and learning process in which there is more study of differing learning styles and more attempt to resource different entry points to the mandated curriculum. Schools could exert efforts to match teaching and learning styles (Gardner 1993), while Heppell observes that some children are better resourced in the home environment than they are in school, which could create a rift in perceptions of the school as a learning environment (Heppell 1995).

The attack on the current education climate is continued in *Learning through Telematics*, which reports:

> Predicting the future of technology is easy. Predicting the way in which the technology will be taken up within education is very difficult. There is a long history of hyperbole about educational technology, characterised by repeated predictions of imminent revolution in methods. Yet there is a strong resistance to change and innovation in the system as a whole. Education is a social and political system and experience should teach us that such systems are not easily changed by developments in technology.
>
> (Mayes 1994: 14)

Yet again the report puts the teacher at the centre of the process:

> A climate of change in which innovation in teaching methods is valued and rewarded, is a necessary precondition for the widespread uptake of educational technology.
>
> (ibid: 16)

Although the report acknowledges the need to spread education more widely, raise the quality and the relevance to industry and supports the need to make teaching more cost effective, it is highly critical of government policies that are reducing the face-to-face opportunities for teaching to such a low level that pupils could be forgiven for believing that they are not being taught at all. Technology should be used to enrich the teaching experience not to replace teachers (Mayes, Coventry, Thompson and Mason 1994; Preston 1997).

Some teachers are hostile to new technologies because they fear replacement. Other barriers are equally complex. Not only must teachers contend with children who have better electronic resources at home than they have in school, but age is another factor that works against the teachers' intuitive understanding of the electronic technologies. Chris Abbott's study has shown that primary children are far better at predicting the end of a cartoon than anyone over twenty-nine (Abbott 1990). However, age is not always a factor. A recent small study shows that innovative teachers in ICT are on average about 45 years old and senior managers. In fact, Information and Communications Technology education for teachers presents more problems than other established curriculum subjects. Few teachers have degree level qualifications (Preston Cox & Cox 2000). The technology changes fast and problems associated with this have made the subject appear to be technocentric. British schools have separated administrative systems from the curriculum systems which means teachers must learn two computer systems. There are not enough senior role models using IT. In 25 schools, which were selected by industry and local authorities because they showed interesting practice in IT, 22 of the heads had a mobile computer or a computer on the desk (Harris and Preston 1993).

In Britain mature teacher entrants bring ICT skills into the profession (Mellar and Jackson 1992). But in a small survey conducted by MirandaNet (Preston 1998) it would seem that teachers have less than two days' ICT training in their initial training year. They are totally dependent on the quality of ICT provision in the school where they do their practice for knowledge and experience. Subsequently, they rely on in-service provision. The opinions of a small sample of teachers who are ICT innovators reveal how in-service training is available especially in subjects like pedagogy and planning. Although most national governments see their investment in ICT in education as a catalyst for change in teaching and learning, less than half the teachers thought that the ICT courses that they had attended addressed this central issue of teaching style. This would suggest that some courses may not help teachers to adopt those new teaching methods which may be needed to accommodate ICT effectively.

According to this small survey these teachers were mainly self taught. Only one per cent had any formal ICT qualifications Most of these competent teachers were training others, although they had been to few courses themselves, and half said they did not feel well informed about the National Grid for Learning (NGfL). Although many of the teachers felt that they had benefited from the training they had received, they wanted to receive more training and also felt that they needed better resources and more technical support and time to use ICT (Preston Cox & Cox 2000). Training is often focused on skills rather than the philosophy, the psychology of learning, and policy issues. Pachler is critical of the prevailing tendency to perceive the value of new technologies in terms of a delivery model perpetuating the view of the pupil as the empty vessel rather than pursuing the opportunities offered for pedagogical innovation. Pachler quotes the DfEE Initial Teacher Training National Curriculum which is intended to teach teachers about 'when, when not, and how to use ICT effectively in teaching particular subjects' (DfEE 1998: 17). He points out the dangers of the lack of pedagogical theory offered in this document (Pachler 1999). The language of this document is didactic which militates against the constructive learning model the government want to introduce. The internet has been tacked onto the end as an extra module for study which makes it look like a study extra rather than a paradigm change in teaching and learning.

Mayes put the alternative view that telecommunications-centred learning environments are central to the achievement of a learning society in the next century. This is based on interactive models of the learner and the teacher engagement in inquiry around design and real problem solving, rather than the dominant didactic model of the teacher as a delivery agent of knowledge through curriculum materials (Mayes 1994).

The New London Group (1996) coined the term, 'multiliteracies' pedagogy. They attempt to describe the four stages of learning that have to be resourced: situated practices, overt instruction, critical framing and transformed practice to take the learner from a situation they know into the ability to recreate their learning in another context.

The New London theorists do not mention the potential of technology in this process particularly in visualisation and modelling. The new technologies are closely woven into the changes that the millennium world is facing. Electronic mediums of communication are the vehicle for powerful messages and for authoritative, public debate. Yet there is an antipathy towards the media amongst teachers, resulting in courses which are critical rather than participative – just as literature and art studies have tended to be (London 1996).

Four centuries of emphasis on reading and writing have disenfranchised other groups of learners who think visually and diminished the value of performance skills (Barlas 1995). Performance and presentation is still a key factor if a teacher is to be effective. Charismatic teachers and communicators have never had a need for props, retouching or amplification whether they are performing in the mediaeval banqueting hall, the theatre, the classroom or in the television studio, but the opportunities for the average teacher to communicate ideas have been transformed by the advent of the electronic media. All teachers and lecturers could use the presentational tools like computer presentation packages which allow them to utilise all the professionalism of the media.

But most teachers at all levels do not use these tools. A dependence on 'schooled literacy' means that the power of presentation tools has not yet struck home. And teachers are part of an educated and powerful class of communicators. The performance skills of these academics, teacher educators, politicians, publishers, editors and government officials are diminished by the reliance on the written text. Many still give lectures devoid of illustration to convey their message. Some speakers read the speech someone else has written for them without making eye contact with their audience. Others read the speech whilst gesturing lamely at the projected bullet points behind them (Preston 1996). In international academic conferences, little use is made of drawings and photographs, still less of sound and animated sequences. Do keynote speakers fear that illustration will trivialise serious thought? That performance skills are somehow offensive? In fact, their ideas may be in danger of being dismissed by an audience used to more effective presentation in the media.

There are some key industrialists who use the full range of multimedia computer tools to make their point. Illustrative computer models and graphs are integral to the argument. Good design helps to underline a cogent point. But then business people will often have the design staff to focus planning and to add the finishing touches which are not so easily found in education support services. These people come from a company culture that values a range of media expression. It may be a company where the visual is highly valued, often a company which is promoting multimedia technologies.

The absence of multimedia presentation in education creates a powerfully negative message for the young learner. Twenty one year old undergraduates studying English were using computers in a newspaper workshop funded by industry. The students were creating paper based and multimedia newspapers on-line. They wrote an anguished editorial.

> With three or four high grade 'A' levels we are labelled 'the top ten percent.' [These young editors went on to say,] But without exception we are computer illiterates. There are primary school displays at this conference on computer education which use better integrated multimedia systems than we presently have at university or have seen during our sixth form. Most highly educated arts students largely do not rate technology beyond the capacity to word process. Can we afford this level of ignorance from our most educated minds?
>
> (Preston, 1995b)

Underlying this statement is the notion that a model of teaching and learning has been employed that will not prepare these high achievers for the Third Millennium.

It is not surprising that the British inspection body, The Office for Standards in Education, is critical of the teaching and use of IT in schools. Resourcing in the classroom is adequate but the inspectors' report for 1994/5 complains that IT is not being taught in sufficient depth across the curriculum. The Department for Education and Employment's longitudinal study on learning with computers, the Impact Report (1993), finds few measurable results from computer use in schools. They conclude that, 'the majority of school pupils are not yet provided with opportunities to take advantage of the potential of the full range of software, a substantial amount of which is currently available in schools'.

Arguably the most important component of a strategy for coping with the demands of the new literacies is the education and training of teachers. In fact they may be a group which has special needs since they have been selected for their prowess in reading and writing, rather than the new literacies required by competent and confident users of technology. In 1998/99 Telematics in initial teacher training remained 'patchy' (Davis 1998). One way of redressing the balance through teacher placement in industry, has resulted in a range of initiatives. One was a publication called *Matching Skills* which looks at literacy and numeracy skills (BT 1993).

In a welcome research trend within teacher education, Heppell has switched his focus from an emphasis on the rapid evolution of software and hardware to studying the evolution of the teachers' and the pupils' learning in technology rich environments. He emphasises the need for observation of children as a means of understanding the emergent capabilities of the ' information generation' (Heppell 1993).

Another hopeful approach to teacher education has been developed by the INTENT project which has now resulted in a book about teachers' experiences. The three themes are: looking at the potential of ICT as a tool that can influence the quality and experience of learning; the ways in which teachers' professional development can help them to use ICT effectively in the classroom and the coordination and management of ICT. The main emphasis in Project Intent is not the technology, nor the teachers' learning process, although they are studied; it is the analysis of the process of change that is involved in engaging teachers in exploration and experimentation. Action research has been the methodology and a rich source of case study material. Not only does this methodology encourage planned change in the learning institutions but it is flexible enough to allow for the adaptations that must take place where change is fast and the learning curve is steep.

They identify the kind of support which is essential for teacher education in telematics: reasonable access to hardware and software that works and is reasonably new; good technical backup so that they can concentrate on teaching and learning; an emphasis in the institutional culture on sharing rather than grudging penny pushing in the competitive fight for resources. Most importantly an institutional culture that is non-judgemental and non-punitive so that experimentation feeds curiosity and leads to learning (Somekh and Davis, 1997).

Conclusion: teachers learning how to learn

Gunther Kress believes that the fundamental aim of education will remain: to make it possible for humans as social beings, to live productive, full and rewarding lives. But there is no way out for those who wish to rest on the past. Each sector of education and each learning institution will have to devise curricular solutions that take account of the local cultural mix and the likely economic future.

Kress also suggests that in order to function the global citizen will need to develop five basic dispositions. The first will be multicultural sensitivity treating diversity as the productive norm. Second, the capacity to view dynamic change as a comfortable stimulus for innovation and transformation. Third, knowledge will be used in the service of new solutions, rather than in the performance of established practices. Fourth, understanding the potential of different modes and media for communication will be significant in a greater emphasis on understanding the target audience and essential for a productive social life. Most importantly Kress raises the question of ethics and the responsibility of each citizen to be articulate in preserving what is best for plural communities (Kress 1998). The shift from mass media to interactive media has increased the power of each individual over institutionalised information whether the source is the church, the nation state, the BBC or Oracle.

Educating people to cope with lifelong learning in the electronic age may be the greatest challenge civilisation ever faces.

Questions

1   What role are you and your school playing in the development of lifelong learning in the local community?
2   How might this role be extended?
3   Are the pupils in your school being prepared for a life where information which might support lifelong learning is on tap?
4   How comfortable are you with Kress's five basic dispositions outlined in the conclusions?

Further reading

Kress, G. (1998) 'Globalisation and education: thoughts on consequences and possible effects'; Hamburg Keynote address: January 1998. Institute of Education, University of London.
Kress outlines the characteristics that citizens of the twenty-first century need to acquire in order to live and work effectively in the information age.
Somekh, B., and Davis, N. (eds) (1997) *Using Information Technology Effectively in Teaching and Learning*, London: Routledge.

References

Abott, C. (1990) *Film and Learning*, PhD dissertation, London: Kings College.
Barlas, C. (1995) 'Is IT doing us any good?', *The Sunday Times*, 14 March.
Beare, H. and Slaughter, R. (1994) *Education for twenty-first Century*, London: Routledge.
BT (previously British Telecom) (1993) 'Matching Skills a question of demand and supply', BT London: BT, 81, Newgate Street, London EC1 7AJ, UK.
Chandler, D. (1984) *Young Learners and the Micro-computer*, Milton Keynes: Open University.
Davis, N. (1998) 'Information Technology for teacher education and professional development: responding to demand', *Journal of Information Technology for Teacher Education*, Vol. 7, No. 2.
Department for Education and Employment (DfEE) (1997) *The National Curriculum Documents*, London: HMSO.
Department for Education and Employment (DfEE) (1998) *A Survey of Telematics within Initial Teacher Training*, London: HMSO.
Department for Education and Employment (DfEE) (1993) *Impact Report 'An Evaluation of the Impact of Information Technology on Children's Achievements in Primary and Secondary Schools'*, London: HMSO.
Fullan, M. and Stiegelbauer, S. (1991) *New Meaning of Educational Change*, London: Cassell Educational Ltd.
Gardner, H. (1993) *The Unschooled Mind: How Children Think and How Schools should Teach*, London: Fontana Press.
Handy, C. (1994) *The Empty Raincoat*, London: Arrow Business Books.
Harris, S. and Preston, C. (1993) 'Software in schools', Slough: National Foundation for Education Research, Nelson.
Heppell, S. (1993) 'Teacher education, learning and the information generation: the

progression and evolution of educational computing against a background of change', *Journal of Information Technology for Teacher Education*, Vol. 2, No. 2, pp. 229–237, Oxon: Triangle Journals.

Heppell, S. (1995) 'Power trips on the SuperHighway', *The Observer* 8 January 1995.

Kress, G. and Van Leeuwen, T. (1996) *Reading Images: The Grammar of Visual Design*, London: Routledge.

Kress, G. (1998) *Globalisation and Education: Thoughts on Consequences and Possible Effects*, Hamburg Keynote address: January 1998.

London, N. (1996) 'A pedagogy of multiliteracies: designing social futures', *Harvard Educational Review*, Spring.

Mayes, T., Coventry, L., Thompson, A. and Mason, R. (1994) *Learning Through Telematics, a Learning Framework for Telecommunications Applications in Higher Education*, London: BT.

Meek, M. (1991) *On Being Literate*, London: The Bodley Head.

Mellar, H. and Jackson, A. (1992) 'Information Technology in post graduate teacher training', *Journal of Computer Assisted Learning*, Oxford: Blackwell Sciences.

New London Group (1996) 'A pedagogy of multiliteracies: designing social futures', *Harvard Educational Review Harvard College*, Vol. 66, No. 1, Spring 1996.

OFSTED Office for Standards in Education (1994/95) *Information Technology – A Review of Inspection Findings*, London: HMSO.

Oracle plc www.think.com

Pachler, N. (1999) 'Theories of learning and ICT' in Leask, M. and Pachler, N. (eds) *Learning to Teach Using ICT in the Secondary School*, London: Routledge.

Preston, C. (1995a) 'Best defence', *The Times Higher Education Supplement*, April 7, p. xii.

Preston, Christina (ed.) (1995b) 'Wired' World Conference for Computer Education (WCCE) newspaper MirandaNet, London: Institute of Education, London University. www.mirandanet.ac.uk.

Preston, C. (1997) 'Review of the Real Time Club on IT in schools', *British Computer Bulletin*, June.

Preston, C. (1998) 'Keynote: Do computers change teachers' attitudes to teaching and learning?' in Votsaka, C. (ed.), *Poskole 98*, Sedmihorsky, CZ: CVUT, Prague.

Preston, C., Cox, M. and Cox, K. (2000) *Teachers as Innovators: an Evaluation of the Motivation of Teachers to use ICT*, London: MirandaNet.

Preston, C. (9 February 1996) 'Teachers lead a revolution in outward mobility after the isolation years', *Multimedia, Times Education Supplement*.

Somekh, B., and Davis, N. (ed.) (1997) *Using Information Technology Effectively in Teaching and Learning*, London: Routledge.

Spencer, D. (1996) *CD Roms and information*, BECTA, Coventry.

Stevenson, D. (1996) *Information and Communications Technology in UK Schools: Independent Inquiry*, London: Pearson Group. Think.com on www.think.com. An Oracle Millenium Initiative.

Wagner, A. (1995) *Hyperstudio Software Handbook*, TAG Developments Limited, 25 Pelham Road, Gravesend, Kent DA11 0HV.

West, T. (1991) *In The Mind's Eye: Visual Thinkers, Gifted People with Learning Difficulties*, New York: Prometheus Books.

15 Developing a 'cognitively flexible literacy'

From an industrial society to the information age

Sarah Younie

Introduction

The coming of the Information Age and the shift from an industrial society to a knowledge economy requires educators to identify the implications for education and the skills pupils will need to cope in an increasingly complex world.

A globalised knowledge economy permeated by information and communication technologies (ICTs), means work patterns are changing, job security is diminishing and old certainties are eroding. In order to manage careers of the future, in the view of the RSA (Royal Society for the encouragement of Arts, Manufactures and Commerce), we need to be equipped with the ability to 'identify and evaluate options for managing risk, hazard and uncertainty' (RSA 1999: 29).

The demands of an emerging information society, saturated by ICT, challenges the future role of education. The need for knowledge workers for the twenty-first century requires school leavers to be equipped with ICT competencies including navigational and research strategies and higher order thinking skills, in short a *cognitively flexible literacy*. We need to create new types of literacy to enable pupils to manage information retrieval, construction and deconstruction, across all types of multimedia technology. Learners need to be able to restructure knowledge and to transfer skills beyond the initial learning situation. To define problems, conceptualise new solutions, requires the ability of critical thinking, which includes abstraction, system thinking, experimentation and collaboration. Implicit within acquiring a *cognitively flexible literacy* is learning how to learn and learning how to think.

For schools the challenge is two fold; one is a matter of ensuring pupil and teacher access to up-to-date technology, the hardware, equipping schools with computers, connecting them to electronic networks, and developing software to meet pedagogical needs. The other is human and infinitely more complex, namely training teachers to use ICTs in pedagogically meaningful ways, and enabling pupils to develop a *cognitively flexible literacy* to live, work and learn with ICTs across a life time.

The challenges posed by the information age require us to examine our responsibilities as educators, and to look at how we should organise education to equip the emerging knowledge workers of the high-tech economy. Among the implications for teachers are ensuring equality of access to technology and an entitlement to develop ICT literacy. This process of restructuring education requires an identification of the dynamics of change and the construction of a framework for analysis, that is a model for understanding the complex relations between pedagogy, technology, teachers and learners. Within schools ICT poses a challenge for our teaching and learning styles: how do we engender the development of technological literacies, that is the ability to read and deconstruct multimedia texts? This requires a *cognitively flexible literacy*, which encourages higher order thinking skills of critical analysis alongside enhanced intra and interpersonal skills. Learners are then equipped with transferable skills including ICT competencies that enable them to restructure their knowledge and under-standing, in order to manage the demand for greater flexibility in a changing world.

The coming of the information age: the worker-less world?

> ... the scary new networks [of] informatics [mark] a movement from an organic, industrial society to a polymorphous, information society.
>
> (Haraway 1991: 161)

The insidious ubiquity of ICTs is changing the economic, political and social world at an unprecedented rate and provide a major challenge as we negotiate new ways of living, working and communicating. Halsey, Brown, Lauder and Wells (1997) argue that global competition and technological innovation have led to an increase in occupational insecurity, redundancy and the demise of traditional career patterns.

> ... the convergence of information technologies and their integration in the workplace, the need to free up and speed up the flow of information and decision making, [means an] increasing emphasis on teamwork and project work, and the need for flexible work practices, along with a new vocabulary of networks [and empowerment . . .]
>
> (Halsey *et al.* 1997: 6)

Technology is integral to this shift 'from an economy based on material, energy, and labour to one based on information and communication' (Rifkin 1995: 236). Schools must prepare pupils to be 'the new professionals, the highly trained symbolic analysts or knowledge workers who manage the new high-tech information economy' (Sheppard and Brown 1999: 158).

This shift from an industrial society to the information age (Webster 1995), can be expected to incur transformations that will be permanent and enduring to the way we organise our lives. This may not happen without casualities, for example, what will be the plight of the techno-illiterate? In the shift to an information based society, people need different skills to those of an economy previously based on manufacturing and manual labour. Selling one's manual power is a shrinking option in a country which has lost the majority of its manufacturing industry. Forty years ago 65 per cent of the workforce in America were employed in manufacturing compared to 13 per cent in 1997, with a prediction of 10 per cent for other western countries, and in 1997, just 24 per cent of America's gross national product was from manufacturing (Dryden and Vos 1997: 55). The need for a manual workforce has declined, whilst an expanding service industry has been largely at the fore front of appropriating ICTs, which demands ICT literacy. A global restructuring of the world's economies means advanced capitalism is dependent upon ICTs in ways previously unknown. For example, the digitisation of the world's stockmarkets has condensed conceptions of time and space.[1] Share prices can be exchanged at the press of a button, across international time zones. 'The instant transfer of money around the globe – $1.3 trillion dollars a day – has altered the very nature of trade and world commerce' (Dryden and Vos 1997: 31) and consequently our working practices.

> The information age has arrived . . . new, more sophisticated software technologies are going to bring civilisation ever closer to a workerless world . . . Redefining opportunities and responsibilities for millions of people in a society absent of mass formal employment is likely to be the single most pressing social issue of the coming century.
>
> (Rifkin in Dryden and Vos 1997: 77)

We need to prepare for working lives that will demand greater flexibility with frequent shifts between employers and roles. This necessitates a high degree of adaptability as people will be expected to define their own career patterns and to take responsibility for their own learning, training and financial security (RSA 1999). Implicit within this analysis is an assumption that individuals know 'how to learn' and can transfer this ability across different situations: a cognitively flexible literacy.

What is our responsibility as educators?

The illusion that it is possible to escape new technologies is diminishing. Whether the technologies are for industrial, biomedical, military, or domestic use, the effects are pervasive. Try a day without technology, increasingly the organisation of daily life is reliant upon ICTs.

Without entering into philosophical debates about whether society has moved into a period of postmodernity, or is experiencing 'the cultural logic of late advanced capitalism' (Jameson 1990), the point is, our lifestyles are not those of our grandparents. The technological differences are evident from phone banking, internet shopping, email to digital TV. Children are becoming more competent in handling electronic technologies through multimedia entertainment (Buckingham 1999). With the developments in video and computer games some children are socialised into using ICTs in seamless ways.[2] The multimedia content may not be educational, in fact it may be controversial. The sexualised appearance and violent behaviour of females in computer games, for example Lara Croft in Tomb Raider II, invites a critical analysis of gender representation and models of conflict management. It is up to schools to develop appropriate critical thinking skills which call into question the validity of the content, also for educational software developers to utilise the strategies used in electronic games for children's engagement such that learning can also be embraced as enjoyable.

What then is our responsibility as educators? Clearly there is a need to equip pupils with the skills needed to live in an information society. Creating competencies with ICT is necessary because pupils will have to work in an economy and labour market penetrated by ICT. ICT developments may require and enable a greater integration of work and education, both merging in ways not seen before. There is the opportunity for new and innovative practices to be developed, for schools to open the space for new connections and to use ICT to realise the potential for life long learning, which can be seen, for example, with the development of the University for Industry and validation of practice-related degrees. Davis (1998) argues that 'the blurring of the boundaries between organisations and sectors is a recurring theme as ICT infuses our society' (Davis 1998: 160). Given the rapid pace of technological development, learning over the whole life span can be more cheaply and effectively incorporated into our daily working practices. Schools may have a critical role in bringing together education and commerce, if they choose to do so. For example Lord Grey School, Bletchley has harnessed a mutually beneficial commercial relationship by having a set of Yamaha keyboards linked to a Music Laboratory System, each with multi-track recording. The school provides Yamaha local industry with a showcase for music technology which benefits the surrounding schools and community.

Organising education for an information age

The RSA (1999) argues for a radical reappraisal of education in light of the knowledge economy where industry and commerce are restructured by new technologies. In order to understand how to manage the risks and uncertainties of the future, it is essential to develop a *cognitively flexible literacy* that engenders an ability *to understand* (knowing that), *to do* (knowing how) and higher order thinking skills of reasoning and analysis in order to solve problems.

There is mounting pressure from the UK government for education to usefully appropriate ICT. There appear to be two agendas from government regarding education and ICT; one for pupils to gain *generic ICT skills* in order to be internationally competitive in a global economy, and two, for ICT to *improve pupil learning*. The two agendas are not synonymous. However the development of a *cognitively flexible literacy* would enable pupils to use ICT to improve learning, because ICT incorporates a variety of mediums which appeal to different learning styles, *and* it allows pupils to transfer their skills into the changing world of work.

In order to create pupil competencies in ICT use, there is the need to adapt the traditional education system to allow greater flexibility in learning patterns. Aviram (1999) at the Centre for Futurism in Education (Israel) argues for a new educational paradigm which reflects the wider changes in society, since the western curricular paradigm has rapidly become obsolete in the digital age.

The 100-year-old organisational and didactic paradigm basic to the modern educational system has been rendered anachronistic by postmodernity.

(Aviram 1999: 164)

Sheppard and Brown (1999) argue the current emphasis on individual learning and performance, once seen as appropriate for the role of the industrial worker, is now outmoded. For the education system to shift from a highly individualised content-led curriculum is a major challenge. Sheppard and Brown (1999) argue that schools have not been successful in their attempts to make such change: 'we have tried almost everything conceivable to improve our schools. We have invested millions of dollars only to watch new skills disappear amidst old routines' (Deal 1990: 6, in Sheppard and Brown 1999: 158). This is why it is essential to realise the role of teachers as the key players in the dynamic process of change.

Emerging knowledge workers

Pupils of the twenty-first century will need to be able to deal effectively with information overload. Whelan (1999) argues that 'internet technologies are at the forefront of the future and are already creating the largest uniformly accessible pool of knowledge ever known' (Whelan 1999: 72). The potential of the internet, to provide enormous amounts of information and link pupils and schools across the world, has boundless possibilities for improving educational practices (Wijngaards 1999).

The internet's rapid and unexpected development, outside of its military conception,[3] challenges the world's education systems to integrate its information and communication potential into the school curriculum. The internet provides new ways of reaching isolated schools, disadvantaged or under-represented groups, like the physically disabled, dissolving the barriers of time and space, allowing connection irrespective of cultural and geographical specificity. Opportunities to interact and create new identities provide spaces for representation free from prejudicial perceptions of age, race, gender, disability. Since there is not parity of access, as access to home computers is linked to soci-economic status, this highlights the role of schools in providing an entitlement to ICT. The success of the internet in schools, however, is dependent on a number of factors: the motivation of teachers, appropriate training, the creation of new pedagogic knowledge, easy access to high quality resources and technical support.

Ensuring equality of access to technology; the implications for teachers

There is the need to examine the complex relations between pedagogy, technology and learners, whilst remembering that technology itself is not neutral. It is embedded in existing social relations which can replicate existing inequalities. We do not come to technology in ideologically neutral ways, we are situated differently to technology if we are disabled, poor, black, female, therefore, using

ICTs in educating pupils from varying ethnic, linguistic and cultural backgrounds means educators need to be sensitive to ways of teaching that do not replicate disadvantage. If, for example, those who are at a socio-economic disadvantage, have limited experience and knowledge of technology, then schools must guarantee equitable access to technology.

Educators need to raise awareness of integrating technology into culturally diverse classrooms. More research is needed on effective teacher use of technology in multicultural settings. Chisholm (1998) argues that 'equitable access to technology requires the infusion of effective multicultural teaching strategies into educational technology use. These strategies must be broad enough to be inclusive of diverse learners, yet specific enough to be valuable as a guide to multicultural teaching' (Chisholm 1998: 274).

Dynamics of implementing change: an analytical framework

In order to understand change it is necessary to understand the different components involved. Change in the classroom is complicated because so many different factors come into play. There is the *pedagogy* which involves teachers and their dominant teaching style. There are the *pupils* who are differentiated in their needs and learning styles. Then there is the *technology* itself, which differs from school to school, depending on finances and amount of resources available. The technology *interfaces* with the teachers and the pupils, and each individual

PEDAGOGY	–	science of teaching	=	classroom practices
TEACHERS	–	learners	=	teachers' personal and professional narratives with technology
TECHNOLOGY	–	medium	=	interfacing relations with learners
PUPILS	–	learners	=	pupils' narratives with technology
POLITICAL	–	institution	=	school management policies
	–	national	=	government ICT initiatives (e.g. NGfL[4], NOF[5], DfEE 4/98)
	–	international	=	inter-government ICT initiatives (e.g. European Schoolnet[6], Montage[7])

Figure 15.1 The dynamics of implementing change in classrooms: an analytical framework

is a learner with a particular relationship to the technology. What this means is each user or learner has a different narrative with the technology, some may be competent users, others may be technophobic. Some (teachers and pupils) may be disadvantaged by the technology, for example if they perceive it to be overtly masculine or technical.

Teachers have their own 'learning relationship' to the technology as well as being responsible for the pupils' learning with technology. Educators need to be aware of the multifaceted nature of the process of learning with technology. The question is how to manage this process, in order to implement change that will be beneficial and lasting to classroom practice. Computers have been in schools for years, however the advent of the internet offers new and exciting possibilities for connecting those computers, to add authentic learning through global curriculum collaboration (see Chapters 6 and 7).

Beyond the dynamics of the classroom there is the added dimension of *politics*. At the level of the school (institution), politics refers to how the school is structured, managed and financed. It is important to identify those management policies of a school which relate to technology. In the UK, those schools with clear aims in their *development plans* relating to technology have made a whole school decision to focus on this, so each department, across all curriculum areas, will teach using technology for some of the time. However, not all schools are funded equally, those receiving *Technology College Trust* status have additional money to focus specifically on introducing technology. Schools which receive this funding must have development plans which show exactly how technology will be implemented into the school. Therefore drives to implement technology into classroom teaching can originate at many different levels; from how the school is financed, the vision of a headteacher, a whole school development plan, to heads of department and individual teachers. Research findings (Leask and Younie 1999 Chapter 16; Leask and Terrell 1997) suggest the role of middle managers is crucial in facilitating the adoption of technology in the classroom.

The dynamics of ICT implementation: an example

The following example of implementing change with ICT in teaching and learning is from an art department in a UK school. The inspiration behind using the internet for art resources came for the head of department. In sharing her *pedagogic* understanding of the value of the internet, the other *teachers* could change their classroom practice (professional narratives) with regards to integrating ICT into art lessons. *Pupils* as learners with ICT were encouraged because the teachers were positive about the technology and the internet (art resources) supported the interfacing relations between teachers (objectives) and pupils (learning). In this art example the internet links to the museums and galleries of Europe and provides pupils with a wealth of visual stimuli. It is easily accessible for pupils, who in turn are motivated by the immediate response of the computer. In their research, the pupils are asked to find out about an artist in the context of an art movement, for example Dali and Surrealism. The pupils are guided to use the internet and other resources to search for relevant information. The pupils select images which they print off for their research portfolios. The teacher then asks the pupils to adapt the design of a prominent building in the UK (the Millennium Dome) in the style of their chosen artist or art movement. The pupils refer to their research portfolio to help them design their Millennium Dome.

The internet is particularly useful for information on contemporary and obscure artists, for example, one teacher used it to teach about Ofili, a relatively unknown artist who won the 1998 Turner Prize. Despite the fact this artist's work was highly publicised, because it used elephant dung, it would take much longer before information about the artist and these images were available in books, in schools.

The use of the internet in the art department in this school can be traced to the teachers who were informed as to the value of the technology. The teachers commented on using the internet for their own classroom preparation and how this acted to inform them about how pupils could use the internet in the classroom. The teachers shared this internet resource with each other, so gaining a momentum to use it in lessons with pupils.

From knowledge transmission to learner-centred education: styles of teaching and learning

There is a variety of approaches to using ICTs in schools which provides an opportunity to place emphasis on learning rather than teaching. This represents a major shift in the ways some teachers conduct their professional lives. It can be seen as a paradigm change from the transmission model of education, where the teacher imparts knowledge to the pupils, whose minds are a *tabula rasa*, to a learner-centred approach which situates the learner as primarily responsible for their own learning in the active construction of knowledge.

Arguably there has always been a tension, since Socrates, between knowledge transmission and interactive learning. The Socratic method favoured by the learner-centred approach can be enhanced with ICT. Initiatives, such as GNVQ, focus on negotiating individual action plans for learning and what is revolutionary is the ability of ICT to support interactive learning, to enhance independent and personalised study. SIMS CAPITA Assessment Manager is a software programme allowing individual profiling of a pupil's achievement across subject areas, which schools are exploiting for target setting on an individual basis. These examples encourage a learner-centred approach which, coupled with the availability of resources on the internet, (at any time and for any number of learners, unlike a traditional library) enhances the opportunity for learners to take responsibility for their own learning.

Where ICT is used to enable pupils to manage their own learning the teacher shifts into the role of resource manager and facilitator. The teacher's role as the expert changes, although this tradition could be seen as a restriction which arose out of conventional practice of knowledge production being in books and transferred through didactic teaching. In interviews for the European Schoolnet

'Learning school' project, teachers have stressed their interest in ICTs, but claim a heavily prescribed curriculum often places teachers under pressure to get through the content, and so they resort reluctantly to didactic methods. Within the constraints of a content-led curriculum we need as teachers to understand how ICT provides an array of tools for acquiring information, communication and thinking that allows more pupils more ways to become successful learners.

ICTs as a new medium, raise questions relating to issues of teaching and learning. It is not the case that ICT just slots into existing methods, rather we need to rethink our teaching and learning strategies, which provides an opportunity to question our pedagogical beliefs. As the teachers' role changes, they lose psychological security. Yet change in educational practice is more likely to happen if it is perceived to be *relevant*, and where there is a *readiness* and the *resources* (Saunders 2000). Greater use of technology opens opportunities for new pedagogies, new approaches to where learning is done, more flexible adaptation of the curriculum to individual learning styles. The fundamental change would be in the relationship between teacher and learner. 'More explicit understandings of the purposes and aims of schooling will bring opportunities for more open and individual negotiation of learning targets and end the link between age and stage' (RSA 1999: 10).

Musker (2000) argues the use of computers in schools provides a motivational enhancement to learning, particularly for pupils whose quality of presentation visibly improves. ICT can support different learning styles because it includes a variety of media which facilitate various ways of learning. Pupils 'should not only be taught how to use ICT they should be using ICT to learn' (Musker 2000: 4). ICT encourages the development of new literacies, that is ways to produce, read and evaluate texts, for example multimedia texts.

The learning revolution; encouraging independent and interactive learners

If pupils are to be equipped with the knowledge and skills needed to meet the demands of the information age, then pupils need to develop a range of abilities that build on Gardner's (1983) multiple intelligences. In short, to develop higher order thinking skills alongside computational skills to create a new *cognitively flexible literacy*. That is to train learners to know how to learn and to take responsibility for that learning which engenders:

- *higher order thinking skills*: abstraction, critical analysis, system thinking, experimentation, problem solving;
- *computation and technical skills*, including navigational and research strategies;
- *intrapersonal and interpersonal intelligences*; building on Gardener's multiple intelligences; and
- *to develop new literacies*; to understand, create and evaluate multimedia texts and participate in the active construction of meaning.

To develop a *cognitively flexible literacy* is to prepare individuals for living and working with ICTs in life long learning contexts. The critical intellectual abilities needed for higher order thinking are reasoning, abstraction, analysis, evaluation and problem solving. Learning with ICTs provides opportunities to develop these skills within a supportive environment of interaction and collaboration with peers and the guidance of the teacher. Encouraging interpersonal development engenders the ability to communicate in a variety of ways with others, which is needed to sustain a *cognitively flexible literacy*. This enables learners to adapt to changing novel situations and new information, which require the spontaneous restructuring of a learner's knowledge.

A world in which technologies are constantly changing requires us to develop new forms of literacy. Literacy is taken to mean an understanding of how to read, create and analyse texts in order to participate in society. Texts are taken to convey meaning, and new ways of producing texts require new ways of reading and processing information, for example multimedia requires understanding the interplay between image, sound and text. Those literacies emerging are multimedia, visual and technical literacies, which involve an understanding of navigational strategies and network literacy (Figure 15.2).

There is a need for a new epistemology in education: one that acknowledges information as commodities, and one that recognises the ontological gap of the current curriculum with respect to assessing interpersonal and intrapersonal skills. Desire for change in this area is not new. See for example the definition of achievement in the Hargreaves Report (1984) reprinted in Goddard and Leask (1992: 220). This vision of the curriculum acknowledges a new and different

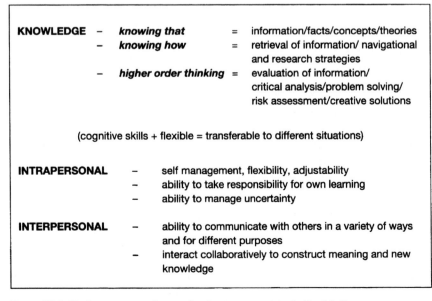

Figure 15.2 Shifting epistemologies: developing a cognitively flexible literacy

balance between knowledge (information content) and learning skills (information handling).

In different socio-historic epochs, the nature of information and knowledge changes. In the industrial era, knowledge was mostly paper based and readily organised into books. Retrieval was dependent on the research skills of knowing how to locate texts; use a library as a physical building, understand referencing, cataloguing, indexing, and so on. Prior to the invention of the printing press, knowledge was a matter of oral convention. With print emerged a literate class, one which knew how to use paper based information. In the next century, information may still be text-based, but electronic and multimedia in nature. This requires a much broader definition of literacy, one which encompasses technological literacy and arguably a new visual literacy and multimedia literacy.

In the information age the nature of knowledge is changing from paper to multimedia and this electronic presentation of knowledge means it is organised in different ways. The linear organisation of a book has been superseded by the non-linear, non-hierarchical organisation of, for example, the world wide web or CD Rom. It is multidimensional and dynamic, making information less static in its storage and retrieval. This makes information more provisional in nature.

The organisation of the internet compared to books has been widely debated, in particular the proposition that hypermedia is better suited to the way the human mind is cognitively organised. However the medium does not guarantee the method: some learners prefer to download and print out websites, thus forcing hot links into a linear sequence for reading on paper. It maybe difficult to discern whether this is habitualised learning or a preferred learning style. If one accepts the work of Buzan (1988) on left and right brained learners, it may be the case that the former is left brained, whereas those who sample books in a random way, rather than read them sequentially, may be right brained. Either way, teachers need to utilise the different multimedias to suit the different learning styles of their pupils (Leask and Meadows 2000).

Knowledge: developing critical analytical skills

In an information age educational epistemology needs to recognise the difference between 'knowing *that*' and 'knowing *how*'. In the classroom the former means teaching pupils to know: information, facts, concepts, theories, mathematical principles, which Jenkins (1999) calls 'learning to know'. This is different to 'knowing *how*', that is, how to get the information in the first instance. This is about information retrieval and key research skills, which Jenkins identifies as 'learning to do'.

Knowing how to search is crucial in an information society, because ICTs make available vast amounts of information which are organised in non-linear ways. Pupils need to be proficient in their technical skills, know how to refine searches, use increasingly sophisticated software, in short, know *how* to research. Pupils also need to be able to evaluate the information once it is retrieved. The ability to discern the quality of the information is dependent upon critical thinking skills.

Given that ICTs can handle so much data, so fast and the world wide web gives no guarantees to the quality of its content, these skills would appear more pressing and paramount than in any other age. Schools have a crucial role to play in developing the higher order thinking skills of critical analysis. Information is meaningless without the cognitive skills to assess its worth.

A world with vast quantities of information, without discerning judgement as to its worth, is a world without knowledge. Knowledge is information, the worth of which is known. Teaching pupils the life long skills of 'knowing that' (information) and 'knowing how' (research skills) must be supplemented with learning to think critically and independently. This is the challenge and it is teachers who are the key players in enabling pupils to realise the full potential of ICTs for educational and creative purposes.

Developing intrapersonal and interpersonal intelligences

The International Commission on Education for the Twenty-first Century (Delors 1996) proposes that pupils learn to 'live together' and 'learn to be'. Taking Gardener's (1983) concept of multiple intelligences, these can be classified as interpersonal and intrapersonal intelligences. This is to address the importance of the communications aspect of ICTs, to strike a balance between the two main assets of the technology: *information* and *communication*.

Global curriculum projects encourage interpersonal communication using the internet and emails to share information. ICT learning environments, like the collaboration projects on the European Schoolnet website (http://www.eun.org), develop pupil competence across different situations and foster team work. This is directly transferable to the work place, for example the service industries, like the travel business, which need interpersonal skills and computer competence. Leisure and tourism are growth industries; half a billion tourists travel each year and this was expected to have doubled by 2000 (Dryden and Vos 1997).

Taking responsibility for oneself and one's own learning is to develop intrapersonal intelligence. For pupils this means 'learning to learn', which computer assisted learning strongly encourages. It also means gaining self-understanding, insight and learning to be self-reliant. This enables individuals to take risks, learn from mistakes, live with insecurity and to trust intuitive leaning, often the most appropriate way to acquire new ICT skills. Similarly, the intrapersonal skills of adjustability and flexibility are recognised as crucial to coping in an unstable world with rapidly changing technology. Developing greater intrapersonal awareness would address the ontological gap in the curriculum. In schools, attention to different ways of being in the world, is often limited to extracurricular activity, like outdoor pursuits, however, these skills also need to be engendered more inside the classroom. If we are to equip pupils with the skills to manage an increasingly complex world with risk and uncertainty, it is imperative that learners have the social skills to cope.

Emphasis on interpersonal skills contributing to a *cognitively flexible literacy* stems from the fact that learning is a social process. Effective communication and collaboration are essential to developing successful learning. Interaction through dialogue plays a critical role in formulating ideas and strategies and interaction enables learners to construct meaning and solve problems. By working collaboratively, learners are able to construct knowledge to a higher level than those working alone. Bruner (1986) argues that learning advances through collaborative interaction. Learners socially construct knowledge and Vygotsky (1978) argues that social interaction plays a crucial part in the development of cognition.

Understanding technology as embedded in social relations

> The machine is not an *it* to be animated, worshipped, and dominated. The machine is us, our processes, an aspect of our embodiment.
>
> (Haraway 1991: 180)

As educators it is necessary to examine the complex relations between pedagogy, technology and users as learners, whilst remembering that technology itself is not neutral. Technology does not appear from nowhere, it comes from the interplay of complex social, economic and political influences, for example, which technologies come to be developed and marketed.

Technology is always embedded in human social relations subject to particular historical circumstances. To understand technology strictly in terms of machines, computers, tools, is illusory because technology always encompasses relationships between designers, machines and users (Terry and Calvert 1997). This approach is to deny any form of technological determinism which assumes technology will bring about change in and of itself, it is not possible to understand technology outside its particular historical, economic and cultural context of design and use. This definition of technology, by exploring the interactive relations between humans and machines, allows for understanding how technologies, designed in specific political and social circumstances, embody or reflect relations of power. Technologies are often created in the interests of military or commercial profit and can reinforce hierarchical social relations. Because this approach seeks to understand how technologies are situated in 'networked social relations' there is the space for creative social agency, for dynamic slippages between intended designs and unintended uses. By understanding technology as contiguous with human activity this effaces any sense of machines as autonomous. It is possible to see how machines and systems can be appropriated differently from their original intended design, and creatively extended or subverted by particular users. The internet's development by the military has the unintended outcome of enhancing community participation by feminists and political eco-activists, and in education, for children to collaborate in global curriculum projects.

With this analysis 'it becomes possible to understand why the internet, originally designed for Cold War strategic military purposes, has a specific format, logic, and programming lexicon rooted in its intended purpose of keeping information decentralised in the face of a nuclear threat' (Terry and Calvert 1997: 4). In realising that we cannot isolate technology from designers and users, this raises fundamental issues about access and control. Given that technology reflects the dominant social relations of production, even allowing for users' creative subversion, equality of access to the technology is paramount in ensuring parity of opportunity. It is here that schools have a crucial role to play, in ensuring technological access and developing an ICT entitlement. If the information age demands a new literacy, one that is technological and multimediaed, educators must prevent a gap between the information rich and information poor and be aware of the costs for the techno-illiterate.

Conclusion: reflections

This chapter considers the shift from an industrial society to a globalised high-tech information economy and considers the implications for education. Education needs to address the challenges by examining the issue of connectivity, that is how schools in a global context are becoming networked; the *hardware* issues regarding ICTs. The *human* issues of how we integrate ICTs into learning requires training teachers to use ICT in pedagogically meaningful ways and to understand the complex and dynamic processes of change in classroom practices. To be an empowered participant in a technologically developed culture means developing a *cognitively flexible literacy*, that is higher order thinking skills of critical analysis and problem solving, which are developed through collaboration and interaction, alongside technical competencies. The development of intra and interpersonal intelligences supports a *cognitively flexible literacy* which enables the learner to transfer skills, actively construct meaning and spontaneously reconstruct knowledge beyond the initial learning situation, in order to be able to evaluate and manage 'risk, hazard and uncertainty' (RSA 1999) in a changing and increasingly complex world.

Notes

1 Strinati (1992) argues that compressions of time and space occur because of global exchanges of information and communication and are a key characteristic of postmodernism. ICTs which enable the condensing of time and space, such as the internet, represent a fundamental shift in the cultural organisation of time and space. These cultural transformations are also reflected in the structure of texts, for example traditional narratives usually represent a linear organisation of time, however, there is a fragmentation or distortion of time and space in postmodern narratives, for example, in the novel *The French Lieutenant's Woman* and films 'Back to the Future' and 'Pulp Fiction'.
2 This reflects the changing nature of how young children are socialised with technological objects, play is more likely to be electronic than a generation ago. These differences are not an excuse for moralising on the value of books versus ICT, which is a fallacious argument, as it is about understanding different mediums for different uses, it is more a matter for understanding how these technologies are increasingly pervasive in daily life.
3 The internet, which developed out of military technology, came about after the Second World War, when America sought a new communications system that was not centralised, in order to withstand possible nuclear attack, because a centralised system can be easily destroyed. By connecting four computers, known as Arpanet, a system

was conceived which had no centre. This was the beginning of the internet; first appropriated by the military and then the academic community. Only recently, from the mid 1990s, has the internet's dissemination been more public and accessible, partly due to falling costs of home computers.

4 NGfL National Grid for Learning http://www.ngfl.gov.uk/
5 NOF New Opportunities Fund: Initiatives in the UK are to connect schools to electronic networks and increase the number of computers in schools (NgFL) and to train teachers to use ICT for learning (NOF). In the UK the government pledges approximately £230 million (330 million euros) from the National Lotteries New Opportunities Fund to train teachers in the use of ICT in schools. There are about 450,000 teachers in the UK, which is approximately $450 per teacher (640 euros). The focus of the training is on the curriculum use of ICT.
6 European Schoolnet Project (http://www.eun.org).
7 Montage Global Curriculum Internet Projects (http://www.montageplus.bc.uk).

Questions

1 How can teachers facilitate pupils to develop a cognitively flexible literacy in order to cope in a changing world?
2 How can the education system develop the skills, knowledge and understanding needed to equip all pupils for living and working with ICTs?

Further reading

RSA (1999) *Opening Minds: Education for the twenty-first Century; The Final Report of the RSA Project Redefining the Curriculum*, London: Futura Printing.
This report is a radical reappraisal of the aims and purposes of education. It argues for a transformation of the way learning is organised in schools and the need to focus on and assess competencies alongside knowledge and learning. Competencies are defined as the ability to understand and to do.

Dryden, G. and Vos, J. (1997) *The Learning Revolution; Your twenty-first Century Passport for Families, Students, Teachers, Managers, Trainers*, New Zealand: The Learning Web.
This text provides a clear and inspirational overview of the issues that will affect education and learning in the twenty-first century. It presents practical suggestions and invites us to rethink our teaching and learning methods in light of research on accelerated learning.

References

Aviram, A. (1999) 'Autonomy-oriented education, or IT in the service of chaos and order', *Shifting Perspectives: The Changing Role and Position of Open and Distance Learning in School Level Education*, Proceedings of the EDEN Third Open Classroom 1999.
Bruner, J. (1986) *Actual Minds, Possible Worlds*, Harvard: Harvard University Press.
Buckingham, D. 'Superhighway or road to nowhere? Children's relationships with digital technology', *English in Education*, Vol. 33, No. 1, Spring 1999, pp. 3–12.
Buzan, T. (1988) *Make the Most of Your Mind*, London: Pan Books.
Chisholm, I. M. (1998) 'Six elements for technology integration in multicultural classrooms', *Journal of Information Technology for Teacher Education*, Vol. 7, No. 2, pp. 268–74.

Commonwealth of Learning Network (http:// www.col.org/cense).

Davis, N. (1998) 'Information technology for teacher education and professional development: responding to demand (Editorial)', *Journal of Information Technology for Teacher Education*, Vol. 7, No. 2, pp. 155–161.

Deal, T. (1990) 'Reframing reform', *Educational leadership*, Vol. 47, No. 8, pp. 6–12, in Sheppard, B. and Brown, J. (1999) 'Overcoming barriers to innovation in schools through organisational learning', *Shifting Perspectives: The Changing Role and Position of Open and Distance Learning in School Level Education*, Proceedings of the EDEN Third Open Classroom 1999.

Delors, J. *et al.* (1996) 'Learning: the treasure within', Report to UNESCO of the International Commission on Education for the 21st Century, Paris: UNESCO.

Department for Education and Employment (DfEE) (1998) 'Requirements for courses of initial teacher training', Circular number 4/98. London: DfEE.

Dryden, G. and Vos, J. (1997) *The Learning Revolution; Your twenty-first Century Passport for Families, Students, Teachers, Managers, Trainers*, New Zealand: The Learning web.

Gardner, H. (1983) *Frames of Mind: The Theory of Multiple Intelligence*, New York: Basic Books.

Goddard, D. and Leask, M. (1992) *Planning for Improvement and Managing Change*, London: Sage/Paul Chapman.

Halsey, A. H., Brown, P., Lauder, H. and Wells, A. (1997) *Education Culture Economy and Society*, Oxford: Oxford University Press.

Haraway, D. (1991) 'A manifesto for cyborgs: science, technology and socialist-feminism in the late twentieth century', in *Simians, Cyborgs and Women*, London: Routledge, pp. 149–81.

Hargreaves Report (1984) *Improving Secondary Schools*, London: ILEA.

Jameson, F. (1991) *Postmodernism, or the Cultural Logic of Late Capitalism*, London: Verso.

Jenkins, J. (1999) 'Teaching for tomorrow: the changing role of teachers in the connected classroom', *Shifting Perspectives: The Changing Role and Position of Open and Distance Learning in School Level Education*, Proceedings of the EDEN Third Open Classroom 1999.

Leask, M. and Meadows, J. (2000) *Teaching and Learning with ICT in the Primary School*, London: Routledge.

Leask, M. and Terrell, I. (1997) *Development Planning and School Improvement for Middle Managers*, London: Kogan Page.

Leask, M. and Younie, S. (1999) 'Characteristics of effective on-line communities for teachers: issues emerging from research', *Shifting Perspectives: The Changing Role and Position of Open and Distance Learning in School Level Education*, Proceedings of the EDEN Third Open Classroom 1999, also adapted and reprinted in this collection, Chapter 16.

Musker, R. (2000) 'Why ICT makes a difference', *Education in Science* February 2000, No. 186, The Association for Science Education, p. 4.

RSA (1999) *Opening Minds: Education for the Twenty-first Century; The Final Report of the RSA Project Redefining the Curriculum*, London: Futura Printing.

Rifkin, J. (1995) *The Work of Restructuring Schools*. New York: Teachers College Press, quoted in Sheppard, B. and Brown, J. (1999) 'Overcoming barriers to innovation in schools through organisational learning', *Shifting Perspectives. The Changing Role and Position of Open and Distance Learning in School Level Education*, Proceedings of the EDEN Third Open Classroom 1999.

Saunders, B. (2000) 'Pedagogical applications of video conferencing', Unpublished MA dissertation, De Montfort University.

Sheppard, B. and Brown, J. (1999) 'Overcoming barriers to innovation in schools through organisational learning', *Shifting Perspectives: The Changing Role and Position of Open and Distance Learning in School Level Education*, Proceedings of the EDEN Third Open Classroom 1999.

Strinati, D. (1992) 'Postmodernism and popular culture', *Sociology Review*, Vol. 1, No. 4, April, p. 2–7.

Terry, J. and Calvert, M. (eds) (1997) *Processed Lives: Gender and Technology in Everyday Life*, London: Routledge.

Vygotsky, L. (1978) *Mind in Society: The Development of Higher Psychological Processes*, Harvard: Harvard University Press.

Webster, F. (1995) *Theories of the Information Society*, London: Routledge.

Whelan, R. (1999) 'The next generation of European RTD&D in Education and Training Technologies', *Shifting Perspectives: The Changing Role and Position of Open and Distance Learning in School Level Education*, Proceedings of the EDEN Third Open Classroom 1999.

Wijngaards, G. (1999) 'Internationalisation of the curriculum: The role of the European Schoolnet', *Shifting Perspectives: The Changing Role and Position of Open and Distance Learning in School Level Education*, Proceedings of the EDEN Third Open Classroom 1999.

16 Building on-line communities for teachers

Issues emerging from research[1]

Marilyn Leask and Sarah Younie

Introduction

This chapter reports findings of research undertaken for the Learning School Project within the European Schoolnet Multimedia Project (EU funded project no MM1010). The schools involved are part of the European Network of Innovative Schools (details on http://www.eun.org). Teachers worked together with researchers across four countries to identify the most effective ways of using electronic networks, and particularly the European Schoolnet EUN, to support professional development and pupil learning across a whole range of curriculum areas. In this chapter we draw on evidence from this project and from other projects investigating the building of on-line professional communities. At the time of writing, the use by teachers of professional on-line communities is one of the underdeveloped aspects of the internet.

Effective on-line communities require teachers to be confident with the technology and this poses a major challenge for those testing out ideas about the functioning and usefulness of effective on-line communities. For this reason, the focus for this chapter is on the identification of user types which aids the analysis of factors which encourage teachers to be confident about using an on-line community for their own professional development. This chapter provides a condensed version of much more detailed and extensive findings which, along with other outcomes of the European Schoolnet project, are published on the website listed above.

Why focus on on-line communities?

In the UK, the government, over a three year period, starting in September 1999, diverted £230 million from the National Lottery into the training of teachers in the use of Information and Communication Technology (ICT) in schools. The expected outcomes were clearly defined (DfEE 1998; Leask and Meadows 2000) and focused particularly on curriculum applications not skill development. This funding worked out at approximately £450 (640 euros) per teacher and there were about 450,000 teachers. This money was not sufficient to provide the amount of training necessary in the traditional manner i.e. face-to-face, daytime or twilight (after 4pm) attendance on courses, even if this was the preferred method. The funders stipulated that as much as possible of the training was to take place in the classroom context. Many trainers (who have been authorised by the Teacher Training Agency, a government agency in England, focusing on teacher supply and training) provided training with on-line and off-line components. The on-line components were essentially on-line communities (the terms 'community' and 'on-line' are defined below) where participants discussed issues related to practice introduced during the training. Research indicates effective communities can be expected to have certain characteristics and these are discussed in the light of user typologies emerging from the research.

At the European level, this question is important as the European Schoolnet initiative (which has gained the support both moral and financial from about 20 ministries of education, the European Union and many educational and commercial organisations) is being developed to provide an on-line community at the European level which provides added European value supplementing national electronic networks, to teachers (http://www.eun.org). Similarly, the Commonwealth of Learning network which has the support of 54 countries http://www.col.org/cense) aims to support a community of teachers linking countries across Africa, North America, Australasia and the Pacific and the Indian sub-continent. These provide examples of the potential of international on-line communities to provide an international network of teachers and other educators which can support a variety of curriculum and professional activities. From the work we have been doing, we also see the potential for various types of communities at local, regional and national level and at the time of writing, experiments are being carried out in the National Leadership College and the General Teaching Council for England.

Definition of terms

What do we mean by 'effective on-line communities'? The concept is new enough to warrant careful definition.

'Effective' on-line communities

Effective communities are those perceived to be of value to teachers and of sufficient value to ensure that teachers return and use the resource regularly whether for their professional development or for purposes directly related to their classroom practice. The variety of background and levels of professional knowledge, skills and understanding of teachers inevitably means that any on-line community will be faced with the needs of a variety of user types and user learning styles. Some may cater for certain user types and others for different user types – each may be effective for its defined clientele.

'Community'

A community is defined as a group with a shared interest/s which is/are strong enough to provide members with motivation to interact. This motivation is critical to the success of the 'community'. If the interaction on-line doesn't happen, then this could be due to two things. The first, and most important in the current context, is that potential users simply do not understand how on-line interaction could be of benefit (see the comment on critical mass below), or how to take part, the second is that the perceived community is, actually, no community at all. In the detailed discussion that follows, we define types of community more closely.

Types of community

'*On-line*': There are a number of web-based tools which can be used to provide on-line services. The ones currently of most use are:

- email – one-to-one, listserves – one-to-many (extension of email);
- discussions;
- conferences/lectures;
- forums;
- informal private or public conversations (often labelled a bar/café/staffroom facility); and
- specially constructed electronic workspaces using software such as First Class, Lotus Notes, BSCW, think.com).

For the purposes of this chapter, on-line communities (for professional development) may be using any form of electronic communication which provides the opportunity for on-line synchronous/asynchronous two-way communication between an individual and their peers, and to which the individual has some commitment and professional involvement over a period of time.

Methodology: data collection

A multi-site case study approach was employed for the research, together with an electronic questionnaire. This method involves, in the UK, visiting a sample of UK schools and gathering data through observation, interviews, (pre- and on going semi-structured interviews) and research diaries. This is supplemented with records kept of all phone conversations, and communications via electronic networks (emails, list serves, and the researchers' virtual workspace on the EUN intranet site, which allows multi-user communication regarding research findings across a European sample of schools). As the research progresses, 'this is coded and reflexively refined into analytic frames. This method involves constant reflection through the observation and interview data that emerges to identify key analytical themes grounded in the data.' (Watson, Blakeley and Abbot 1998: 17).

An emerging typology of users of on-line communities: developing personal narratives with technology

The need for users to be comfortable with computer technology is clearly a necessary prerequisite for effective on-line communities. This need can be analysed on two levels (which interface), on the one hand there is the need to be psychologically comfortable with the technology, (maybe needing to overcome techno-phobia) and secondly there is the need to be technically competent . The question then is, what is the emotional hook for users/teachers to use electronic networks, particularly when time is always pressing with the demands of everyday teaching? What is the motivating force that drives teachers to use this technology?

Teachers do not come to computer technology in emotionally neutral ways. Each user has their own individual life history, or personal narrative with technology. Inevitably, as individuals, they bring this with them; each has a life story or narrative of their relationship with technology based on past experiences, which may be successful or not. The residue memories of an individual's competencies is a narrative which gets retold each time the individual comes to a new piece of learning with technology. Consequently, users vary in their needs and methods of use of on-line communities. Those developing on-line communities need to be aware that each user has a personal career with technology which influences their relationship to that technology. 'Lurkers' in on-line communities are those who log-on and read messages but do not contribute. Reasons for lurking are various. For instance, a less psychologically confident user may be a 'lurker' compared to a fully participating on-line member who can competently (technically and psychologically) move discussions/debates forward. Alternatively, the evidence is that some 'lurkers' are satisfied with being involved in this way.

The next logical question is how do users develop their technological narrative? The mechanisms found to enhance a user's individual development with technology can be described by *networked relations*, an emerging concept which seems the most appropriate to describe the initial research findings. Almost all those individual users with a clear competence in terms of ICT skills and sense of psychological confidence (which includes accepting that making mistakes and needing to ask questions is part of working effectively with the technology), reported access to family members or friends from whom they felt comfortable to learn. These users would commonly describe a similar process, or personal narrative, which explained their individual technical progression with ICT.

From the interviews conducted, these users reported using the technology *at home*; an environment in which it felt safe to learn, and most importantly, access to the advice of the 'networked relation'. This appears crucial in the learner becoming familiar with the technology in order to gain the confidence to move to the public domain of the on-line discussion space. The evidence for this narrative of personal progression with technology is most strongly documented in the interviews with teachers who were part of the 'UK lap top for teachers' initiative. This provides a basis for understanding how teachers as users develop their personal narrative of competence with ICT, which allows them to advance in their use of technology, and increase their psychological confidence in their relationship with on-line communities.

In terms of a continuum of ICT user competence, individuals can be placed on a scale, ranging from illiterate, possibly phobic, to highly skilled or fully integrated (see Figure 16.1). Clearly participating in an on-line community would necessitate a certain amount of competence, both technically and psychologically. In order to understand an individual's relationship between their personal development (through networked relations and progressive life narrative with technology) and their professional development (using on-line communities), further research is being conducted following our initial findings. One model that could be usefully employed to elaborate this learning relationship is *BASIS*, developed by Alistair Smith (1998), who argues that for effective learning to take place, the learner needs the following: a sense of belonging, aspirations, safety, identity and success. Richard Millwood (2000) who has worked extensively in this field, identifies the creation of a sense of identity among participants in the on-line community as crucial to success and his findings mirror the ideas of Smith. Initially it is possible to see how the notion of networked relations/or family provides a sense of belonging, safety and identity (personal narrative), which allows for ICT aspirations and success.

Typology of users – a continuum of user type

Given that users vary and have different personal narratives with technology, it is possible to develop a typology of users, ranging from phobic, and including lurkers who read but don't contribute to on-line communities, to those who are fully integrated users of on-line communities.

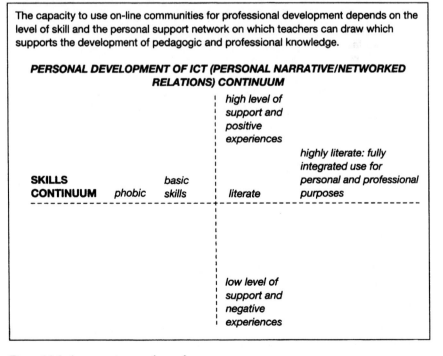

Figure 16.1 An emerging typology of users

From the initial interviews conducted for the research there appears to be an emerging relationship between an individual's personal development of ICT and their professional use of ICT. Gaining confidence in the former seems to be an essential element in understanding which factors are supportive to developing on-line communities. Similarly, a lack of access to *networked relations* (informal personal facilitators) can be seen to be a prohibitive factor in developing participation in on-line communities. Dawes (2000) has undertaken extensive research which backs up these findings. This is touched on in Chapter 5.

The typology could be fleshed out using the CASK model of analysis as applied to individual users (i.e. what Concepts, Attitudes, Skills, and Knowledge are needed for a user to be fully integrated?). The answers to these questions would indicate where on the continuum one would place themselves. The idea of subjective placement is very important, because it is the individual's perception which is the crucial factor here. For instance, the time required to take part in an on-line community is purely subjective, as Davis and Denning (1997) argue,

> I now saw respondents' perception of time as a key. Within the interviews I had found particular instances of people who, say, were regularly working at weekends but still found the time to contribute on-line, while there were some people who seemed under less pressure at work but were 'unable to find the time to take part'. I remembered a colleague, who worked incredibly long hours to a degree of professionalism which went beyond what anyone could have expected from him, who was unable to re-structure his priorities to commit himself to a forum for his own professional development needs. I could then see that my interpretation of participation needed to show that time was indeed a subjective concept but I wanted to reject the voluntarist approach that implied everyone could make the time if they wanted, or at least could find the time at little cost. I knew from talking to friends and colleagues that they were having enormous difficulty juggling the demands of work, family and personal and professional interests.
>
> (Davis and Denning 1997: 2–3)

On-line community – a killer application supporting professional development?

From evidence collected from users involved with on-line communities, it is clearly important that the notion of being part of a community potentially provides a *killer application* which would be attractive to reluctant ICT users i.e. the notion of community provides strong reasons to initially participate and continue participating. A detailed analysis following five years' innovative research and development of the potential of an on-line professional community to support the professionalism of teachers in England, in particular, was presented by the TeacherNet organisation (http://www.teachernetuk.org.uk) to the newly formed General Teaching Council in England (Leask 2000a,b). It remains to be seen to what extent this organisation can realise this vision over the first decade of the twenty-first century.

The necessary pre-requisites for teachers currently appear to be, firstly the motivation to become ICT literate, then there is the need to relate one's learning to *real world tasks*, which offer authentic uses of these skills. Joining an on-line community is one such example of an *authentic project*, a concept developed by John Dewey in 1916, 'according to Dewey (1916) the form of experience that is most educative is participation in shared enquiry' (Mashhadi 1996). It could be the case that the psychological motivators for learning remain the same, with different skills (ICT) in different environments/contexts. The point is, the emotional hooks have to be there in order for teachers to become initially involved and there has to be a return on the investment, otherwise there is no killer application.

The added value of on-line communities is *sharing information* in a spirit of collaboration. The community is by definition a group of professionals with shared interests. Vygotsky (1986) emphasised the *social contexts* for learning, and on-line communities offer professionally, supportive spaces. This allows for the development of a 'critical community' (Selinger 1998), which dissolves the professional isolation of the reflective practitioner, who is busy reflecting alone. The concept of critical community when applied to on-line communities means

- knowledge is socially constructed through action, communication and reflection;
- learning is situated within the domains or communities of practice;
- teaching is the process of facilitating learning through expert practice and promoting learning conversations.

(Selinger 1998: 24)

The benefits of an on-line community are evident when Richard Pring emphasises how ' – by thinking and reflecting in a group, and exposing one's ideas to scrutiny – one's ideas are refined and one's efforts are supported. The practice of thinking and deliberating in concert with others also makes possible greater confidence in the provisional conclusions that are arrived at' (Pring 1995: 126).

Effective communities

Riel and Levin (1990) quoted in Davis and Denning (1997: 2–3) give a list of what they consider necessary to get a good, successful network to function effectively: to enable participants to recognise a presence behind their computer screen. Their criteria were as follows:

- Does the group already exist?
- Is there a need for communication?
- Is there a shared goal or task with a specified outcome?
- Will access to the technology be easy and effective?
- Will all participants have regular patterns of mail access?
- Is there a person who will facilitate group planning and work?

Our experience with a number of emerging communities in the UK supports these criteria and we support the notion that these points should guide the construction of on-line communities with some additions as discussed above. The on-line community should generate : 'a sense of belonging, aspirations, safety, identity and success' (Smith ibid).

We are not unaware of the dangers of people working on-line which Rangecroft (1998: 75–76) identifies as 'isolation, lack of the group interaction, lessening of social interaction'. But these have not appeared as issues raised by the research as yet, possibly because few teachers in the sample are long-term users.

Conclusion: the need to create a critical mass of users

In this chapter, we have not discussed in depth the positive outcomes identified by teachers who are using electronic networks for professional rather than curriculum purposes. There is sufficient evidence from our research about the professional gains (e.g. in the dissemination of new pedagogic knowledge see Leask 2000c) to be achieved through networking teachers for us to support further development and deployment of funding in this area. However, the availability of professionally run sites, including both interactive and passive content of relevance to teachers and publicity about what is possible, is critical if the shift in professional practice required to use the technology effectively is to be achieved within an acceptable timescale. The building of a critical mass of users is an essential factor in the success of initiatives such as the European Schoolnet mentioned earlier.

Hammond (1997: 4) suggests that face-to-face training is required to develop a critical mass in every school who understand how on-line communities work – others can then be relatively easily inducted into these ways of working as they join the school.

> Often the argument for on-line discussion is lost by default – learners know that they can use email and hence imagine they know how an on-line forum works. One way forward in developing participation within on-line forums is to discuss the principles of on-line working at face to face sessions and illustrate these principles through hands on working at machines.
>
> (Hammond 1997: 4)

At the time of writing, this creation of the critical mass of users is just beginning. The training of teachers as discussed at the beginning of the chapter plus the National Curriculum in IT for Initial Teacher Training, i.e. the required IT curriculum for student teachers (see the appendix in Leask and Meadows, 2000), is beginning to have the effect that knowledge about ways of using the internet for professional development through on-line communities is becoming widespread. The Oracle Corporation's initiative in providing free for the education community, think.com, a web-based interactive and individually responsive community building software, is likely to have a significant impact as it becomes widely known and used. Readers interested in this initiative and the others mentioned in this chapter should contact the authors for further details.

Note

1 This chapter is adapted from Leask, M. and Younie, S. 'Characteristics of effective on-line communities for teachers', published in the conference proceedings from: Shifting Perspectives, Changing Role and Position of Open and Distance Learning in School Level Education, European Distance Education Network (EDEN) Open Classroom III Conference, European Distance Education Network, March 1999, Balatonfured, Hungary 1999.

Questions

1 Can on-line communities for teachers provide new spaces for teachers' continuing professional development?
2 Consider the use of on-line communities in your subject area and for the pupils you teach. Does the technology provide opportunities to enrich your pupils' work? What has to happen for the technology to be useful to you as a teacher? Who might undertake this development and how could this be done?

Further reading

The following web sites support on-line communities of different types. We suggest you consider the value of what they offer to you in terms of interactivity and opportunities for professional dialogue:

- General Teaching Council http://www.gtce.org.uk/
- Virtual Teacher Centre http://www.vtc.ngfl.gov.uk/
- TeacherNet UK http://www.teachernetuk.org.uk/
- European Schoolnet http://www.en.eun.org/
- Global Schoolhouse http://www.gsn.org/
- TeacherNet http://www.dfee.gov.uk

References

Davis, M. and Denning, K. (1997) *Learning in virtual space: potential and pitfalls in electronic communication*, Paper given at the 28th Annual SCUTREA Conference.

Dawes, L. (2000) *The National Grid for Learning: Outcomes of an Opportunity for Change*, PhD thesis, Bedford: De Montfort University.

Dewey, J. (1916) *Democracy and Education*, New York: Macmillan.

DfEE (1998) Initial Teacher Training National Curriculum for the use of Information and Communications Technology in Subject Teaching, London: DfEE.

Hammond, M. (1997) *Making links between teaching and research; an example from an inquiry into networked learning*, Paper presented at the 28th Annual SCUTREA Conference.

Leask, M. (2000a) 'Ways in which a website could support the GTCE in the realisation of the organisations' key roles: views from TeacherNet members' Briefing paper 2 for the 17 February 2000 seminar, mimeo, Bedford: De Montfort University.

Leask, M. (2000b) 'The GTC website: Purposes, content, services, stages of development', Report from the seminar 17 February 2000, mimeo, Bedford: De Montfort University.

Leask, M. (2000c) 'European Knowledge Centre within the European Schoolnet', seminar

2 report: 'Classroom practice and educational research: using ICT to build European networks for innovation and change', mimeo, Bedford: De Montfort University.

Leask, M. and Meadows, J. (eds) (2000) *Learning to teach with ICT in the Primary School*, London: Routledge.

Mashhadi, A. (1996) *Educational research and the Internet*: Paper presented at the Singapore Educational Research Association Conference, at the National Institute of Education: Nanyang Technological University 25–29 November 1996.

Millwood, R. (2000) 'Presentation to the European Knowledge Centre UK', seminar 2, March 7 2000 published in Leask, M. (2000c ibid.) seminar 2 report: 'Classroom practice and educational research: using ICT to build European networks for innovation and change', mimeo, Bedford: De Montfort University.

Pring, R. (1995) 'The community of educated people', *British Journal of Educational Studies*, Vol. XXXXIII, No. 2, pp. 125–145 cited in Mashhadi op cit.

Rangecroft, M. (1998) 'Interpersonal Communication in Distance Education', *Journal of Education for Teaching*, Vol. 24, No. 1, 1998, pp. 75–6.

Selinger, M. (1998) 'Forming a critical community through telematics', *Computers and Education*, Vol. 30, No. 1/2, pp. 23–30.

Smith, A. (1998) *Accelerated Learning in the Classroom Network*, Stafford: Network Educational Press Ltd.

Vygotsky, L. (1986) *Thought and Language*, Cambridge, MA: MIT Press.

Watson, D., Blakeley, B. and Abbott, C. (1998) 'Researching the use of communication technologies in teacher education', *Computers and Education*, Vol. 30, No. 1/2, 1998, pp. 15–22.

Author Index

Subject Index